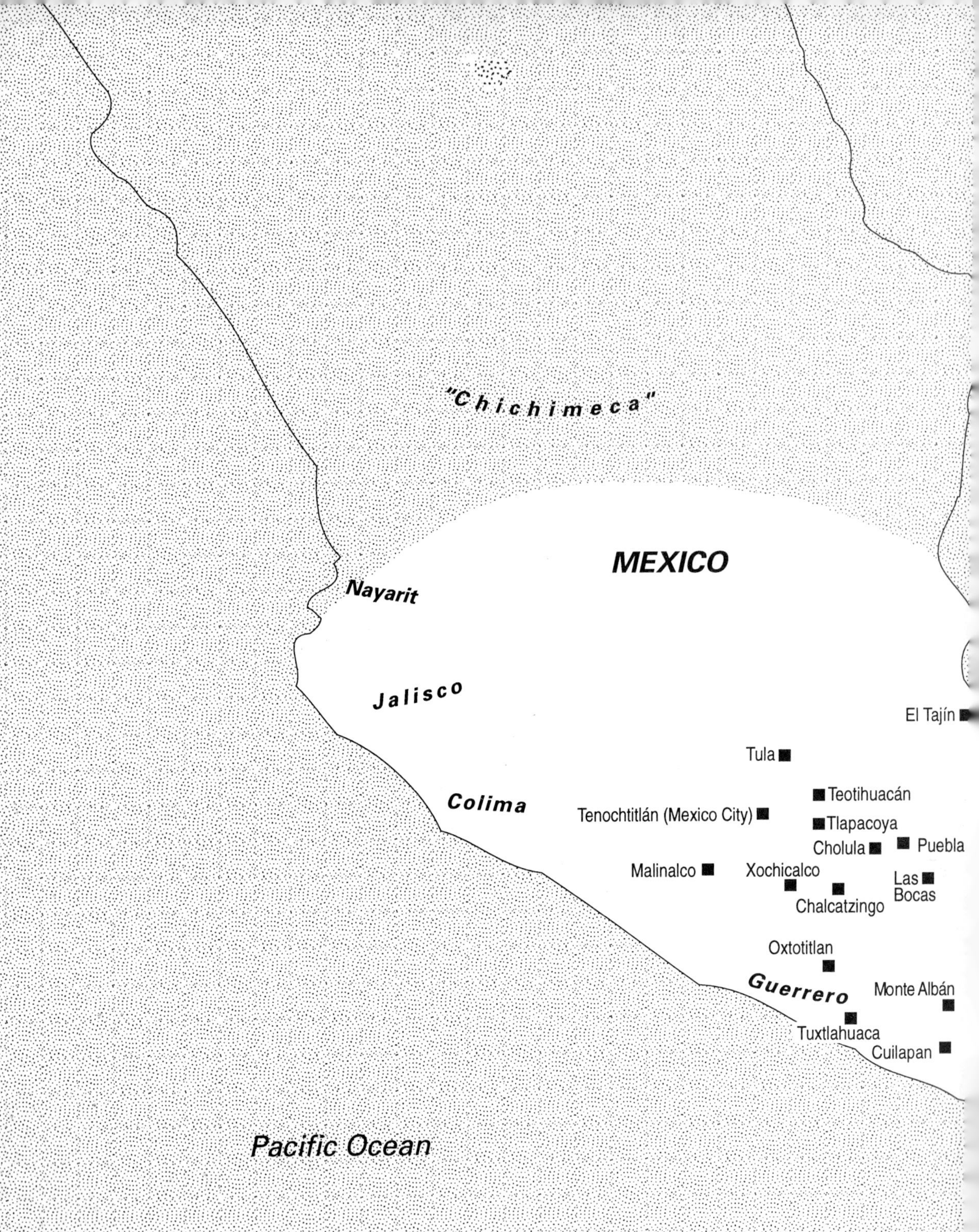
"Chichimeca"
MEXICO
Nayarit
Jalisco
Colima
Guerrero
Pacific Ocean
El Tajín
Tula
Teotihuacán
Tenochtitlán (Mexico City)
Tlapacoya
Cholula
Puebla
Malinalco
Xochicalco
Las Bocas
Chalcatzingo
Oxtotitlan
Monte Albán
Tuxtlahuaca
Cuilapan

Mesoamerica

Selected archaeological sites

Gulf of Mexico

ANCIENT MEXICO

Cultural Traditions in the Land of the Feathered Serpent

Jacqueline Phillips Lathrop

Fifth Edition

KENDALL/HUNT PUBLISHING COMPANY
4050 Westmark Drive Dubuque, Iowa 52002

Cover and interior layout design by Robin Collet.
Cover illustration is based on photos (*Medieval American Art*, by Kelemen) of bas relief at Xochicalco, Mexico, and a drawing of same by Miguel Covarrubias.
Chapter head illustrations are from *Design Motifs of Ancient Mexico*, by Encisco.

ISBN 0-7872-1305-5

Library of Congress Catalog Card Number 95-78854

Printed in the United States of America
10 9 8 7 6 5 4 3 2 1

Contents

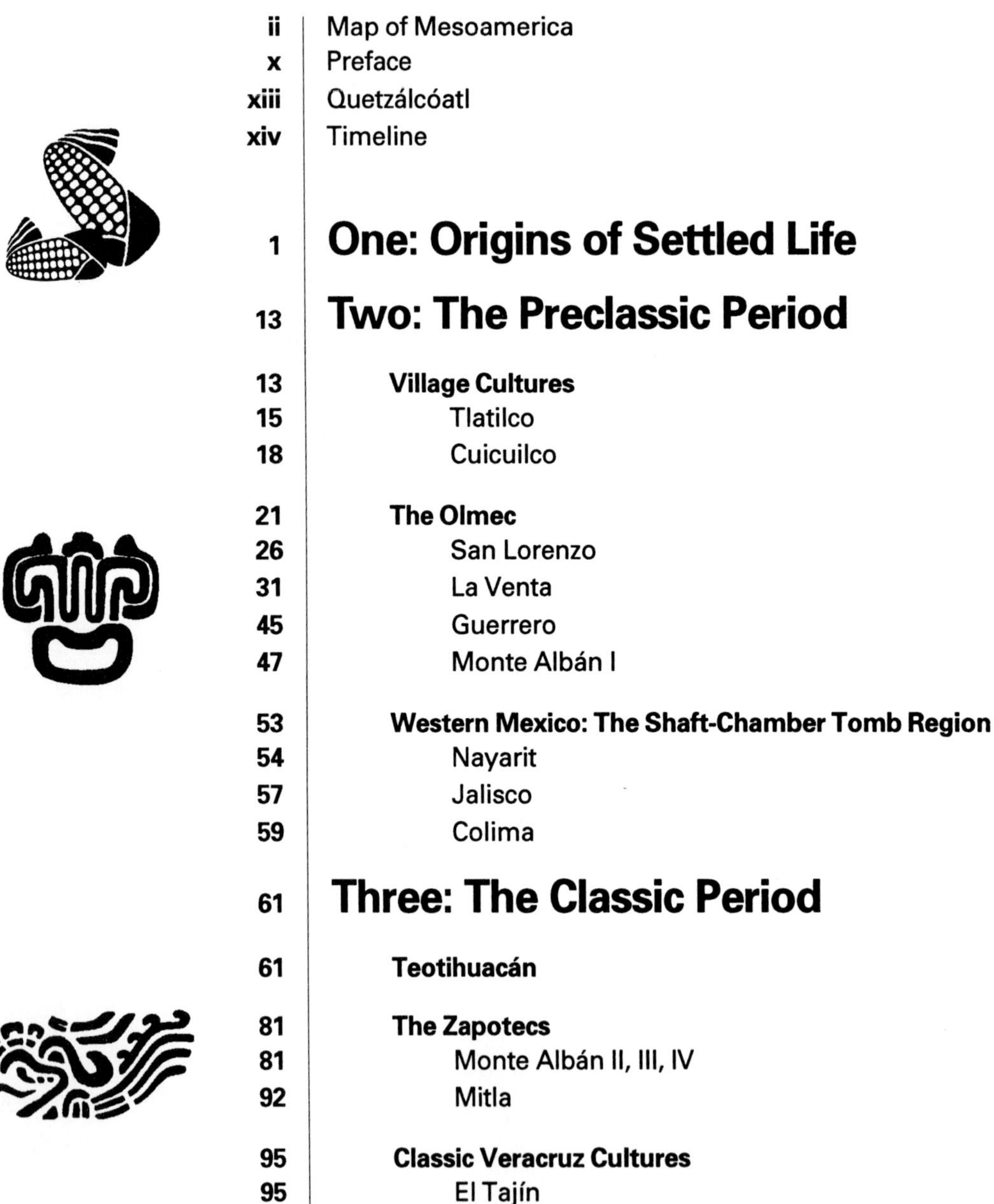

Preface

Ancient Mexico surveys major cultural developments in Mexico from Prehistory to the Conquest of Mexico in the 16th century. Highlighting major sites in Mexico and Central America, the book focuses on the important achievements at each location and provides a base of information for the reader who has little or no prior knowledge of the country's early history. Although appropriate time periods are clearly identified in each section, I have chosen to keep specific dates to a minimum, so that the reader can focus upon the achievements of each cultural group without feeling the need to memorize a myriad of uncertain and sometimes conflicting dates. A more detailed timeline is included at the beginning of the text for reference. In addition, an updated bibliography will be helpful to the reader who wishes to further explore early Mesoamerican cultures.

Our knowledge of Mexico's ancient past is expanding rapidly; new discoveries and more highly refined dating techniques continue to give us a fuller understanding of early Mesoamerican cultures. This edition revises former text material that has become outdated, and retains invaluable and timeless archaeological data. New illustrations and timelines are included. These improvements should give a more complete picture of the chronological sequence of events in Mesoamerica.

Despite the expansion of text material in this new edition, one thing has remained the same: I have tried to write an introduction to a most exciting field of study for the lay-person. I hope the book will be enjoyed as a chronological survey of Mexico's remarkable cultural history. It is intended for all who feel in need of some orientation in a beautiful and fascinating land.

All photographs were taken by the author on location, or with special permission at the following museums: the Instituto Nacional de Anthropologia Historia, Mexico, D.F. (INAH); Cicom Museum in Villahermosa, Tabasco (CC); the Leland Stanford University Museum, Stanford, California (LSUM); the

M.H.DeYoung Museum in San Francisco (DYM); the Boston Museum of Fine Arts (BMFA), and the Metropolitan Museum of Art in New York City (MMNYC).

Special thanks to two reviewers who helped to shape this text: Gerald Kohs, and Jay Leibold; each graciously sharing his expertise in the critical editing of past and current editions. Both read proof pages and offered many helpful suggestions. Jerry critiqued earlier manuscripts, Jay helped in the expansion of this new, fifth edition. Their ongoing support, friendship, and encouragement have helped me immeasurably. Last, but far from least, I am indebted to Robin Collet who creatively formatted the text and photos, and designed the striking and very relevant cover. All three were wonderful to work with. Their dependability and strict adherence to personal "deadlines" made the timely completion of this book possible.

As in previous editions, I wish to extend my heartfelt thanks to the many people in Mexico with whom I have had contact. Their friendship, courtesy, and willingness to help a stranger fills my mind and my heart with wonderful memories.

Finally, I wish to thank my husband, Donald Branum Lathrop, for his infinite patience and gentle good humor. He lovingly supports me in all endeavors, including this one.
I dedicate this book to him.

Quetzálcóatl

Quetzálcóatl, the "Plumed" or "Feathered" Serpent, was one of the most important deities in Mesoamerica. No one knows the exact origin of this god, but there is evidence that he may have been worshipped during early Preclassic times by the Olmec. Quetzálcóatl brought man knowledge of the arts, agriculture, and science. He was the god of learning and the priesthood—and he was the morning and evening star. Primarily, however, he was the creation god: he symbolized the concept that life blended into death and continued uninterruptedly onto another spiritual plane.

The name Quetzálcóatl, itself, describes this blending of earthly existence and heavenly afterworld: Quetzál, the name of a sacred bird that flew freely from the earth to the sky, and Coatl, an Indian word for the revered serpent which, in shedding its skin, represented rebirth and eternal life.

In the 10th century A.D. a powerful leader who ruled the Toltecs at Tula, in the Valley of Mexico, took the name of the ancient deity Quetzálcóatl as his own, and became his earthly representative; he worshipped only this one god. This was in striking contrast to the belief held by all of the Indian groups at this time that many gods existed and controlled all aspects of one's destiny on earth. Quetzálcóatl's god taught that all life was sacred, and Quetzálcóatl tried to please his god by abolishing human sacrifice. In addition, this influential leader encouraged the development of the arts and sciences among his people and all people of the Postclassic era. He was a gentle and just ruler who brought prestige and respect to the Toltec name.

According to historical accounts, the ruler Quetzálcóatl always wore black. He was described as being fair skinned and bearded—both of which were not common physical characteristics of the people. Five hundred years after Quetzálcóatl's reign, a man arrived by ship from a far distant land. This newcomer believed in only one god, he wore black, and he was fair skinned and bearded. This man's name was Cortes.

Archaic
7000 - 2000 B.C.

Preclassic
2000 B.C. - A.D. 200

Early Preclassic 2000 B.C. - 900 B.C.
Mid Preclassic 900 B.C - 400 B.C.
Late Preclassic 400 B.C. - A.D. 200

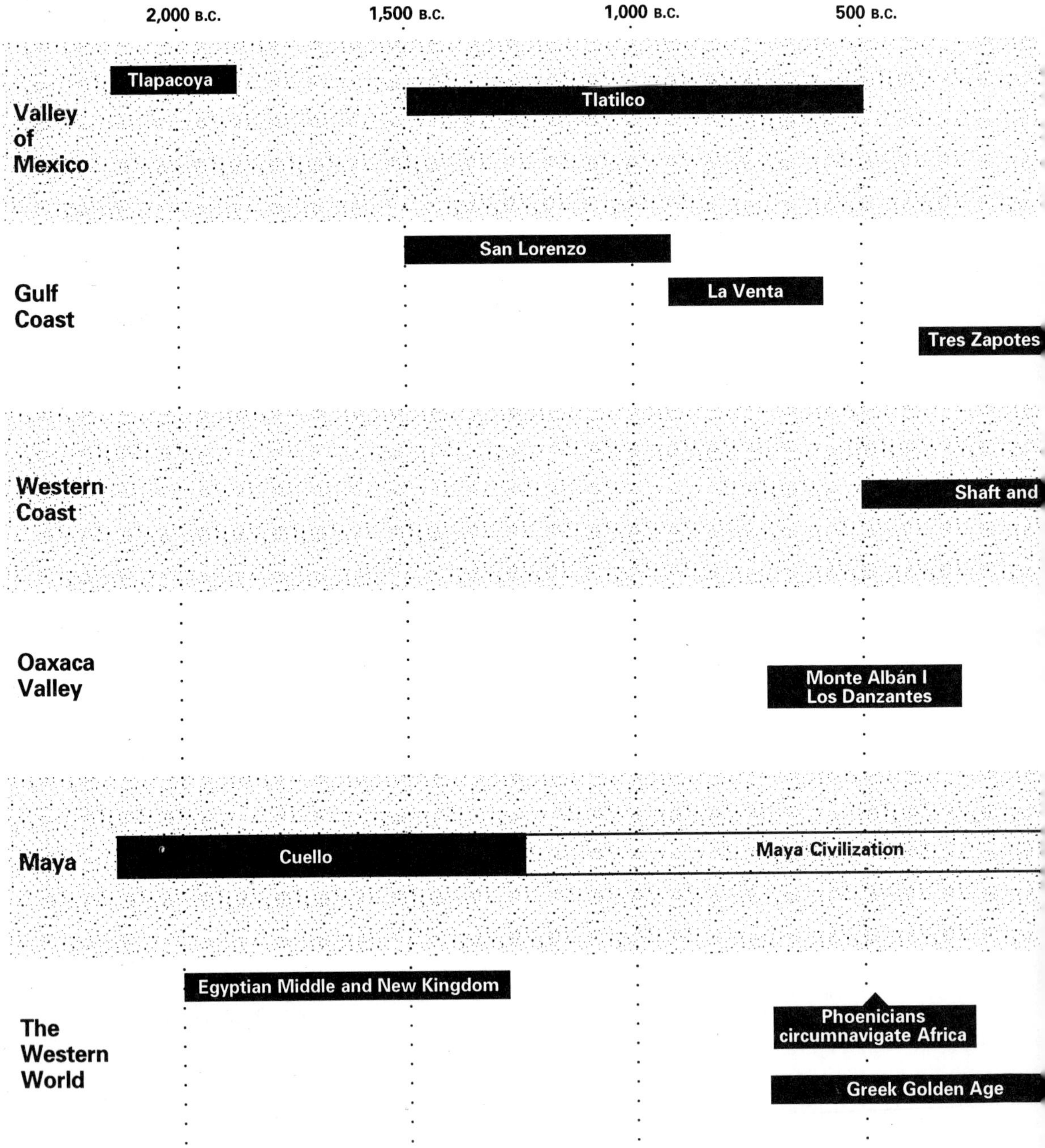

2,000 B.C. | 1,500 B.C. | 1,000 B.C. | 500 B.C.

Valley of Mexico
Tlapacoya
Tlatilco

Gulf Coast
San Lorenzo
La Venta
Tres Zapotes

Western Coast
Shaft and

Oaxaca Valley
Monte Albán I
Los Danzantes

Maya
Cuello
Maya Civilization

The Western World
Egyptian Middle and New Kingdom
Phoenicians circumnavigate Africa
Greek Golden Age

Classic

A.D. 200 - A.D. 900

Early Classic A.D. 200 - 600
Late Classic A.D. 600 - 900

Postclassic

A.D. 900 - 1521

Early Postclassic A.D. 900 - 1200
Late Postclassic A.D.1200 - 1521

Conquest

A.D. 1521

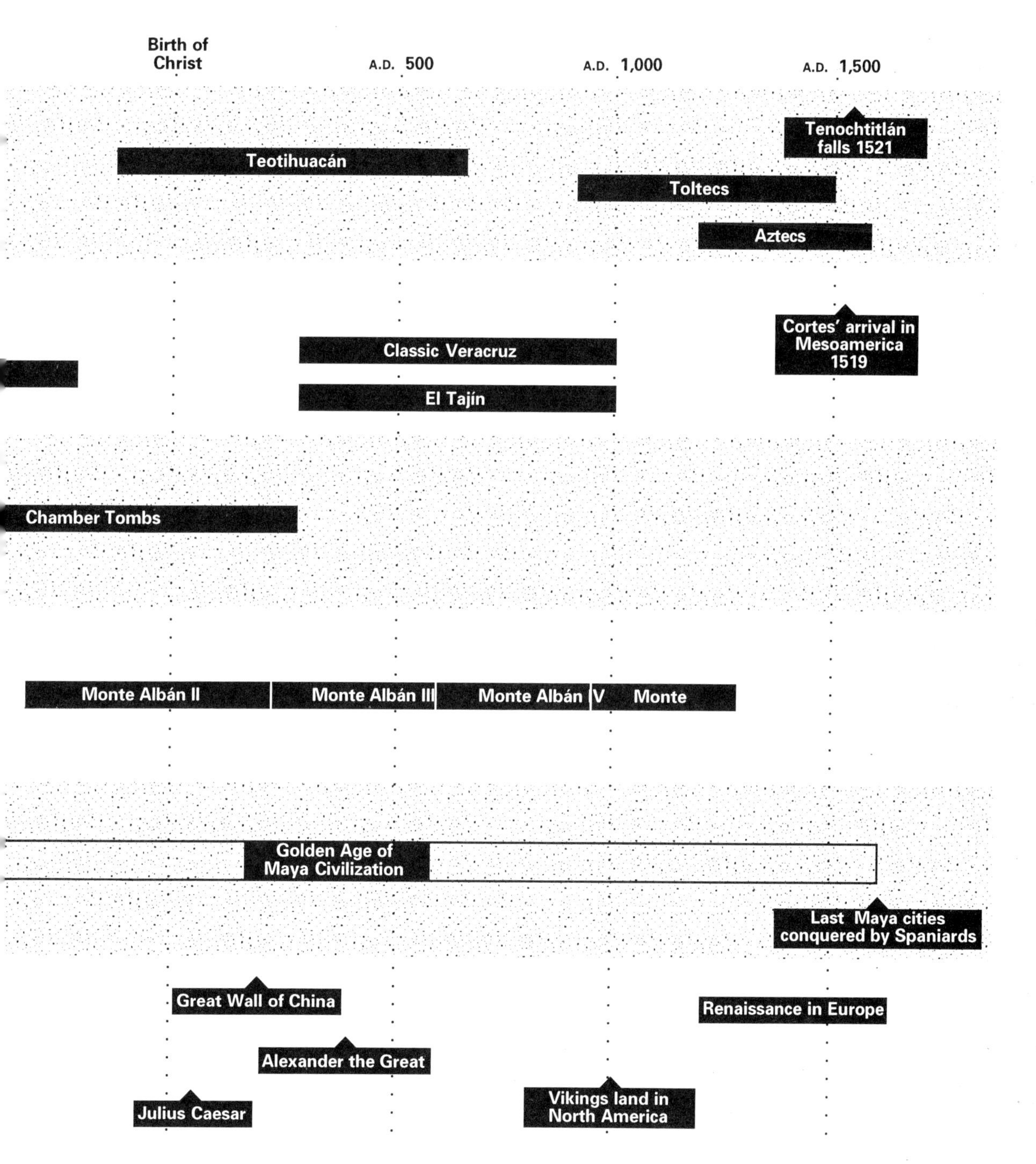

Arctic Ocean
Chukchi Sea
Siberia
Chukchi Peninsula
Bering Strait
Seward Peninsula
Onion Portage
Alaska
Bering Sea
Aleutian Islands
Pacific Ocean

Origins of Settled Life

I raise my songs,
I, Macuilxochitl,
with these I gladden the Giver of Life,
may the dance begin.

Macuilxochitl, daughter of Tlacaelel
(Translation by Leon-Portilla 1967)

Early Migrations

It is generally accepted that humans first crossed from northeast Asia to Alaska by means of a wide strip of land called the Beringia Land Bridge in the Bering Strait region. This land mass was exposed at the height of the Wisconsin Glaciation, the fourth and last major ice advance to occur during the Pleistocene period (1.8 million to 10,000 years ago). Sometime after 75,000 B.C., the sea level was lowered by several hundred feet because much of the water was contained in great ice sheets. Due to the lowered water level, a wide strip of land was exposed, and Asia and Alaska were united (fig. 1). Large animals were able to move freely across Beringia during this final phase of the Wisconsin Glaciation. Early hunters could have followed these game animals without even being aware that they were leaving one continent and entering another, as climatic conditions were the same on both sides of the strait.

Migrations from Asia to Alaska could easily have taken place for as long as the great sheets of ice existed. Unfortunately, all evidence of these journeys lies under the present-day strait. The physical remains that may still exist would be covered not only by 300 feet or more of water, but also by as much as 100 feet of sediment. For this reason, tangible evidence of these crossings from one continent to another in the Bering Strait region will

1. *Opposite.* Map of Bering Strait Region during the final phase of the Wisconsin Glaciation; shaded area indicates ice sheets linking the two continents. Humans and animals could travel between the two land masses during this time.

probably never be found. Any new information that we might obtain must come from the adjacent land areas in Siberia or Alaska.

According to some archaeologists, there is evidence that nomadic hunters crossed Beringia from northeast Asia to Alaska at least 25,000 years ago when optimum conditions prevailed.

We do not know exactly when it was that the first migrations into the Western Hemisphere began. The **Land Bridge** could have been crossed as early as 50,000 years ago when climatic conditions became more favorable, but there is no physical proof to substantiate this early date. The migrations could have continued from that time until approximately 8000 B.C. when the Ice Age ended, the great ice sheets melted, and the Land Bridge was once again covered by water.

Very little tangible evidence of human presence has been found near the coastal areas of Alaska or Siberia dating from before 5000 B.C. The reason is that when the massive glaciers began to melt, the water rose to a point close to its present level, flooding the settlements that may have existed close to the sea. Some inland sites have been found, but because of the barren terrain and the harsh conditions that exist away from the sea, excavations of most of the interior locations have generally yielded sparse and infrequent remains. The inland environment simply could not continuously support the game animals that were needed to nourish the early hunters.

However, one very important early site was discovered by the late J.L. Giddings of Brown University. The settlement is called Onion Portage, and it lies on the Kobuk River just 125 miles inland from the Chukchi Sea (refer to fig. 1). Onion Portage is the oldest coastal site that has ever been discovered north of the Aleutian Islands, and artifacts that have been found at the deepest levels of excavation may prove to be as much as 15,000 years old. Some of the tools that were discovered here closely resemble those from sites around Lake Baikal, in Siberia, that were occupied some 15,000 years ago, thus providing some evidence of a link between the two continents.

Cultural Remains

The earliest nomadic tribes that entered the Western Hemisphere were constantly moving in order to survive; they followed the big game animals, which were their major food source. Their weapons and implements were flint-tipped spears, knives, and crude skin scrapers, some of which appear to be quite similar in design and function to those used in Asia during the same time period. These tools and weapons have been found all the way from Alaska to the southern tip of South America; many have been found at sites in the Central Highlands area of Mexico, a region rich in cultural remains that date from the earliest Paleolithic Indian occupation, perhaps as much as 20,000 years ago, up to the time of the Aztecs in the 16th century. These tools and weapons have provided us with some understanding of the New World's earliest inhabitants and their continuing struggle to survive.

New Theories

Although the Beringia Land Bridge was exposed from 25,000 to 8000 B.C., some geologists now suggest that it may also have been exposed as early as 170,000 years ago, and again 70,000 years ago. Newly dated fossils give evidence of an earlier Beringia crossing (Goodman 1981). For example, new techniques have been developed that enable us to date fossil remains far more accurately than with the more conservative Carbon 14 process, which has a 40,000 year limit. As a result, many newly tested bone fragments have proven to be far older than once believed. One such new dating technique, developed by Dr. Jeffrey Bada, a geochemist at the Scripps Institute of Oceanography in LaJolla, California, measures a natural biological process called "racemization," whereby amino acids in living organisms gradually racemize, or change, after death. Using this technique, Bada established that two fully "modern" skulls discovered in the San Diego area are at least 50,000 years old, which is 25,000 years older than the conservative Beringia crossing time frame of 25,000-8000 B.C. Another skull, unearthed in Sunnyvale, California, has been tentatively dated to be 70,000 years old. After publishing his findings in *Science* (May 17, 1974), Bada dated three other Paleo-Indian bones with ages of 39,000 years or more. Conclusive evidence of early human presence in the Americas at least 40,000 years ago was also established on Santa Rosa Island, off the coast of Santa Barbara, California. At this site, Dr. Rainer Berger, a UCLA archaeologist and geophysicist, confirmed that an ancient, stone lined cooking pit with burned fragments of animal bones dated from more than 40,000 years ago (Berger 1975).

Recent archaeological digging in Brazil's remote backlands have also led scientists to push back the probable date of early settlers in the New World. A stone chopper—the most primitive tool used by humans— and fossilized bone fragments were found buried in layers of sediment beneath the rock floor of a cave. The layer in which the fossils were discovered is believed to be at least 300,000 years old. Although the discovery has not been conclusively confirmed, Dr. Jacques Labeyrie, physicist and founder of the Center of Weak Radiation at the National Scientific Research Center in Gif-Sur-Yvette, France said, "We are 90 percent certain of the age of these bones. If confirmed, it would be the first positive proof of pre-Neanderthal groups in the New World. In addition, it would refute the prevailing belief that migrations to the Americas from Asia occurred only 10,000 to 25,000 years ago" (*Science* 1994). Although the evidence of an earlier dating for human presence in the Americas is limited and somewhat speculative at this point, new discoveries might ultimately prove more conclusively that migrations into the New World occurred far earlier than previously believed.

The Central Highlands of Mexico

The oldest living site yet discovered in Mexico has been found at **Tlapacoya**, which lies approximately forty miles east of Mexico City in the Central Highlands region. A tentative dating of some of the cultural remains found at this location indicates that the sites may have been inhabited as early as 19,000 B.C. **Animal bones** discarded by hunters have been discovered here, as well as some cooking hearths and stone implements. Because of the extreme antiquity of the site, however, the cultural evidence that would provide a more complete picture of human existence at this location is extremely limited.

Animal bones, cooking hearths and stone implements from Tlapacoyo date from 19,000 B.C.

Near Tequixquiac, an area just north of present-day Mexico City, rich fossil beds have yielded important remnants of early human presence in Mexico, most of which are buried some forty feet underground. Some of the remains date from as early as 10,000 B.C. The most unusual fossil found at this location is the sacrum of an extinct llama, which had carefully and deliberately been changed to look like the head of a wild boar. Indeed, 12,000 years ago, with just a few alterations to a bone, early humans left us evidence of timeless creativity very much like the impulses that we experience today.

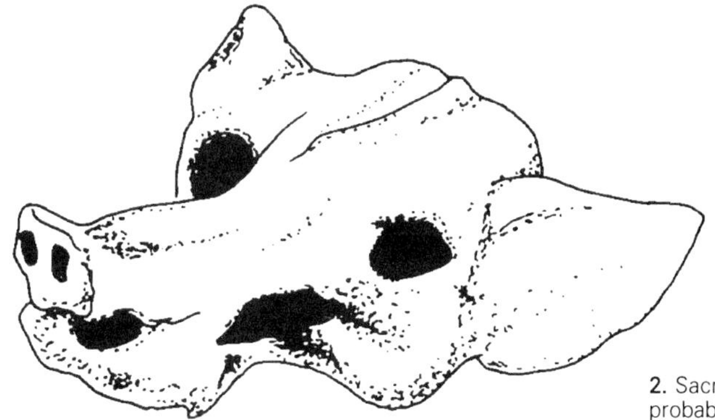

2. Sacrum bone of extinct animal, probably a Llama, Tequixquiac, Mexico. c. 10,000 B.C.

In 1947, an important discovery was made at Tepexpán, which is located in the Valley of Mexico near Mexico City. As construction workers prepared a site for a new hospital, they discovered the fossilized skull of a large, now extinct mammoth, and a well-worn flint. Geologists were called to investigate the site, and the entire area was scanned with a device that directs electrical currents into the ground with linear electrodes. The impulses from the electrodes identify areas of resistance in the earth where foreign objects lie. The first two scans at the site were unsuccessful. The third attempt pinpointed an area just 46 inches below the surface of the ground where parts of a human figure were found. Archaeologists named the figure "Tepexpán Man." Fluorine analysis of the remains dates them to roughly 9000 B.C. The skull, the long bones of the arms and legs, and parts of the spinal column and ribs were found facing down, in a crouching position. Because of the unusual position of the body, and the fact that only those parts of the skeleton facing the once swampy area were disturbed, it appears that the person who died here was found by animals that ate those portions of the remains projecting above the mud. The remaining bones were intact and undisturbed because they were covered with a deposit of calcium carbonate. The skull was especially well preserved, and studies identify many characteristics shared with present day American Indians and some East Asian groups.

It has not been conclusively proven whether Tepexpán Man was a man or a woman. At first, the remains were thought to be of a male of about 55 to 60 years old. More recent studies indicate that Tepexpán "Man" may have been a woman of

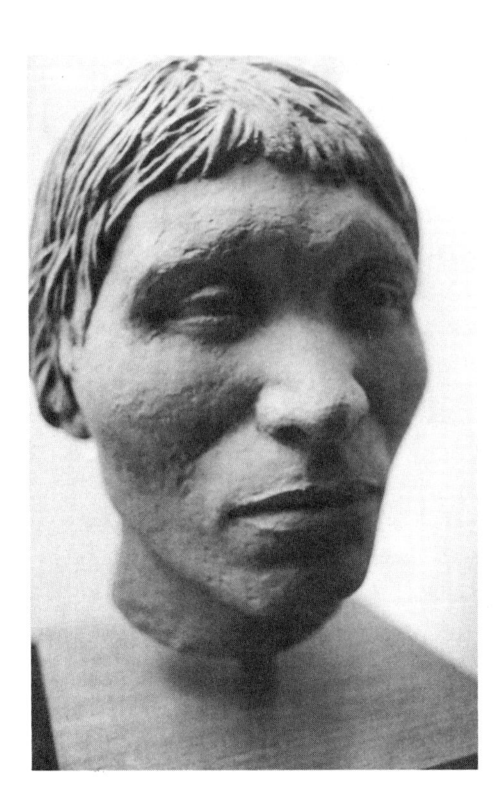

3. Reconstruction of Tepexpán Man. The skull was discovered at Tepexpán in a once swampy area of Lake Texcoco, Valley of Mexico. c. 9000 to 8000 B.C.

about 5 foot 7 inches in height and approximately thirty years of age. Despite the controversy, this important discovery clearly shows human presence in the Americas at an early time. In addition, some of the East Asian physical characteristics of the skull seem to support the Beringia crossing theory.

The Transition from Nomadic to Settled Life

Little is known about the earliest communities in Mesoamerica other than that they were established as a result of a dramatic change in lifestyle. This change came about sometime between the end of the Pleistocene epoch, some 10,000 years ago, and 5000 B.C., when it was discovered that the seeds of some plants could be planted and then nurtured long enough to produce an edible product. This discovery marked the end of nomadic life and ushered in a more settled phase in human development when permanent communities were established. Then, as a result of an increasingly plentiful food supply, the early inhabitants began to devote more time to activities other than hunting and gathering. Permanent shelters were built, and a wider variety of tools and cooking implements were made.

Since there have been no discoveries of houses built prior to 3000 B.C., it is assumed that the earliest inhabitants must have lived in makeshift shelters. Then, sometime after 1350 B.C., the one-room, thatched-roof house made an appearance (Flannery 1976). These simple structures had a framework of four corner posts and a floor made of clay which was stamped into a smooth, compacted surface. The exterior of the house was faced with finger-sized reeds or canes, called "wattle," which were then covered with a thick layer, or "daubs," of clay. This type of house is referred to as a "wattle-and-daub" structure. Some of the houses were left this way, others were given a final application of whitewash, mud plaster, or limestone. A general inventory of the kinds of objects that were found inside each house includes a variety of tools, bone needles for sewing, cutting tools, and fragments of pottery, grinding stones, and jars. Corn kernels, beans, avocado pits, and bones of small animals have also been found in these first formal dwellings. By 1000 B.C., the wattle-and-daub houses were common and abundant (Flannery 1976).

Agriculture

The most important agricultural discoveries in Mexico were made during the years 1960-64 when the American archaeologist Richard S. MacNeish began to explore the dry caves of Tehuacan, Puebla, in the highlands area of central Mexico in order to establish the presence of early food cultivation. MacNeish distinguished two kinds of settlements in Tehuacan: "macroband" camps which were occupied by 15-25 persons, and "microband" camps, which were small units of two to five individuals. These groups were most probably family units, since both men's and women's tools were found. Some of the earliest occupied sites were in caves, while others were in more open areas; they were not villages, in the traditional sense, but rather temporary huts and windbreaks that provided shelter to the semi-nomadic groups (MacNeish 1964-72).

During these years of excavation, MacNeish discovered the preserved remains of many of Mesoamerica's most important

We now know that the use and cultivation of corn was preceded by a wide variety of plants such as beans, peppers, pumpkins, tomatoes, avocados, and a variety of squashes.

and earliest food crops, including corn, in the dry caves of Tehuacan. Since it was originally believed that corn was the **first major domesticated plant** in the New World, there has been an ongoing search to find the oldest preserved remains of the plant. Logically, the discarded remains of an early and important food source such as corn would also identify the areas where the first small communities, called hamlets, were built. Corn, as we know it, is a cultivated product that bears little resemblance to its original, wild form. It is a unique plant in that its pollen is located in the tassels, and the seeds that must be pollinated are enclosed in a tough and fibrous husk. Thus, to reach its present size and quality, corn must have been pollinated and cross-bred by humans many times. This could only have occurred when there was some knowledge of the principles of pollination and other agricultural techniques.

Richard MacNeish excavated five caves in the Tehuacan Valley during the 1960-64 diggings, and reconstructed the incidence and frequency of food production spanning a lengthy time period. He discovered food specimens in different levels in the caves and dated and placed them in a proper time sequence. This became the story of the domestication of corn and the move toward settled life. According to MacNeish, the earliest evidence of plant domestication occurred somewhere between 10,000 and 6500 B.C., when the Valley of Mexico was somewhat different than it is today. As the valley recovered from the effects of the last Ice Age, it was covered by a mesquite-like grass, and the climate was cool. The people were engaged in communal hunting for small game animals such as rabbits and antelope. This stage in development is referred to as the *Ajuereado* phase which ended around 6500 B.C. (MacNeish 1964).

During the subsequent *El Riego* phase, which was sometime between 6500 and 5000 B.C., the climate in the Valley of Mexico began to change to more closely resemble what we see today. The early settlers gathered in larger groups, and communities were harvesting the edible seeds of the wild squash. The people also planted seeds in the ground and returned at a later time to harvest their crops. This was the beginning of plant domestication and the so-called Food-Producing Revolution of the New World.

By the *Coxcatlan* phase (5000-3500 B.C.), a wide variety of plant foods were cultivated. In addition, wild corn, a rather fragile grass with long glumes similar to the hulls of pod corn, made its appearance. This had two husks which parted easily so that the small, hard seeds could disburse. Although the origin of domestic corn has not been conclusively traced, we do know that it first made its appearance in the Western Hemisphere. The two most widely accepted theories about corn's early ancestors are as follows:

1) corn descended from a now extinct wild pod-popcorn in which individual kernels were enclosed in and protected by chaff rather than by a cupulate fruit base (Mangelsdorf 1974).

2) corn may be descended from the widespread Mexican grass teosinte (Mangelsdorf, MacNeish, Galinat 1964).

Despite the debate, the most important issue is to recognize the agricultural achievements of the *Coxcatlan*-phase people, who made the most important discovery ever attained by the

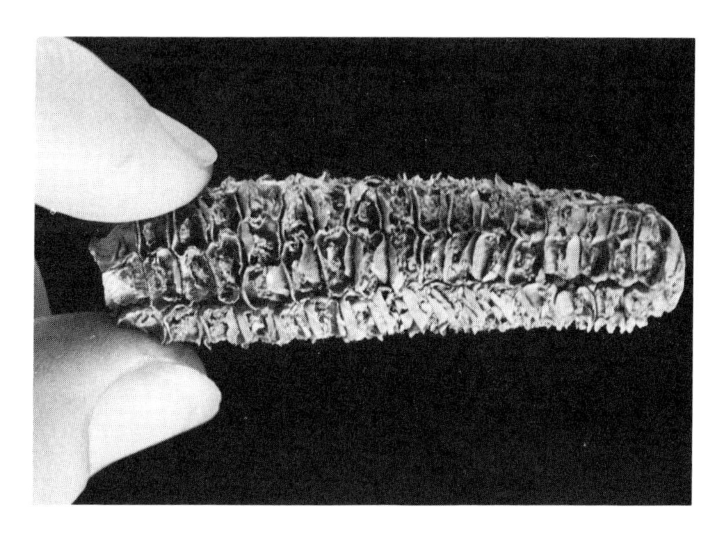

4. Corn cob found approximately fifteen feet below ground in the Valley of Mexico. c. 1500 to 1000 B.C. Estimated age based on size, development, and burial level.

American Indians. More than any other domesticated food, corn created and fed the native New World civilization.

At the time of the *Abejas* phase (3500-2300 B.C.), enough food was harvested to allow for the establishment of small hamlets consisting of circular pit houses that probably had pole and thatch roofs.

Richard MacNeish proved how increased food production allowed the early inhabitants of this valley to remain in one location and gradually develop into more complex societies. In addition, it was noted by MacNeish that sometime between 5000 and 2000 B.C., certain changes that undoubtedly were a result of early agricultural experiments occurred in some of the major plants. The genetic structure of beans changed at an early date to make them more edible, and maize (corn) underwent a series of changes that resulted in a steady increase in quality and cob size. These two basic foods provided the nutrients that were essential to the well being of the early peoples in this region. Maize provided the necessary carbohydrates in the diet, and beans the plant protein. Fats and oils came from small animals that were snared, as well as from an abundant supply of avocados. Other plants underwent similar changes which improved their size and quality (Mangelsdorf, MacNeish, Galinat 1964).

Thus, a nutritional breakthrough occurred. As a result, the nomadic peoples began to establish permanent settlements. In time, the small groups merged with one another to form larger, agriculturally oriented communities with more diversified activities. The small communities, or hamlets, increased in size and population and became organized villages. In effect, the onset and development of a non-nomadic lifestyle was made possible by agricultural production (Flannery 1976).

Summary

The search for the earliest inhabitants of Mesoamerica continues today. Although few skeletal remains of great antiquity have been discovered, an ample selection of tools, weapons, and other cultural artifacts have been found in various locations between Alaska and South America, establishing human presence in the Western Hemisphere sometime between 25,000 and 8000 B.C. Some early sites may have existed in central Mexico as early as 19,000 B.C., but there is little cultural evidence to substantiate this early date; the final step toward settled life did not come about until agricultural skills were firmly established. Corn, which was a major food source, was domesticated by 5000 B.C. At this time, small groups of people began to live together in settled, productive, agricultural hamlets. As farming techniques became even more sophisticated, food production increased. Because of this, the small settlements expanded in territorial size, population, and occupational diversity. They became the earliest village communities. Although very little is known about this early period, future excavations will continue to provide information that will increase our limited base of knowledge about the first settled communities in Mesoamerica.

The Preclassic Period

2000 B.C. to A.D. 200

Village Cultures

In the earliest phase of the Preclassic period, people lived in established villages where they cultivated a great variety of foodstuffs. These small communities were occupied on a permanent basis and life became more sedentary; there was time for the gradual addition of the arts to settled village life. By 2000 B.C., these simple farming communities were spread throughout Mesoamerica. Although food production was the most essential concern of the people, the villagers also made objects that were necessary for everyday activities. Simple but functional pottery has been found, as well as other objects of a possible religious or ritual purpose. Many pieces dating from this early time have been found in the remains of ancient villages in the Valley of Tehuacan, at Puerto Marques on the Pacific Coast, and at numerous sites in the Valley of Mexico. In the Valley of Mexico, near the present-day cities of El Arbolillo, Zacatenco, and Ticoman, many of these villages were clustered along the shores of the great lakes which existed there at that time. One of the largest was Tlatilco, which means "where things are hidden." A high level of artistic achievement was reached by the artists of Preclassic Tlatilco.

5. *Opposite.* Clay figure displays agility often associated with acrobats or dancers. Tlatilco, Valley of Mexico. Early Preclassic period. (INAH)

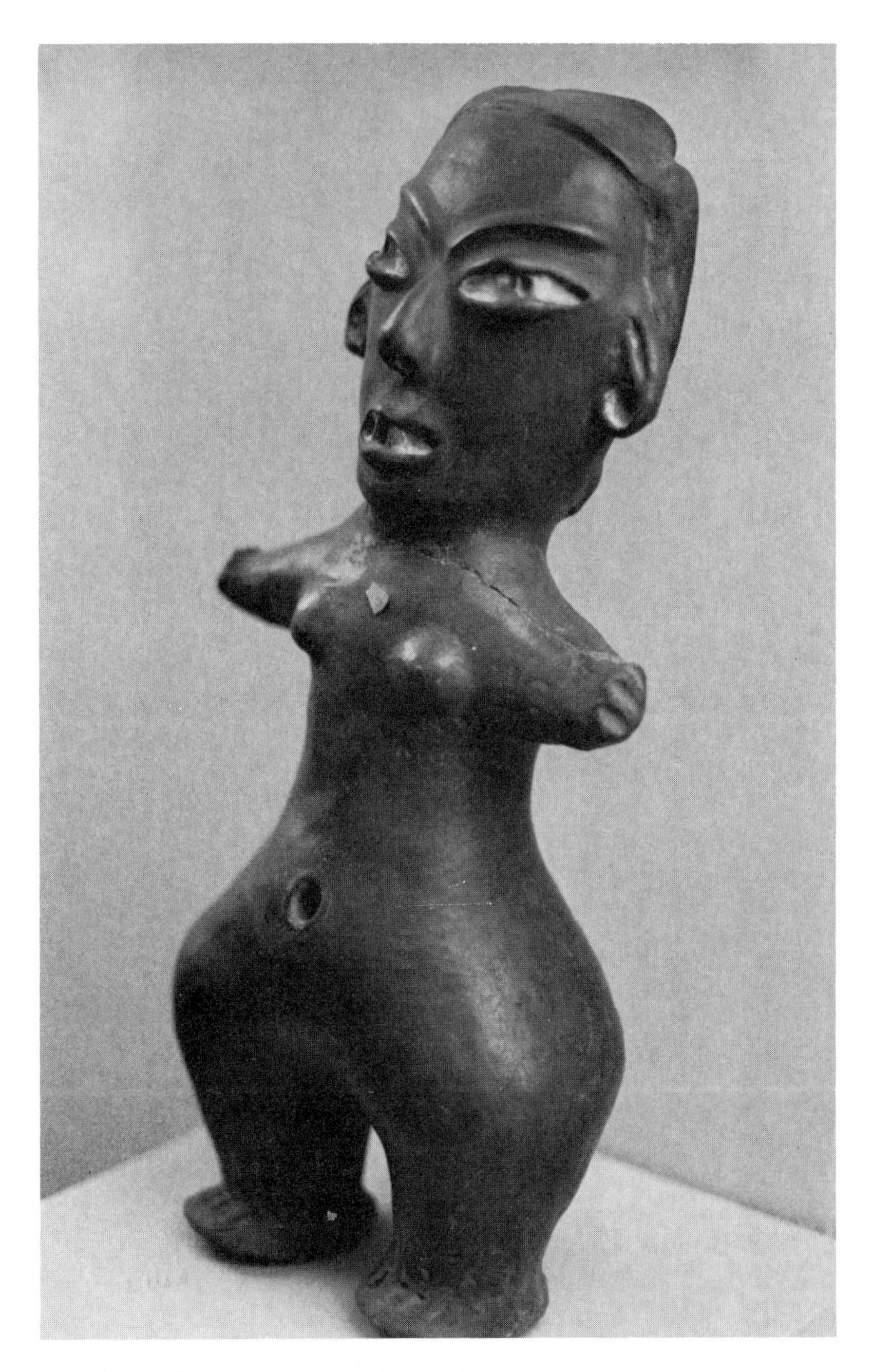

6. Female figure, Tlatilco. Once called "pretty ladies," these figures were probably meant to ensure fertility in the afterlife. Height: 5 inches. (INAH.)

Tlatilco

Tlatilco lay hidden under a thriving brickyard on the outskirts of Mexico City until around 1940, when workers began to find figurines and pottery in the clay they used to make bricks. The figurines were attractive, but no thought was given to their possible value. It soon became apparent, however, that these objects were of great antiquity and of value to collectors and scholars. In 1942, a full-scale scientific excavation was undertaken under the direction of the Mexican artist and archaeologist Miguel Covarrubias. Some two hundred graves, complete with burial offerings, were excavated. It was the real beginning of our knowledge of this important village.

Tlatilco was a large village, but there was no monumental or religious architecture found there; there was only evidence of a simple wattle-and-daub type house construction. Tlatilco's most unique feature was that it contained hundreds of burials within the residential complex. Many of the graves and some refuse debris were analyzed, and documentation of a long occupation of the site was made. Most of the burials were complete with elaborate funerary offerings. There were bowls and long-necked jars of great beauty. Many figurines displayed a wide range of activities: there were ballplayers, dancers, acrobats, and musicians. However, female figurines were more frequently represented than other figural types found in the graves. It is believed that they were **fertility fetishes** of the utmost importance in burial rites.

A fetish is an object that is believed to have magical powers.

Although most of the offerings found in the graves were of interest to scholars, the female figurines attracted the greatest attention. The late American archaeologist, George Vaillant, took an interest in the figures from Tlatilco and the other nearby village sites, and classified them in the first Preclassic chronology ever devised (Vaillant 1930). This early work was later refined by Pina Chan and Paul Tolstoy, resulting in a complete picture of ceramic traits in the Preclassic period.

The female figurines of Tlatilco, and other valley sites, are between three to five inches tall and are hand-molded from clay. Most exhibit exaggerated sexual characteristics, with wide hips and clearly detailed breasts; many depict women who are pregnant or holding a small child. For the most part, they are unclothed. Occasionally, they wear skirts along with elaborate collars (they are usually bare-breasted), necklaces, and earrings. The hair is always arranged artistically in a variety of styles, and their heads are often covered by a turban or a small hat. The womens' faces display similar characteristics: slashes for eyes, a pinched-clay nose, and filed teeth. The arms and feet of the Tlatilco figurines are greatly simplified. This lack of detail would seem to suggest that they were not important details in the representation of the female body. We are not absolutely sure that these figures were intended to represent fertility, but evidence points in that direction. Assuming they were fertility fetishes, one can understand their profound value as funerary offerings, and the role they could play in the concept of continuing life after death.

In addition to the female figurines that were found here, there were also masked individuals, and joined figures that may represent Siamese twins. There were human images with three eyes, two noses, and two mouths: each mouth, nose, outer eye and shared central eye forms a separate image that faces away from the other, thus presenting a dual identity. Another important dual image is of a man who is divided from the crown of his head through the center of his body. One side of his body is a skeleton, and the other side depicts a living man. These unusual representations appear to be important symbolic expressions of **duality**. The concept of duality is the belief that all things have an opposite: good and evil exist side by side as traits that exist in everyone; light is followed by darkness; night is followed by day; life leads to death and in death one begins life again, etc. This concept of duality in all aspects of life on earth is inherent in ancient Mexican thought and culture.

Duality: the belief that all things have an opposite.

Although Tlatilco was active about 2000 B.C., the highest level of artistic achievement appears to have occurred from about 1000 B.C. to 500 B.C. when occupational specialization began. At this later date, the most talented artisans were able to devote all of their creative energy to the making of fine pottery and votive figures. They reached a high level of technical accomplishment without interference from outside sources. The quality of their products was maintained, and the artisans produced work of the highest level of aesthetic sophistication and technique for as long as the site was inhabited. During later

7. Female figure with two faces, Valley of Mexico. One central, shared eye creates both right and left face. Clay. (INAH.)

centuries increasing religious pressure developed, and the arts were forced to follow the dictates of the priests who came to power. Never again would artistic freedom exist as it did at Tlatilco, and the other Valley of Mexico sites, during the Preclassic period.

Tlatilco, Arbolillo, and Zacatenco are truly representative of the typical early Preclassic Mesoamerican village. They were agriculturally productive communities that used milling stones to grind their grain, hand-woven baskets to store their food-stuffs, and clay pottery for both functional and ritual use. Community life was relatively permanent, and most of the inhabitants lived in wattle-and-daub houses; there were no temples or pyramids. As the Preclassic period drew to a close, however, important changes began to occur. The small villages gradually advanced toward a way of life that was both urban and

8. Female figure with mirror on chest, Tlatilco. Early Preclassic mirrors made from magnetite and ilmenite are highly polished, and can reflect images or produce fire. (INAH.)

9. Standing female figure, Las Bocas, Puebla. Clay. Height: 20".

ceremonial. By 400 B.C. small, densely populated villages, whose population now concentrated around a temple-pyramid nucleus, began to make their appearance. This development is reflective of the expanding importance of the priestly class, and it anticipates the Priest-ruled cities of the Classic Period in Mesoamerica. It is best represented at Cuicuilco, in the Valley of Mexico.

Cuicuilco

The massive, circular platform at Cuicuilco was constructed at the end of the Preclassic period, when early village civilization in the Valley of Mexico first began to give way to the building of cities with monumental, religious architecture. It was built with stone slabs which were firmly mortared together with clay. The diameter of the structure measured 370 feet, and four circular stages rose about 65 feet in height. The two lower stages were built with an altar on top, and stairs on the west and east led to the uppermost platform. The stairs prefigured the later temple stairways of Classic period pyramids. Near the close of the Preclassic era, a river of lava from a nearby erupting volcano buried the platform and adjoining burial grounds. Fortunately, 20th century excavations at the site have revealed much of the original structure, confirming Cuicuilco's importance as the most prominent early example of monumental architecture in Mexico. Whether the priestly class or family dynasties ruled in the Valley of Mexico at this time is still under discussion. The relevant fact is that there was a growth of a new, elite leadership that had near total control over the decision making processes at each major site. The establishment of a new class structure, and the subsequent construction of religious architecture and ceremonial buildings began to change life in Mesoamerica for all time.

10. Monument I, Olmec colossal head from La Venta.
Parque La Venta, Villahermosa,Tabasco.

The Olmec

It would appear that there was a gradual and predictable evolution of man in Mesoamerica, from earliest times well into the Preclassic period—but this was not so. The first hint of a different culture existing during the Preclassic came in the early 1930's from excavations of a site about fifty miles south of Mexico City. This was Gualupita, and it was the last Preclassic village to be excavated by George and Susannah Vaillant.

It was found that Gualupita was a **stratified** village and burial ground. It was initially discovered, as Tlatilco had been, by brick-yard operations. When the Vaillants excavated the site, they found that the topmost levels dated to the Postclassic period. Below, was a Preclassic level of occupation which contained figurine types of superior workmanship, and of a style that was not typical of the Valley of Mexico sites. Of particular interest were two large, hollow clay figurines that were unlike anything yet seen. They had full cheeks, infantile facial features and down-turned mouths. The Vaillants identified them as representing an unusual "babyface type of sculpture in Southern Mexico" (Vaillant and Vaillant 1934). These were among the earliest Olmec-style objects found in a preclassic settlement.

Stratified means that evidence of occupation was found in successive layers or "strata" of earth dating from different periods of time.

The first official recognition of this style had been the accomplishment of Marshall Saville, who was head of the Museum of the American Indian in New York City in 1929. He noted that there were many objects found in southern Veracruz that had infantile features, oval eyes, and snarling mouths . Since this Gulf Coast region is rich in rubber tree forests, Saville called the culture "Olmeca," meaning "people from the land of rubber." When Covarubbias later excavated at Tlatilco, he found similar Olmec-style figurines in the graves. It was apparent that both Tlatilco and Gualupita were villages that had been influenced and perhaps even inhabited in earliest times by a vastly different culture. Subsequent investigations in Central Mexico have confirmed this picture of early, preclassic Olmec influence on the early village cultures.

History of Olmec discoveries, 1869-1945

In 1869, the Mexican scholar Jose Melgar y Serrano submitted a brief notice to the bulletin of the Mexican Society of Geography and Statistics. It read:

> In 1862, I was in the region of San Andres Tuxtla, a town of the state of Veracruz, in Mexico. During my excursions, I learned that a colossal head had been unearthed a few years before, in the

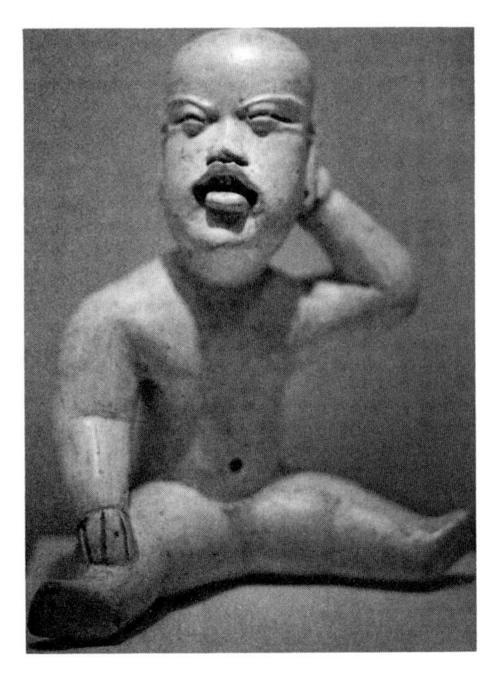

11. Olmec Baby figure. Height: 11 inches. (MNYC.)

12. Baby figure with ball. Early Preclassic period. (DYM.)

> following manner. Some one-and-a-half leagues from a sugar-cane hacienda, on the western slopes of the Sierra of San Martin, a laborer of this hacienda, while cutting the forest for his field, discovered on the surface of the ground what looked like the bottom of a great iron kettle turned upside down. He notified the owner of the hacienda, who ordered its excavation. And in place of the kettle was discovered the above-mentioned head. It was left in the excavation as one would not think to move it, being of granite and measuring two yards in height with corresponding proportions...On my arrival at the hacienda I asked the owner to take me to look at it. We went, and I was struck with surprise: as a work of art, it is without exaggeration a magnificent sculpture...but what astonished me was the Ethiopic type represented. I reflected that there had undoubtedly been Africans in this country, and that this had been in the first epoch of the world.

This article was accompanied by an engraving of what we now know as Monument A at Tres Zapotes.

In 1925, the Danish archaeologist Frans Blom and American anthropologist Oliver La Farge journeyed through the Gulf

Coast jungles of Veracruz and Tabasco. They proceeded overland along the Veracruz Coast and then made their way up the Tonala River in Western Tabasco. After branching off into a tributary stream, they finally arrived at the swampy island of La Venta, the greatest of all the Olmec ceremonial centers. The site was complete with magnificent stone sculpture and giant stone heads. Unfortunately, Blom and LaFarge did not realize the significance of their discovery, and attributed the ruins to the ancient Maya culture.

Two years later, the German archaeologist Hermann Beyer, read a report written by Blom and LaFarge describing an Olmec-style monument they had discovered on their journey to La Venta. Beyer saw at once the unmistakable similarity between a small stone carving that had been in his possession and the monument described in the article. He proposed that these similar objects be ascribed to the Olmec style. However, as previously noted, Marshall Saville was the first to formally recognize the Olmec style in 1929.

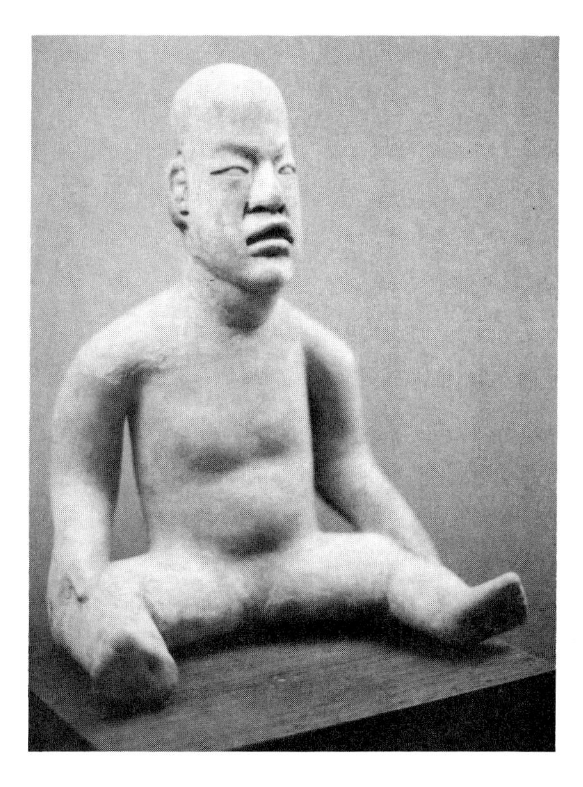

13. Olmec Baby figure. (INAH.)

14. Hollow Baby figure, Las Bocas, Puebla. Clay. Height: 30 inches. (MNYC.)

In 1932, George Vaillant published a paper describing strange, almost Oriental-like pieces from the Gulf Coast regions, and again applied the name "Olmec" to this unique style.

Matthew Stirling made the greatest discoveries of all in the jungles of the southern Gulf Coast region. In 1938, Stirling visited Melgar's colossal head at Tres Zapotes. As impressed as he was by his first view of the head, he was more intrigued by the number of great earthen mounds located in this area. Stirling began a massive, two-year excavation of the site, at which time he discovered the extraordinary monument we now call Stela C, which is the oldest dated artifact that can be attributed to the Olmec culture. On one side of the stone, there is carved a date using the same Long Count system used by the Classic Period Maya. On the other side is carved an Olmec-style, **were-jaguar** face. Using J. Eric Thompson's correlation of Maya and Christian calendars, Stirling was able to date Stela C in the year 31 B.C. This was three hundred years before the beginning of the Classic Maya civilization. The immediate implication was that the Olmec civilization pre-dated the Maya, and that the calendrical aspect of Maya culture may have been

Were-Jaguar: part human, part jaguar.

15. Olmec Were-Jaguar. The combination of feline-like mouth, paws, and human body form identifies this were-jaguar image. Parque La Venta.

invented by the Olmec. From 1939 to 1945, Stirling continued his excavations throughout the Gulf Coast regions.

The area called San Lorenzo Tenochtitlán was first explored by Matthew Stirling and Philip Drucker for the Smithsonian Institute and the National Geographic Society in 1945 and 1946. Although Stirling maintained that the Olmec culture was the first high civilization of Mexico, it was not until 1957, when radiocarbon testing at La Venta established dates ranging from at least 1000 to 400 B.C., that Stirling's theory was positively confirmed. It would appear that highly developed civilization had existed in Mexico long before the Maya. This civilization is often referred to as the "Mother Culture" of all of Mesoamerica.

The Olmec Heartland

Major centers were established by the Olmec at San Lorenzo, La Venta, Laguna de los Cerros, and Tres Zapotes in what is now southern Veracruz and western Tabasco. This region is known as the Olmec heartland, because it was the center of Olmec activity in the Preclassic period. The heartland is a hot and humid lowland region with a very high annual rainfall; it is a rich agricultural area that must have offered the Preclassic Olmec an almost inexhaustible food supply.

San Lorenzo

San Lorenzo is situated on a plateau that rises above a densely forested jungle in southern Veracruz. It is the oldest of the heartland sites, dating from about 1500 B.C., with Olmec presence appearing about 1250 B.C. As noted above, it was first explored by Stirling and Drucker in 1945 and 1946. Early explorers believed that the elevated site was natural in origin and that the ravines and ridges which cut into the site on the north, west, and south sides were the result of erosion. The excavations led by Richard Diehl and Michael Coe in the late 1960s, however, proved that most of the ridges were man-made because they are mirror images of opposing formations. The symmetry is displayed in other ground irregularities as well, and it appears that almost all of the ridges and ravines at the site were deliberately formed by the early Olmec.

On top of the San Lorenzo plateau are rectangular courts, small pyramidal mounds, and an earth and clay pyramid approximately twenty feet in height. Nearby are over 200 rectangular mounds that

16. Map of Mesoamerica showing Olmec heartland: San Lorenzo, La Venta, and Tres Zapotes.

are believed to be platform bases of ancient Olmec structures (Coe, Diehl 1980). These mounds were astronomically aligned, and they date from the earliest Olmec times. A little over two feet in height, they are sometimes grouped so that two will form a right angle, or three will cluster around a small court. It is estimated from the number of mounds uncovered that at least one thousand people could have lived at San Lorenzo. Since it would have taken a larger work force than this to build San Lorenzo and to move the major monuments, it seems apparent that the city's support area, where builders and stone cutters lived, must have been much larger than San Lorenzo itself (Coe, Diehl 1980).

Between 1966 and 1968, Michael Coe directed what is known as the Yale University Project, which involved the exploration and excavation of San Lorenzo. The Yale team mapped the entire site and discovered 65 monuments made of basalt from the Tuxtla Mountains some 60 miles away. Since basalt is a highly magnetic rock, the project crew used portable

17. The "Wrestler." Three-dimensional basalt portrait sculpture, Veracruz. Height: 26 inches. (INAH.)

search magnometers, which measure magnetic materials in the earth, to aid them in their search for stone monuments. The basalt monuments that were discovered during these and subsequent excavations include so-called "altars," columns, complete human figures, were-jaguar figures, and ten colossal heads. All of the colossal heads, as well as the faces on many of the large figures and basalt monuments, exhibit typical Olmec features: fleshy cheeks, raised irises of the eyes, broad noses with flaring nostrils, ridged lines around fleshy lips, deep depressions at the corners of the mouth and between the eyes, and a helmet-like head covering. The were-jaguar figures combine human and animal features. Many of the altars resemble those from La Venta. One in particular, Monument 14 at San Lorenzo, is remarkably similar to Altar 4 at La Venta. The front surface of each monument shows an Olmec man seated cross-legged within a deeply recessed niche. Both figures hold ropes which extend across the front of the stone and around the side, where they wrap around the hand of another figure. It is apparent that both altars depict an event, or ritual, that was universally important to the Olmec.

In 1967, midway through the Yale Project excavations, Matthew Stirling discovered several drain stones in a depression close to the principal mound at San Lorenzo. A small area was excavated and 21 meters of an intact drain line was discovered. Coe and Diehl continued Stirling's excavations, and found evidence of a deeply buried stone aqueduct or drain line. It was soon determined that the small section of drain was part of a lengthy and highly efficient graded drain line which extended almost 600 feet along the west side of the San Lorenzo plateau. It was made of U-shaped basalt stone sections with flat lids which extended east-west in a straight line; three branch lines intersected at right angles. Some of the U-shaped troughs had small drain holes or wide openings along the side walls which would have allowed some degree of flow control. One large basalt monument, called Monument 52, was found near the intake end of the system. It is a seated human/feline figure with paws, a snarling cat-like mouth, slanted human eyes, and wide nose, all of which are typical features of the Olmec style. The head covering is elaborate, and there is a cleft at the top of the head. The back of the figure has a deep, hollow, U-shaped space similar to the shape of the trough stones of the drain itself. Because of its close proximity to the end of the drain line, the monument may be an early example of the Olmec rain god (Coe, Diehl 1980). The drain provided an extremely efficient system of water control for the lower ponds located within the ceremonial complex.

Highly acidic soils and high rainfall in the Olmec heartland make preservation of human bones difficult, if not impossible; not one Olmec burial was discovered at San Lorenzo during the Yale expedition. Not only is there an absence of ancient human remains (other than infrequent pieces of human bone found along with animal bones), but burial offerings are nonexistent. This would suggest that the Olmec at San Lorenzo buried their dead in other places. Fortunately, the stone monuments provide a clear description of Olmec dress and ornamentation during the Preclassic period. According to Coe and Diehl (1980), the Olmec had deformed heads (probably a result of head binding), and the heads appear to have been shaved, probably with obsidian blades. The head was covered with a type of helmet, or head covering, possibly made from leather. Some of the headpieces display jaguar paws or jaguar skin patterns, rope or bead designs, or claws. The headpiece was held in place with a cloth headband which was knotted at the back. In front of the ears were long tabs of cloth or leather; pierced ears held earspools, or curved or circular ear ornaments. Each headdress pattern was different, as was each colossal head, which supports the theory that the heads were individual portraits of important rulers. Complete Olmec figures wore a type of loincloth or brief pants, capes, armbands of cloth, and sometimes leg bands of rope. **Concave mirrors** were often displayed on the chests as ornaments.

Concave mirrors of iron ore materials such as magnetite, hermatite, and ilmenite were worked, sliced and ground to an oval or concave surface; they are highly polished, and can reflect images and create fire by focusing the sun's rays.

There is unmistakable evidence that around A.D. 900, most of the carved stones at San Lorenzo were deliberately mutilated. The monument's surfaces show evidence of pounding with stones to obliterate features; some were fractured by breaking and chipping large flakes and chunks from the monuments, or entire heads from full figures (Coe 1965). There is no way to explain how most of the mutilation was done, since much of the destruction was inflicted with a force more powerful than that which could have been caused by man alone. According to Coe, "In our bewilderment, we have postulated large tree trunks being lashed together into huge tripods, from which great pieces of already shattered monuments could be suspended by ropes and sent oscillating to smash into their appointed targets. In no other way can we account for the power of these blows." After the colossal heads were deliberately pitted, they were buried along a line, deep in the man-made ridges and ravines, and then covered with earth. Smaller monuments were also defaced and buried. The seated figure known as Monument 34 was decapitated and then positioned facing east, directly on a gravel floor deep in the ground. Offerings were placed between the legs and around the left foot, and the monument was covered with limestone fill (Coe, Diehl 1980).

Although the earliest occupation of San Lorenzo dates from about 1500 B.C., **monumental Olmec stone sculpture** does not appear until around 1250. There is no explanation for the sudden florescence of the Olmec style at this time; it seems likely that a complete range of Olmec stone sculptures from the earliest times has not yet been discovered.

Heizer (1971) has proposed that Olmec sculpture may have been sent to various sites from one central location. The numbers of duplicate sculptures found supports the central workshop theory (for example, Monument 4 at La Venta, and Monument 14 at San Lorenzo). In addition, stone workshops have not been found at any of the Olmec sites. Clewlow (1970) suggests that the monuments were carved in the Tuxtla Mountains and then transported to their respective locations. Although several Olmec sculptures have been discovered in the Tuxtla area, it is unlikely that we can conclusively prove the existence of workshops there because of ongoing volcanic activity.

From 1250 until 900 B.C., the greatest phase of San Lorenzo unfolded. After 900 B.C., Olmec activity at San Lorenzo came to an end. Although we can only speculate what the master plan was intended to be, it is possible that completion here was interrupted and the site abandoned because of the same destructive forces that were responsible for the mutilation and burial of many of the stone monuments. One theory is that an internal revolt may have taken place around 900 B.C. at San Lorenzo; there is no evidence of an outside invasion (Coe 1965). The stone images were deliberately destroyed—and then carefully hidden from human sight for almost three thousand years.

La Venta

La Venta is located on a small swampy island in the Tonala River in western Tabasco, seven miles inland from the Gulf of Mexico. Until recent times, it has been believed that La Venta was strictly a "ceremonial" city, occupied by a small group of priestly rulers and supported by workers and craftsmen who lived nearby. New evidence has proven this to be incorrect. Test excavations completed by a team of anthropologists from the University of Pennsylvania in 1986 and 1987 identified previously unknown settlement patterns at La Venta and located nine "support" communities nearby. House floors, storage pits, urn burials with pottery offerings, and a workshop for making serpentine and clay artifacts were found during these excavations; the nine support communities were discovered by means of aerial photography. Settled by the Olmec at least 600 years before La Venta became a major center, the peripheral sites date as early as 1750 B.C. They were small communities that clustered along the Rio Bari, an abandoned, silt-filled, twin-channeled river that once wound its way to the Gulf, through the marshy countryside around La Venta. The earliest domestic objects found at these locations include necklaces, grinding

Pottery shards found at the Rio Bari sites date from c. 1750-1400 B.C. La Venta was not developed at this early date.

stones of basalt, and **pottery fragments.** It was further determined by aerial photography and geological analysis that the Rio Bari was an active river; therefore, the transportation system of these communities was most likely river-based. In addition, there were ten to twelve foot high levees along the river banks that provided protection from seasonal floods. Transporting goods by water would have been a practical and expedient method of distributing daily necessities and ceremonial monuments to the Olmec communities. It would also have been expedient to transport goods by raft to La Venta since the Rio Bari passed close to the island's ceremonial center. This is a much shorter and more direct route than the previously suggested Rio Tonala access to La Venta.

The discovery and subsequent dating of the Rio Bari settlements confirm that a sizeable population lived along the river before La Venta became a major ceremonial center. This is the first tangible evidence for local antecedents to the development of La Venta and the emergence of Olmec influence in this region. The new data indicate that simple population growth in this resource-rich early Preclassic environment preceded the structured social hierarchy that dominated during middle Preclassic times. The excavations also established the existence of domestic occupation near the ceremonial core at La Venta. As a result, we now know that La Venta was not just a "ceremonial city" that was inhabited only by the ruling priest-leaders. It was a temple town composed of a civic-ceremonial complex surrounded by a permanent domestic settlement (Redman1978).

In summary, it can be stated that as early as 1750 B.C. small communities existed along the Rio Bari River. Sometime between that date and 1200 B.C., a major change in social and political emphasis shifted to the site that became La Venta. By 900 B.C., La Venta was a major decision-making center, as well as the nucleus of an active cultural and commercial exchange network between communities. This continued until around 400 B.C., when finally all activity abruptly ceased and La Venta was abandoned.

During the period from 900 to 400 B.C. La Venta was an important center—perhaps the most important of all the Olmec sites. Here, the Olmecs built a well-planned ceremonial complex that deviated just 8° west of true north. It is believed that this alignment reflected true north as determined by the position of the stars as they were when viewed over 3000 years ago. The largest structure in the complex is an earthen pyramid that is approximately 110 feet high; this is the largest Olmec pyramid in existence. It has an unusual form, with ten ridges and ten ravines alternating around the mass like a deeply fluted cone. It has been suggested that the pyramid was deliberately made to look like a giant volcano, similar to those in the nearby Tuxtla Range. Just north of the pyramid lies a Great Court flanked by two long, low mounds. Deep in the ground, at the northern entrance to the court, stylized masks were formed from serpentine and basalt. A short distance away, between this court and the Great Pyramid, another mosaic mask was found, also buried deep within the earth, and made of green serpentine stones assembled to suggest the image of a great face. Although there has been some dispute over the identification of the masks, the accepted opinion is that they represent the image of the Jaguar. Since they were carefully buried soon after they were completed,

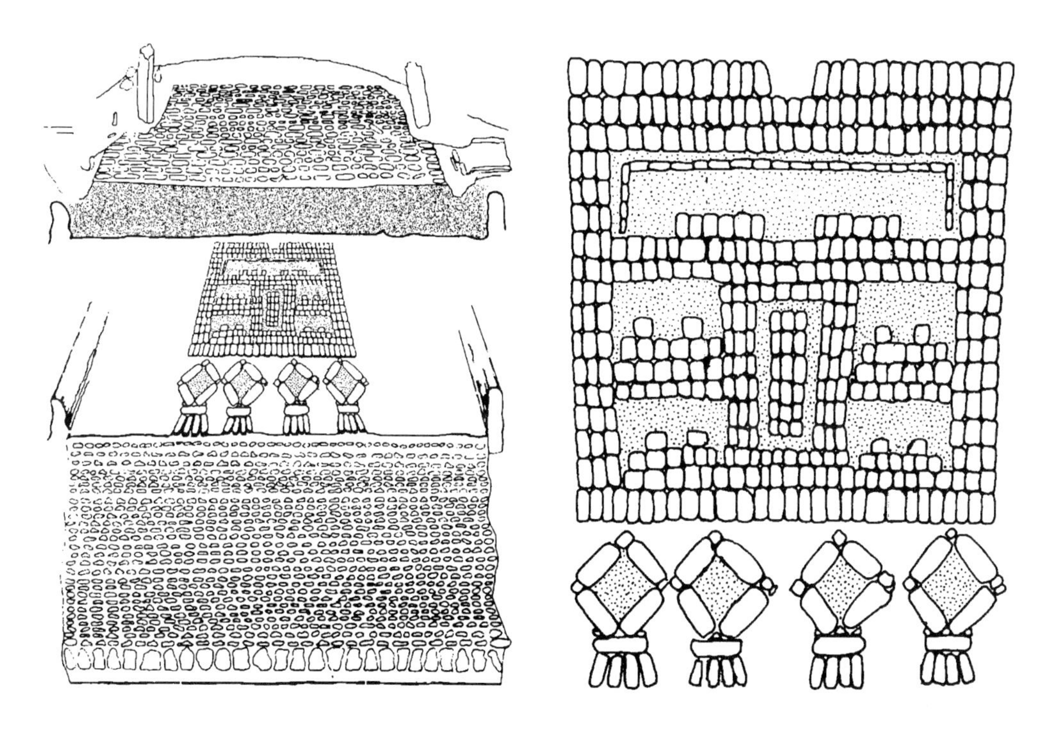

18. Reconstruction of pit at La Venta. Image may depict the face of a Jaguar. Colored earth, clay, and hand-cut serpentine stones. *Right:* Detail of stylized Jaguar face.

the masks may have been intended as ritual offerings to this powerful animal. Beyond the Great Court is another rectangular court that had originally been enclosed by seven foot high basaltic stone columns. Just southeast are additional mounds, courts, and columns that have not yet been completely excavated.

Four colossal heads were found at La Venta. Each head weighs from ten to twenty-five tons and was carved from basaltic stone that was quarried in the Tuxtla Mountains some 80 miles away. The massive heads portray men with typical Olmec features: thick, clearly defined lips, wide nostrils, full faces, and a peculiar type of close-fitting head covering (refer to fig. 10). The helmet-like head coverings have wide bands and some display unusual markings. The significance of the enormous heads, whose height ranges from four and one half to almost ten feet, has never been clearly understood. It is possible that they may have been associated with beheading rites or the ritual ballgame, since they always existed as heads alone and never had bodies. It could also be that they were portraits of great leaders or warriors. Whatever their meaning, it must have been of great importance to the Olmec to create these portraits in stone considering the enormous planning and expenditure of energy required to obtain and carve the massive blocks of basalt. Seven massive basalt monuments were also uncovered. One of them, called Altar 5 (sometimes referred to as the Altar of Infant Sacrifice) is carved on three sides. On its front, an important looking personage, wearing a headdress with jaguar symbols, sits crosslegged within a niche. He leans slightly forward, holding a cleft-headed jaguar-human child in his arms. This is the were-jaguar baby, the hallmark of Olmec art. On one side of the monument are two impressively dressed male figures who hold two wildly gesturing were-jaguar babies. On the opposite side are two more adult males, each with a child in his arms. This monument is a powerful visual description of an ancient ritual or ceremony that was of utmost importance to the Olmec.

Altar 4 is the best preserved of all of the so-called "altars" that were found at La Venta. The male figure on the front of the stone leans slightly forward out of a deeply carved niche; he is almost completely separated from the massive stone block. The elaborate headdress he wears displays the face of a jaguar whose

19. Altar 5. (Sometimes called the Altar of Infant Sacrifice.) Parque La Venta, Villahermosa.

muzzle-like mouth has the X, or crossed-band symbol, so conspicuous in Olmec art. (The X symbol may have been a reference to the pattern made by the spots on the jaguar. During the Classic period, the Maya used the symbol to represent "sky" or "serpent".) The man holds a long, rope-like object that extends around the side of the altar and ends coiled around the wrist of a second, smaller figure. This person looks towards the man and points to him, directing the observer's gaze back to the front of the monument. In prehispanic symbolism this could represent union, submission, or dependence. It is possible, albeit speculative, that this scene may represent the union of two different groups, since the features of the second figure are totally different from the typical physical characteristics of the Olmec.

The Ambassador Stone, or Monument 13, is a flat, basaltic stone carved in bas-relief. It displays the earliest known examples of glyph expression. The figure depicted is shown with one foot extended, in a walking position; he holds a flag or

20. *Top.* Altar 4. An Olmec ruler emerges from this large basalt stone. He holds a twisted object (perhaps a rope) in his right hand which wraps around the wrist of a smaller figure on the end panel. Parque La Venta.

21. *Bottom.* Detail, end panel Altar 4. (Note pointing finger and "rope.")

22. *Left.* Monument 19. Man sitting within the curve of a Serpent's body, Parque La Venta.

23. *Right.* Monument 13, "The Ambassador Stone," Parque La Venta. A round form, cloverleaf, bird's head, and foot in front of and behind the bearded man may be early hieroglyphs.

banner in his left hand. Below, and to his right, is the raised image of a bare foot, a common convention in later Mesoamerican manuscripts for "journey." Under the flag are three additional raised glyphs: an oval shape, a cloverleaf-like image, and a bird's head. Some researchers have suggested that these symbols may identify the figure on the monument.

There was frequent use of basalt columns at La Venta and Tres Zapotes. They were used in front of religious and ceremonial compounds and as a form of sculptural architecture. The Tomb of Basaltic Columns, or Monument 7 at La Venta, is an example of the use of basalt for architectural purposes. The tomb, which was discovered in 1942, was built with 44 columns, ten of which form the roof; the floor inside is covered with tiles. Offerings placed inside the tomb include a female figurine with a pyrite mirror on her chest, two obsidian discs, a mirror, two human hands carved from jade, a shark's tooth, and some bone fragments. All of this was covered with red cinnabar powder.

In addition to the large monuments and colossal heads found at La Venta, there are also a number of intricately carved basalt stelae. Two noteworthy examples are stelae 2 and 3, both of which are in rather poor condition. Stela 2 has an important looking personage carved on the front. He wears a tall and elaborately detailed headdress, similar to those worn by Maya priests hundreds of years later. Stela 3 focuses on two major figures who face each other in earnest confrontation. The features of one are almost completely obliterated, but the face of the other is intact and exhibits non-Olmec features: a prominent nasal bridge, high cheek bones, and a long, thin face and full beard. Six secondary figures, resembling chubby little children, surround the central images. These may be Chaneques, who were believed to be old dwarfs with the faces of children. They supposedly lived in waterfalls and were able to foresee rain; and so are always connected with a water spirit. Although the specific meaning of this unusual tableau is still rather interpretive, the arrangement of figures, elaborate dress and headdress

24. Basalt tomb. Elaborate burial offerings and partial physical remains indicate important status of this burial. Parque La Venta.

25. *Left.* Stela 3. Two elaborately dressed men face each other; six small figures hover above. Parque La Venta.

26. *Above.* Detail, Stela 3.

style, and unusual facial features may provide clues that will someday unlock the secrets of Olmec life.

By around 400 B.C. La Venta was no longer a major ceremonial site. There was deliberate destruction of many of the major monuments and the site was abandoned by the ruling class. Tres Zapotes now became the center of Olmec activity. It lies near the foot of the Tuxtla Mountains, about 100 miles northwest of La Venta. Some Olmec-style figurines and small jades were found here, as well as a small pyramid that had been faced with cut stones. There were also two colossal heads, one of which is described earlier under the History of Olmec Discoveries. In 1939, Matthew Stirling located the lower half of an extraordinary monument known as Stela C. On the front of the monument was a "jaguar mask" panel; on the back appeared a vertical column of bars and dots, the numbering system previously attributed to the Maya. Although the numbers are not accompanied by glyphs that would identify days, months, or years, Stirling reconstructed a Long Count date that would correspond to 31 B.C. Stirling's dating was positively confirmed in the early 1970s, when the missing top portion of Stela C was found (Cohn1972.) The only other dated Olmec monument is the small jade Tuxtla Statuette, which was discovered a few miles south of the present town of San Andres Tuxtla in the heart of the Tuxtla Mountains. Although its origin and the circumstances of its discovery are unknown, the Tuxtla Statuette appears to be Olmec in style, and the calendrical inscriptions closely resemble the later Maya Long Count system.

The Olmecs preferred to work with jade and hard stones in their quest for symbolic expression. Although they mastered the art of making magnificent hollow ceramic figurines, it was the hard stones and jades that were carved in the greatest numbers by the Olmec artisans at La Venta and Tres Zapotes. (Although many basalt monuments were found at San Lorenzo, jade was not discovered in the excavations at that site.) Among the most beautiful Olmec objects are the jade and stone masks, celts, and complete figurines that range in size from one to ten inches in height. The masks and figures represent two distinct Olmec physical types: one has the full face and thick lips that are seen on the colossal heads, and the other is distinguished by a high-bridged aquiline nose and finely modeled lips as seen on one of the principal figures on Stela 3 at La Venta. The faces that fall into this second category are always long and thin, and the eyes are usually oval in shape.

One of the earliest Olmec jades discovered was the Kunz Axe, which was acquired late in the 19th century in Oaxaca, far from its probable place of origin in the heartland region. The celt is an eleven inch tall, blue-green jade figure. More than half of the celt is taken up with the head, which displays the open, howling mouth and slightly oval eyes that are so characteristic of the Olmec style. The lower half is more simply carved in a blocky, geometric format, with incised lines providing details of the body. The arms cross in front and clutch a smaller version of itself close to its chest. Another impressive Olmec stone sculpture is the Las Limas figure, discovered in 1965. It shows an adult Olmec holding a were-jaguar baby. The face and parts of the body of the larger figure are incised with undecipherable marks and strange faces which may be deities or other spiritual beings.

In addition to the many individual jades found in the heartland region, a magnificent cache of sixteen figures was discovered in a shallow pit at La Venta. It is known as Offering 4, and it includes fifteen jade and serpentine figurines, one granite figure, and six jade celts. Fourteen of the jade and serpentine figures stand in rapt attention in front of their spokesperson, a commanding presence who stands with mouth slightly open, as if talking; his back is to the single granite figure who stands directly in front of the upright celts, somewhat apart from the larger group. Is the lone granite figure about to be judged by the others, or is he is about to be accepted into some privileged group? Perhaps this is an initiation ritual; we can only

27. Offering 4. Sixteen figures and six celts. Jade, serpentine, and basalt. (INAH.)

28. Detail, Offering 4.

speculate as to the meaning of this important tableau. About 100 years after their burial, the figures were carefully exposed, and then reburied with great care.

Social Structure

It is significant that all of the art forms which have been found throughout the heartland region relate in some way to religion or ceremony, or represent a priestly ruling class that was the dominant force in Olmec society. Still, while Olmec stone carvings have been interpreted as having religious content, much more may be learned from them than merely an understanding of the culture's religion or governing priests. These monuments and art objects are highly representative of the development of certain social and political factors in Olmec society that were nonexistent in earlier or in contemporary cultures. We can clearly see that the political rulers also served as priests, who probably acted as intermediaries between gods and men. They

29. Monument 56. Olmec figure gazing skyward. Approximately 6' high basalt stela, Parque La Venta.

established a theocracy which brought about a division of labor and the development of a clearly defined social order.

In order to separate the politico-religious responsibilities of the Olmec leaders from those of the lower classes, clearly defined tasks had to be allocated. The rulers maintained order and purpose in Olmec centers and directed the laborers in the moving of basaltic stones from the Tuxtla Mountains to the heartland cities for use as ceremonial sculpture. The great scale of operations involved in floating these massive stones on rafts down rivers to the sites reveals much about the absolute authority and power of these priest-leaders to motivate the people. In addition, there is evidence of social differentiation seen on the stelae, which depict some male figures with elaborate headdresses and clothing and other men who are more simply dressed. Although positive identification of the elaborately clothed figures is not possible, it may be that the ornate headdresses carry symbols that identify important rulers. For example, a motif on the headdress of the figure on the side of San Lorenzo Monument 14 is repeated on La Venta's Colossal Head No. 4, and both figures display prominent teeth (Grove 1981). Teeth are rarely depicted in bas-relief carvings.

The Olmec represented a highly sophisticated and unique early civilization that provided a religious and political foundation upon which subsequent cultures were to pattern themselves. Although much of what is known about their beliefs and customs is purely conjectural, their stone sculpture provides tangible clues as to the structure of their ruling class and their religion. This culture, as it can be viewed through the iconography of its stone sculpture, represents the end of fetish worship and the less structured social order of the early agricultural communities. Thus, the Olmec provide an important link between the village communities of Preclassic times and the fully developed civilizations which were soon to follow. In many ways, Olmec influence is evident not only in other Preclassic cultures, but also in the accomplishments of future generations that were to pattern their art, social structure, and base of fundamental knowledge after this remarkable and mysterious people.

30. Olmec stone mask. (DYM.)

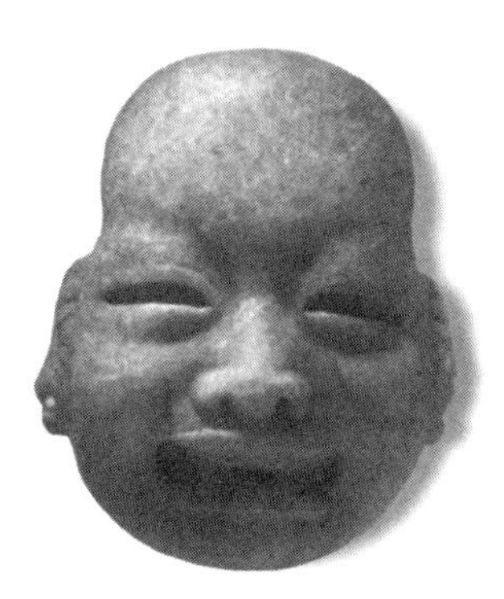

31. Greenstone mask. (MNYC)

32. Small jade mask. Height 6 3/4 inches. (INAH.)

33. *Top.* Ceramic bowl made of finely textured clay. (MNYC.)

34. *Bottom.* Olmec bowl. Bird's head and beak create dramatic composition. Height 4 1/2 inches. (MNYC.)

The Olmec Outside the Heartland

As a result of ongoing explorations and spectacular discoveries in Veracruz and Tabasco, we know that the most advanced centers of Olmec culture lie within these two states. All of the objects that have been found there are of a superior quality and exhibit sophisticated methods of production.

The Olmecs had widely developed trade routes which they used to distribute their products and maintain contact with other peoples in Mesoamerica. Olmec-style pottery has been found as far west as the state of Guerrero on the Pacific Coast, throughout the Highlands of south-central Mexico, at Copán in Honduras, and in the Guatemala Highlands. Despite this wide distribution of Olmec products, the highest stage of cultural and artistic development took place within the Gulf Coast region.

Guerrero

Although many Olmec-style artifacts have been found throughout Mesoamerica, more have been found in the western state of Guerrero than anywhere else outside the Gulf Coast region. Green stone plaques, jade figures, life-like clay figurines, masks, and celts have been found in the central part of the state and along the banks of the Mezcala River and its tributary streams; **one great wooden mask in Olmec style** was found in a high, dry cave near Iguala. No other region has yielded as many Olmec art treasures. Since Guerrero was a probable source of the prized jade that was sought by the Olmec, it would explain Olmec presence in this remote area so rich in natural resources. In Xochipala, Guerrero, extremely realistic solid clay figurines that date as early as 1500 B.C. have been found (Miller 1986). Their realism and natural forms are equal in beauty to ceramics throughout the ancient world. Many of the objects from Guerrero are equal in quality and workmanship to similar objects from the heartland region, while others exhibit the workmanship that is generally associated with an earlier phase of cultural development. Despite this intriguing disparity there is not enough evidence available to draw any positive conclusions. We are still not certain if the Olmec expanded towards Guerrero after reaching peak activity in Veracruz and Tabasco, with formative centers still undiscovered, or if Olmec activity originated in Guerrero and expanded toward the heartland region. Regardless of any chronological speculation, the evidence draws

The discovery of this elegant mask tells us that the Olmec were also masterful wood carvers. Unfortunately, because of the hot, humid climate and acid soil, no carvings of wood or other perishable materials have been found in the Gulf Coast region.

35. Standing figure, Mezcala-style, Guerrero. Height: 7 inches. Stone. (MNYC.)

attention to the fact that at some time during the Early Preclassic period Olmec activity and influence extended far beyond the boundaries of the Gulf Coast region. Widespread trade by the Olmec included the importation of obsidian from Guatemala, Valley of Mexico, and Puebla; serpentine is believed to have come from the Isthmus, on the border of Oaxaca and Chiapas, or from Puebla and Guerrero. Suggested sources for Olmec jade are Guerrero and the Isthmus (Coe 1968; Heizer 1971). The active trading and strong economy may have facilitated the spread of Olmec art to other areas.

In addition to the small objects found in Guerrero, caves have been found decorated with remarkable paintings in pure Olmec style. These are the caves of Juxlahuaca and Oxtotitlan, some of which are located nearly one mile inside a mountain and are believed to be over 3000 years old. In the major cave at Juxlahuaca, a large figure is shown wearing a tunic, cape, Quetzál headdress, and leggings of jaguar skins; near him crouches a smaller figure. In an adjoining chamber is a bright red serpent which faces a smaller cat-like creature. At Oxtotitlan, some twenty

36. Stone temple with figure on top. Mezcala. (MNYC.)

miles to the north, the paintings are located near the entrance to a cave. They show a human figure seated on a jaguar head. At both locations, the cave paintings are executed in shades of red and black and portray jaguars, "baby-face" figures, and the earliest known examples of the speech scroll.

Cave paintings in pure Olmec style have also been found at Chalcatzingo, located just southeast of Mexico City in the central highland state of Morelos. The pictographs and rock carvings here provide tangible evidence of Olmec activity far from the Gulf Coast heartland. The walls of the caves at Chalcatzingo are covered with red painted pictographs; there are also Olmec-style reliefs carved in stone, two free-standing monuments and twenty altars (Gay 1971). Figures made of serpentine and stone, pendants, and jewelry have also been found.

Monte Albán I

Monte Albán is situated over 1000 feet above the nearby present-day city of Oaxaca. There are many small valleys here that nestle between mountain peaks, joining together in the center of the state to form the Valley of Oaxaca. Some 500 years

37. *Gallery of the Danzantes.* Monte Albán I.

Identification of public architecture from this early period is difficult because of later construction over the original buildings.

before the birth of Christ, people came here and began to prepare a building site. We do not know who the earliest inhabitants were or where they came from. We only know that during its Preclassic period of occupation, Monte Albán experienced a very high level of artistic and cultural development; it is here that we see the first glyphs and evidence of calendric notation. The site itself shows **signs of careful planning from earliest times**, and at least one building, known as the Building of the Danzantes, was constructed during this Preclassic period. The Building of the Danzantes was first described by Guillermo Dupaix in 1806, at which time drawings of five of the carved slabs that were set into the side of the building were made by his site artist, Castaneda. Between 1931 and 1958, Alfonzo Caso directed additional excavations. Over 140 carved slabs from the Danzantes building have been identified (Marcus 1974). The slabs are flat, carved stones placed side by side in ascending rows that display life-sized nude male figures, each in a different

38. Detail, Danzantes figure. Distinctive facial features and helmet-like head coverings suggest early Olmec influence. Monte Albán I.

position. The figures have been named "Los Danzantes" (the dancers) because of their extremely varied and contorted positions. The faces of the Danzantes display Olmec-like features, especially in the full, fleshy lips, the wide nose, and the peculiar helmet-type covering upon their heads. The figures at the lower level display elaborate necklaces and earplugs. Second row figures lay parallel to the ground, their heads pointing north. The figures on the third and fourth tiers are simpler, with very little, if any, ornamentation. Each is unique and distinct from the other because of the unusual positions of their bodies, arms, and legs. Two unusual aspects of these carvings are that the eyes of the men are closed and the mouths are open (a symbol of death in many early cultures), and distorted or mutilated genitals are displayed. Displaying the sexual organs is an uncommon feature in traditional Olmec art.

Although there is some controversy surrounding the identification of these figures, Miller (1991) suggests that the figures may be sacrificed captives of war. Other theories postulate dancers, swimmers, priests, important political prisoners, or participants in religious blood-letting ceremonies. Indeed, the Danzantes have been subjected to every conceivable interpretation. According to Marcus, the only interpretation consistent with iconographic conventions elsewhere in Mesoamerica is Michael Coe's. He points out that "nudity was 'scandalous' in Monte Albán; it was used to humiliate captives. Important personages were never shown naked, or in awkward, distorted, sprawling positions, but such depictions were standard for captives" (Coe 1962). Marcus further suggests that the stones represent a "symbolic display of power which coincided with the time when Monte Albán's rulers would have felt the greatest need for propaganda to intimidate their enemies and reassure their supporters" (Marcus 1974).

Olmec symbols have been identified on clay vessels that date from the San Jose phase ceramics in Oaxaca (1150-850 B.C.), where stylized fire-serpents and were-jaguars, and jaguar-paw-wing motifs, have been found on housepots (Drennan, Flannery and Marcus 1983). Despite our inability to attribute positive identification of the Danzantes figures, the presence of the earlier Olmec motifs, as well as the unmistakable Olmec features of the Danzantes figures cannot be ignored. For this reason, it may be said that the Danzantes figures, far from the Heartland region, can most assuredly be placed within the Olmec world.

Summary

The early power and sophistication of the Olmecs is quite apparent in the remains found at San Lorenzo and La Venta; this was indeed, the earliest "high" civilization in Mesoamerica. In addition to the heartland region, Olmec presence has been found in the highland states and as far west as Guerrero, where they worshipped in caves and searched for jade. It is apparent that the Olmecs' trade routes extended far into western and southern Mexico; perhaps as far as Central America. The Olmec influence was strongest during the mid-Preclassic era, but by late Preclassic times the power of the Jaguar People began to fade. At this later time, the great city of Teotihuacán was under construction, and its growing influence and strength was soon to influence all of Mesoamerica; in addition, hundreds of other important sites were being planned in areas where villages had formerly flourished. As a foundation, however, the Olmecs had already established patterns that were destined to forever influence other peoples and to distinguish them from all other cultures in Mesoamerica.

Although we do not understand why this great power came to an end or why its influence diminished, the end of the Preclassic Olmec world really signalled the beginning of even higher levels of development that were soon to follow; the people of the Classic period were to build upon the Olmec inheritance. In this respect, then, as Miguel Covarrubias once proposed, we can say that the Olmec may have been the "Mother Culture" of all subsequent cultures of Mesoamerica.

39. Seated figure, Jalisco. Early Classic period. Height: 20 inches. (MNYC.)

Western Mexico

The Shaft-Chamber Tomb Region

The western coastal states of Nayarit, Jalisco, and Colima consist primarily of a mountainous region averaging about 5000 feet above sea level, and a rather narrow lowland plain extending over 2500 miles along the Pacific Coast. The majority of western Mexico's shaft-chamber tombs are located in the highland region.

The western highlands have a relatively temperate climate with adequate rainfall and fertile soil in most areas. The temperate climate would have provided ideal conditions for food production during the time when funerary offerings for the shaft tombs were being made by the villagers. During this time, west Mexico did not follow the trends that were developing in the rest of Mesoamerica; its communities were generally smaller and lacked the large pyramid construction and sophisticated religious architecture that were making their appearance in other areas. There is no evidence of writing, nor the use of calendrical systems. There was only the production of clay objects for the numerous shaft-chamber tombs that extended north from Colima, through southern and central Jalisco, and into south-central Nayarit.

The size and shape of the tombs varies considerably. Ranging in depth from about twelve to eighteen feet, the shafts connect to the burial chamber by means of a short entrance passageway. Most of the tombs were carved into a volcanic material called *tepetate*. After burial, the shafts were filled to the surface opening with fine dirt. A stone slab usually covered the chamber entrance. According to some experts (Furst 1966), certain tombs in southern Nayarit contain clarboyas, which are small shafts that connect the chambers to the surface of the earth. Furst has suggested that the latter were constructed for supplying food to the dead in the afterlife. A small shrine may have been built over the tomb, where ceremonies could then have been held in honor of the dead below.

On the basis of Carbon 14 dating, we can date most of the tombs from about 500 B.C. to A.D. 350, when this type of tomb construction ended. Perhaps the introduction of new religious-ritual systems, along with a change in basic socio-economic patterns throughout the rest of Mesoamerica, was responsible for the termination of the shaft-chamber construction.

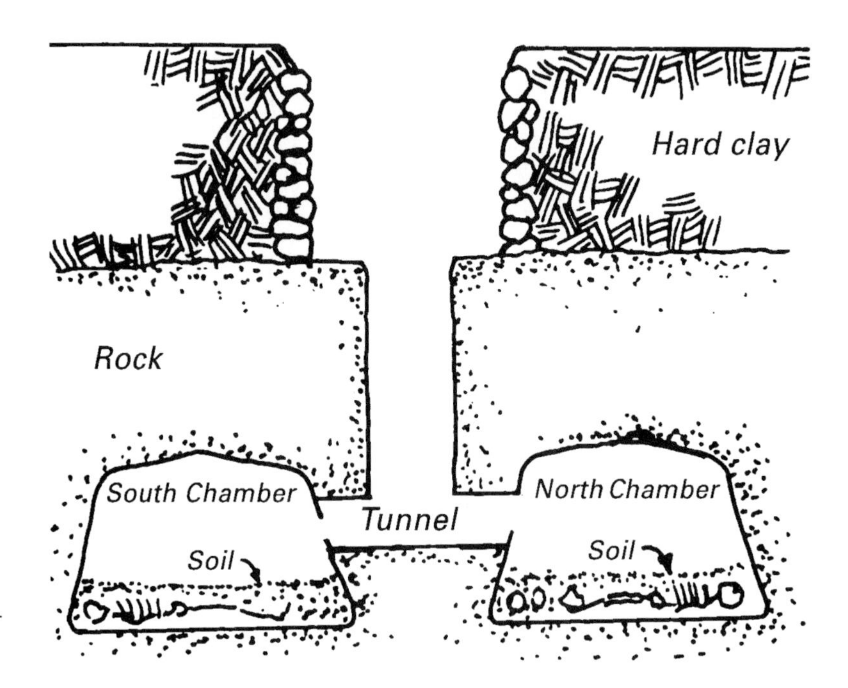

40. Reconstruction of typical Shaft-Chamber Tomb. Western Mexico.

Nayarit

The figures from the state of Nayarit display both positive and negative painting. The most descriptive details of Nayarit figures show arms as long thin ropes of clay, with little realism or anatomical detail. The hair of the Nayarit figure is clearly described by the application of many fine incised lines. Both males and females wear elaborate earrings and nose ornaments; some exhibit facial markings of long vertical lines on the cheeks. The high status of the individuals represented is indicated by their elaborate dress and adornment. Highly characteristic of Nayarit figurines are the "elephantine-like" legs and enormous feet. These figures display the greatest variation and range of activity of any west Mexican figure style. Of particular interest, too, are the small figures grouped around a house or temple structure. These so-called "house-scenes" seem to provide a visual narrative of everyday life as it existed here in ancient times. Although clay models of ballcourts are included in these "house-scenes," actual ballcourts have not yet been discovered.

41. Seated figure, Nayarit. Early Classic period. Height: 12 inches. (MNYC.)

42. House scene. These figure groupings provide a visual narrative of everyday life. Nayarit. (DYM.)

43. House scene. Nayarit.

Jalisco

Small solid figurines, some with pointed heads, have been found in the Jalisco tombs. Many are of musicians and performers who are often shown in community or ceremonial activity. In addition, there are large realistic figures that are usually between one to three feet high. Although there are several stylistic variations of the figurines here, the classic Jalisco style, known as "Ameca Grey," is most characteristic of this region. Ameca Greys are figures that are either cream, red slipped, or a combination of both. The distinguishing features of the figures in this category include a raised design which crosses the extremely elongated head; some of the male figures wear a crested helmet. The breasts of the female figures are often tattooed with spiral designs. Ameca Grey figures are also distinguished by their staring eyes, thick brows, sharp, hatchet-like nose, and large open mouth which displays clearly defined teeth.

44. Seated figure with nose ring. (INAH.)

45. Gesturing figure, Jalisco.

46. *Top.* Clay Dog, Colima, Western Mexico.

47. *Left.* Dancing Dogs, Colima, Western Mexico.

Colima

Colima ceramics can be identified by their light orange to deep red color with a splattering of black patina on the surface. Classic Colima figures, though represented in a wide range of positions, are most often seen in a highly mannered pose. These large, hollow, three dimensional figures were formed from a light brown clay, to which an orange-red slip was applied over the entire surface, with clothing detail added in dark red colors. The pieces would then be polished, often with a smooth stone or animal skin on the unbaked surface, to produce a richly glowing sheen. Some of the Colima figures have one or two horns rising from the center of the head. Furst (1965) believes that these horns symbolize the presence of supernatural powers and were worn only by priests and shamans who possessed this power. In support of this theory, one must note that many of these horned figures face left, which was the direction associated with death, and believed by the ancients to be the direction of the entrance to the underworld.

There are a wide range of forms to be seen in Colima ceramics, from figural representations to effigy vessels and beautiful pots. Lovely examples of animals, fruits and vegetables are also important contributions of the Colima potters. Among the most famous of the animals and of Colima pottery in general are the dogs, which are thought by some scholars to represent the emissaries of Xolotl, the God of Death, who guided the souls of the dead across the river on their journey through the underworld. The importance of the dog is indicated by the fact that it is frequently represented wearing a human mask.

The art of the western village cultures was largely ignored until recent times, when modern artists began to appreciate and collect these expressive ceramics. Until this happened, when objects were found in newly plowed fields, ranchers used them as targets for shooting practice. Fortunately, we now realize the value of this unique and meaningful art, and cherish it for the insight it gives us into the lives and customs of the people of these ancient villages.

The Classic Period

A.D. 200 - 900

Teotihuacán

By the end of the Late Preclassic period, some of the small villages that populated the high, green Valley of Mexico merged together to form larger settlements. Major population centers began to emerge. Teotihuacán was the largest and most influential of all. What is remarkable about Teotihuacán is that it may have been the first time in the history of Mesoamerica that all levels of society lived and worked together within one settlement. It was a true city in the literal definition of the word.

Sometime between 100 B.C. and A.D. 150 construction began at Teotihuacán, and ceremonial architecture appeared for the first time in the highland Valley of Mexico. It is believed that the Pyramids of the Sun and Moon were built during the earliest phase of this construction period, and that the city was divided into four main quadrants. The main residential area (the Old City) was in the northwest quadrant; the temples and palaces of priests and officials were grouped toward the center of the city. Located around the periphery were the houses and workshops of the craftsmen and artisans. All of the streets were laid out in straight and precise lines in a grid pattern. This allowed for growth and reflected the ingenuity and foresight of the architects of the city.

48. *Opposite.* Teotihuacán, Valley of Mexico.

49. Courtyard area, Palace of Quetzálpapálótl at Teotihuacán. Sculpted columns depict butterflies and Quetzál birds.

After A.D. 200, no new pyramids were constructed, but small-scale building continued at an accelerated pace. A shift in the settlement pattern caused hundreds of permanent stone-walled residences to be built in various parts of the city. There were palaces for the priesthood and aristocracy; there were also large apartment compounds with communal living areas for the rest of the population. At its peak, Teotihuacán had an estimated population of at least 200,000 people. No less than 4000 major structures were spread over eight square miles. There were no clearly defined defensive fortifications or walls, only walled areas within the city itself. Large complexes on the "Street of the Dead" were walled, and great elevated platforms around the periphery of the massive 38 acre Ciudadela would have provided protection from aggression.

There is, however, little to suggest that large-scale warfare ever involved the populace of Teotihuacán. Indeed, throughout most of its history, Teotihuacán's power was unchallenged. Politically, it was the most influential city in central Mexico, and most likely it was the nucleus of a kingdom whose influence in politics, religion, and trade extended throughout most of Mesoamerica. Yet despite this apparent strength, sometime around A.D. 650-700 Teotihuacán was destroyed by fire, and most of its inhabitants left the city. Burned areas around temples indicate a devastating holocaust: the Palace of Quetzálpapálótl was discovered with its roof collapsed, and charred remains of wooden beams were found lying on the stucco floor. We do not know if hostile invaders attacked the city or if it was accidentally destroyed by fire; we only know that after the fire, the city was abandoned. About fifty years after its abandonment and devastation, some few small dwellings were constructed; the temples and compounds along the Street of the Dead were never rebuilt. The glory days of Teotihuacán were over, and never again would the power and influence of this great city reappear.

City Plan

One major street dominates the site. It extends through the city in a north-south line just 15.5° east of north. The Aztec called it "Miccaotli," or the Avenue, or Street of the Dead, and it is over two miles long. Although very few burials have been found along the avenue, it is possible that there are tombs in some of the unexcavated buildings lining it.

At the northern end of the avenue is the Pyramid of the Moon. The entire plan of the ancient city is aligned with this pyramid and with Cerro Gordo, the volcanic peak which rises behind it; water for Teotihuacán originates from springs linked to Cerro Gordo. The Teotihuacános believed that the mountain was the source of their all-important water, and much of their art contains symbols suggesting mountains and water. It is significant to note that the shape of the pyramid approximates Cerro Gordo's massive form. The Pyramid of the Moon is approximately 95 feet in height. Four massive, graduated tiers form the shape of the structure and a wide stairway provides access to the top. Directly in front of the Moon Pyramid is a large open plaza. Eleven stepped pyramid bases frame the open area and an elevated platform dominates the center. On the west side of the Plaza is the Palace of Quetzálpapálótl, or the Quetzál-Butterfly Palace, with its room murals and large inner patio adorned with square pillars sculpted in bas-relief.

A short distance to the south, on the eastern side of the Avenue of the Dead, is the Pyramid of the Sun. Both the Pyramid of the Moon and the Sun Pyramid were built with sun-dried clay bricks faced with volcanic stones set in a clay-like mortar and finished with a smooth coating of lime plaster. The sacred temples for worship were at the top. The Sun Pyramid was built over an earlier structure that had a base almost as large as the one we see today (Millon: Barrin, Pasztory 1993). Tunneling projects in 1920 and 1933 exposed a passageway under the pyramid that led to a cloverleaf-shaped cave buried twenty feet under the center line of the structure. It was complete with ritual offerings dating from the first century A.D.

The Pyramid of the Sun rises high above Teotihuacán, and is the largest architectural form in the city. It is interesting to compare its dimensions with those of the Pyramid of Cheops, the largest pyramid in Egypt. The base of the Sun Pyramid measures 246.66 yards on each side, and the Egyptian Pyramid measures 247.33 yards, a difference of only 2/3 of a yard (Tompkins 1976). Despite the similarity in base measurement the Pyramid of the Sun is only 210 feet high while the Cheops

50. Pyramid of the Sun at Teotihuacán.

Pyramid measures 490 feet. The position of the Pyramid of the Sun marks the east-west movement of the sun each day, and the appearance of the Pleiades on days of equinox (Aveni 1980).

The avenue continues past the Pyramid of the Sun in a southerly direction, past endless numbers of structural remains and partial foundations, and ends just south of two massive enclosures: the Great Compound on the west side of the avenue, which served as the city's main marketplace and bureaucratic center; and the Ciudadela, or Citadel, covering 38 acres on the east side of the avenue. The Ciudadela, with its magnificent Pyramid of Quetzálcóatl, appears to have been the religious and ritual center of the city. The Pyramid of Quetzálcóatl is a six-tiered structure with a wide, frontal stairway. The entire exposed surface of the pyramid is covered with a thick layer of plaster bearing traces of red paint. Carved heads project from the face of the structure: serpent heads that emerge from a feathered, or petaled, ring, and heads with square lower jaws and circular eyes. While it is obvious that the serpent head is symbolic of the ancient god Quetzálcóatl, the identification of the other is more

51. Pyramid of Quetzálcóatl at Teotihuacán. Carved facade depicts two tenoned heads, shells and marine motifs.

tentative. Some investigators believe that the second style represents Fire Serpents, the Old Fire God, or the Storm God (later called Tlaloc by the Aztec), especially since water symbols are lavishly displayed on the building's facade.

The Pyramid of Quetzálcóatl has been excavated extensively, and approximately 120 human skeletons, buried in groups of four, eight, nine, eighteen, and twenty, have so far been exhumed. The mathematical ratio may indicate that additional burials exist within the pyramid (Cabrera: Berrin, Pasztory 1993). From 1980-1986, a group of skeletons in the north and south ends of the building were found on their backs with their hands behind them, as if they had been tied at the time of death. These were male warriors with elaborate necklaces, some with human-like teeth and upper jaws made from shell. One single burial was of a man with a necklace made from real teeth and a human upper jawbone. The warriors were sacrificed when

52. Detail, Feathered Serpent head projects from pyramid's facade.

53. Detail of alternate head type, possibly the Storm God.

construction of the pyramid began. Some female skeletons with small shell earspools and simple shell necklaces were sacrificed; male sacrifices, however, greatly outnumbered female burials. Directly in the center of the pyramid twenty skeletons and burial offerings were placed on the ground and covered with semi-flat stones. Foundation stones covered the remains. There was no precise orientation to the bodies, nor were their hands behind them.

No tombs or identifiable burial sites for Teotihuacános have been discovered in the city. The dead were buried where they lived. They were tightly wrapped and placed in hollowed out depressions under courtyards or floors of their living quarters.

A short distance west of the Ciudadela, in an excavated area called the "Oaxaca barrio," two Zapotec urns, hundreds of Oaxaca-style shards, and **a tomb complete with Zapotec hieroglyphs** were found (Millon 1973). In addition to the Oaxaca-style pottery, ceramics from Veracruz and quantities of Maya pottery have been found in the city, suggesting widespread trading with these areas during the Classic period.

About 30 out of a possible 2000 communal apartment compounds designed for urban living have recently been excavated; each compound housed at least 30, and possibly 100, individuals. There were rooms for food preparation, sleeping, or group activity; individual units were joined by long passages. The living quarters opened onto interior courtyards that provided light and air and insured privacy from the street. The compounds were built around A.D. 250, replacing previous temporary structures. After A.D. 250, no large structures were built at Teotihuacán.

Although most of the residences and shops were built in a traditional post and lintel style, the dominant architectural theme at Teotihuacán for the large-scale buildings and pyramids is the Talud-Tablero profile. This design can be observed in seemingly endless repetition throughout the site, on every pyramid, platform, shrine, and altar. The repetition of this unique form emphasizes its importance and is significant in that the profile appears to be restricted to religious and ceremonial structures.

Astronomy

In 1912, Sansbury Hagar, Secretary of the Department of Ethnology at the Brooklyn Institute of Arts and Sciences, was one of the first to suggest the astronomical nature of the Mexican monuments at Teotihuacán. He stated his belief that the Citadel had been a solar temple, and that its two enclosures

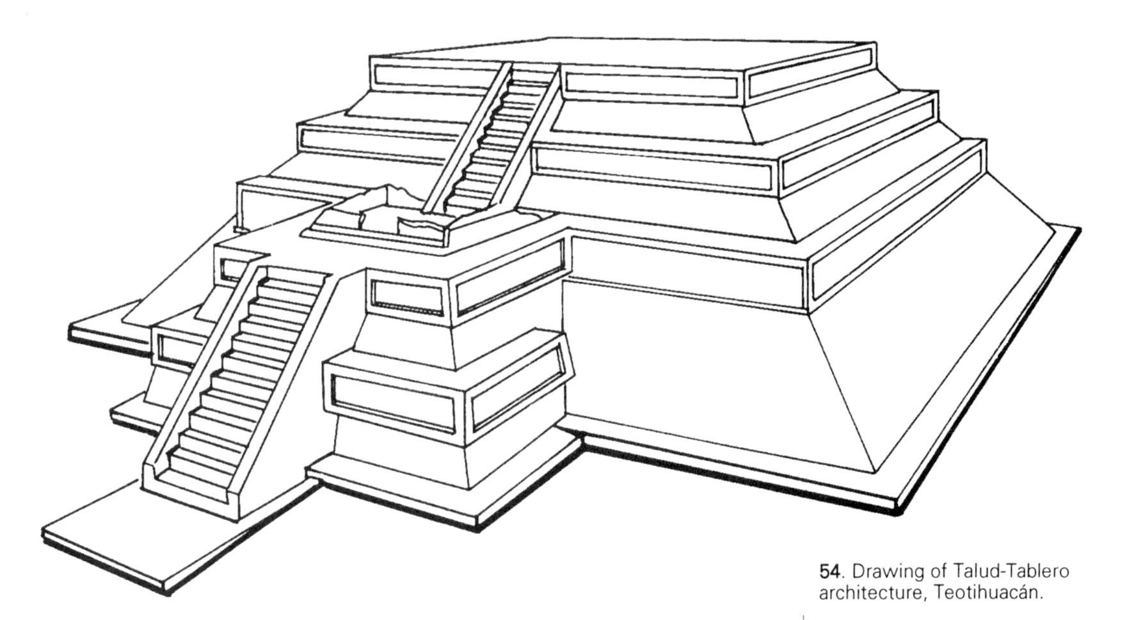

54. Drawing of Talud-Tablero architecture, Teotihuacán.

related mathematically to the solstices and equinoxes. He further suggested that the smaller mounds may have been intended to represent the planets or other stars, and that the Avenue of the Dead paralleled the position of the Milky Way. Hagar's theories were not widely accepted at that time. But Aveni (1980) describes in detail the cosmic orientation of Teotihuacán, and describes ancient petroglyphs that bear markings used in the initial orientation and plan of the city. Peter Tompkins also suggests that the master plan of Teotihuacán was more than just precise and orderly. He postulated that the buildings were placed along the Avenue of the Dead in a deliberate pattern ingeniously parallel to the position of the planets in our solar system. Tompkins cites specific data, especially the research by Hugh Harleston, an American engineer (Tompkins 1976).

According to Harleston, the distances between the structures at Teotihuacán correspond to the orbits of the known planets in our solar system. In order to prove his theory, Harleston first had to establish the basic unit of measurement that was used when the city was built. By determining ratios of large to small-scale measurements, Harleston was able to establish a unit of measurement equivalent to 1.059 meters. He named this unit a hunab, after the Mayan word for unified measure. Harleston then studied the various structures along the Avenue of the

Dead, trying to determine a possible function for their placement. He used the axis of the Avenue of the Dead as a kind of astronomical yardstick, with the Citadel, on the east side of the avenue, representing the sun. He then assigned a value of 96 hunabs to the earth's orbital distance from the sun and compared this to a drawing of the solar system. Given these conditions, he found a correlation of distances between major walls and platform centers inside the Citadel, as well as some major structures along the avenue, to the orbital distances of Mercury, Venus, Earth, and Mars from the sun. He noted an intriguing coincidence involving the distances between the structures in hunabs (beginning from the center point of the Pyramid of Quetzálcóatl in the Citadel) and the distances of the planets from the sun in astronomical units (A.U.). The measurement comparisons are as follows:

Planet	Hunabs	A.U.
Mercury	36	0.39
Venus	72	0.72
Earth	96	1.00
Mars	144	1.52
Jupiter	520	5.20
Saturn	945	9.54
Uranus	1895	19.20
Neptune	2880	30.60
Pluto	3780	39.40

The similarity between the numbers is striking. If the values given for the orbital distances of the planets in astronomical units were multiplied by 100, the resulting products would closely match the values given in hunabs. In order to determine the distance of the planets from the sun, the ancient astronomers would have had to have been competent mathematicians, and would also have understood that the sun was at the center of the solar system, not the earth. Western Europeans did not come to this realization until the sixteenth century, long after Teotihuacán was abandoned (Tompkins 1976).

The mathematical relationships of the structures along the Great Avenue suggest an orderly and deliberate plan, yet we have no conclusive evidence that would suggest the purpose of this design. According to Millon (Berrin, Pasztory 1993), "The Street of the Dead has a distinctive orientation—15.5 degrees east of north. I contend that this orientation was based on astronomical observations related to the cave (under the Sun Pyramid). These observations also determined the location of the 'Street' and explain why the pyramids are where they are."

Art

The great numbers of small clay figurines that have been found at Teotihuacán suggest their importance as ritual or trade objects. Some were hand modeled but most were made from clay molds formed from the original piece. Thousands of figurines were produced in this manner and widely distributed; many have been found as far south as Guatemala, indicating their possible use as widespread trade items. Specific characteristics of the figurines include wide foreheads, aquiline noses, and well-formed mouths. The general effect is of a triangular-shaped face that is most frequently topped by a flat rectangular headdress. There are also large sculptural pieces, such as the tenoned heads that project from the front of the Pyramid of Quetzálcóatl, the massive basalt female figure discovered in front of the Pyramid of the Moon (believed to be a water goddess, similar to the Aztec Chalchiuhtlicue), and the massive Storm God in front of the Museum of Anthropology in Mexico City. These geometric forms exhibit the same clarity and mathematical precision seen in the architecture of the city.

Numerous masks of serpentine, onyx, greenstone, and obsidian were made by the Teotihuacános. These are usually near life-sized and expertly carved. Eyes and teeth are often designated by inset bits of shell or mica, and facial features are defined only to the hairline. It has been suggested that these life-like images may be elaborate funerary masks that were tied to the cloth in which the dead were wrapped, and that an elaborate headdress may have been attached to the top of the mask to emphasize the importance of each individual, or as a means of identification. It is possible that the mask served both purposes.

55. Xipe Totec, the Flayed Lord. Snakeskin belt fits around this god's waist. Loose skin turned inside out at the neck simulates the snake shedding its skin. (INAH.)

56. Clay mask. Distinctive design under nose is reminiscent of Talud-Tablero form, or stylized butterfly wings. (INAH.)

Simple clay masks were found in household rubbish, and are believed to have also been part of the burial ritual of commoners.

Quantities of mass produced ceramics, as well as elaborately decorated vessels, have been found at Teotihuacán. The most well known styles are Thin Orange ware, Plano Relief, and stuccoed vessels; Orange ware was the most widely used. The name comes from the bright orange color of the clay, which is determined by certain combinations of minerals and other elements in the material. Plano Relief vessels have raised motifs carved into the clay when dry, then overpainted with color or stucco after firing. The stucco pieces are extremely fragile, and they are covered with thin layers of stucco and paint. The thinness and lightness of these ceramics is a striking contrast to the blocky, heavy quality of the large sculptural pieces and architecture at Teotihuacán. There were also large polychromed urns and elaborately decorated censers.

The profoundly symbolic and religious art of Teotihuacán reached its apogee in the murals that have been found in many of the temples and palaces. In contrast to Aztec art, which often focuses on frightening imagery, or Olmec art that describes elaborately dressed leaders and monumental altar-like scenes, the imagery at Teotihuacán (specifically the Late Classic murals) frequently

57. Clay and shell mask. The realism of this mask suggests portrait sculpture. (INAH.)

58. Mask, Teotihuacán.

59. Mask, Teotihuacán. Early Classic period. Height: 10 inches. (INAH.)

60. Censer, Teotihuacán. Ceramic and mica.
Height: 24 inches. (MNYC.)

61. Reproduction of Tlalocan mural from the Tapantitla compound at Teotihuacán. Sometimes called the Paradise of Tlaloc. Agustin Villagra: INAH, Mexico City.

depicts scenes of nature's bounty and paradisiacal events. The mural known to us as the Tlalocan painting (often called the Paradise of Tlaloc) from the Tepantitla compound at Teotihuacán, is an excellent example of the Teotihuacáno's reverence for beauty, nature, and the spiritual world. Caso (1959) was the first to suggest that this was the Tlalocan of the Aztecs, a mural dedicated to the rain god they called Tlaloc, describing a paradise for those whose death was in some way associated with water.

A large figure wearing a half mask dominates the top section of the mural. Plants sprout from the head, and droplets of water and pieces of jade flow from the hands and fingertips. Two

62. Detail, newly arrived souls in the paradise of the Water God.

elegantly dressed men face the central figure. In the back is a strange tree-like form with seashells and butterflies flowing through its branches. The bottom portion of the mural is covered with little figures dancing and joyfully moving about in the land where the spirits of the dead meet. There is a mountain rising out of the water, and many of the figures are swimming or joyfully playing. New arrivals to the watery paradise are assisted by friendly souls. Some of them play ball, wave tree branches above their heads, or ride piggyback on the others. Painted speech scrolls suggest singing or continuous conversation. They are surrounded by butterflies, flowers, and water motifs. All of this symbolism appears to relate to the religious beliefs of the ancient Teotihuacános.

Teotihuacán was the most powerful city in Mesoamerica during the Classic period; its influence in trade and commerce extended south as far as Guatemala, and embraced both the west and east coastal regions. Rulers were royal leaders who made religious as well as administrative decisions; the people were actively engaged in a wide spectrum of work activities. Many of

63. Detail, small figures in various joyful activities.

64. Stela 71, Teotihuacán. Stone with traces of red paint. 41" (MNYC)

the known Mesoamerican gods were worshipped here: the Feathered Serpent god, whose importance is emphasized by the sacrificial rituals that accompanied the dedication of the pyramid that bears his name, and the Storm God, a major deity who in later times was called Tlaloc by the Aztec in the Valley of Mexico, are two examples. There is also an elusive, masked female deity on many of the murals whom we simply call "The Goddess." She is always masked, or her face is missing; her hands are usually outstretched, and from her fingertips flow streams of water and precious objects. It has recently been suggested that she is the figure that dominates the Tlalocan mural's upper band (Pasztory 1993). According to Pasztory, "The Goddess, a mysteriously masked being, seems to be entirely local, primarily involved with the city and its population at large; her image did not last much beyond the fall of the city." Pasztory postulates that the large number of caves in and around Teotihuacán, particularly the cave beneath the Pyramid of the Sun, supported the emergence myths in which a female deity is associated with the place where human beings emerged at the beginning of creation.

Despite the volume of cultural remains discovered at Teotihuacán, there are still many unanswered questions. For examples: why did large-scale construction stop after A.D. 250? How powerful was The Goddess and what role she play? And the ultimate question: How was this powerful city destroyed, and by whom? We do not know what language the people at Teotihuacán spoke, nor do we know to which ethnic group they belonged. Unlike the Maya, who left hundreds of stelae inscribed with names, dates, and information about their rulers, the Teotihuacános left no inscriptions.

Teotihuacán was partially destroyed and abandoned by its people more than 1200 years ago, yet its buildings and pyramids still stand. The architectural grandeur and the profound symbolism of its art bear silent tribute to this remarkable city, the first great metropolis in Mesoamerica.

65. Seated Deity, Monte Albán III. Clay. Height: 18 1/2 inches. (MNYC.)

The Zapotec

Monte Albán II, II, IV

Toward the end of the Preclassic period, and continuing some 800 to 900 years, Monte Albán underwent a period of new and extensive construction under the Zapotec who lived in the surrounding mountains and valleys. Hundreds of acres of mountaintop were leveled, administrative and ceremonial buildings were constructed, and several residential enclaves were established; Monte Albán was slowly molded into a magnificent city. It was to become the greatest urban center to dominate the Valley of Oaxaca for more than 800 years. The area may have been selected as the site of a great administrative center because of its strategic location at the junction of three arms of the Valley of Oaxaca. Its position high above the rich, agriculturally productive areas in the valley and the absence of water on the mountaintop supports the theory that the site was chosen for political, administrative, and/or religious reasons. There are remains of early walls around part of the city that may have served as a defense against rebellious subjects or aggressive groups from outside the valley, or simply as a reminder to the population below of the Zapotecs' formidable power during the Classic period. However, by A.D. 900 the population began to diminish, and large portions of the city fell into disrepair. Some small groups of Zapotec and Mixtec continued to inhabit the site, but the power and influence of the earlier Classic period rulers is no longer evident.

Chronology and Development of Monte Albán

Monte Albán I: 500 B.C. Some simple tombs date from the early Preclassic period, as well as many burials that contained pottery of a fine paste grey ware. There were solid figurine types of the Tlatilco style, and ceramics that compare in form and decorative motifs to similar pieces from the Valley of Mexico, Chiapas, and Veracruz. There is some evidence that the inner buildings of the Northern Platform may have been built at this early date. However, the architecture of this time is poorly represented because of later construction over the original buildings (Flannery & Marcus 1983).

Phase I is the earliest period of development at Monte Albán, and it dates from early Preclassic times to about 500-400 B.C. The Temple of the Danzantes is believed to have been the first permanent structure built during this early period. It is a large flat platform, faced with stones carved with images of nude male figures. Although there is some disagreement as to the ethnicity of the figures, the features appear to be Olmecoid, and the full, fleshy mouths display the characteristic droop at the corners so identifiable with the Olmec culture (refer to the Olmec section for full description). Fine paste grey ware for ceremonial use continued to be favored, although a variety of pottery styles for both ceremonial and everyday purposes was made. Particularly noteworthy of the Phase I ceramics are the small vessels with a fine polish and slip with bridged spouts.

Many Mesoamerican groups used the Calendar Round, but only the Maya developed it in such a way that there was never any danger of confusing a date from this calendar with any other.

In addition to the Danzantes building and the existing ceramic activity, there is abundant evidence from hieroglyphs, numerals, and calendric inscriptions on carved stones that the 52 year calendar cycle, known as the **Calendar Round**, was in use (refer to page 114); glyphs from more recent time periods are recognizable in an early form in Phase I. According to Marcus (1983), "The writing system of Phase I appears fully developed with single and double columns, day signs, possible month signs, and noncalendric glyphs which may be verbs."

Monte Albán II: 200 B.C.-A.D.100 Public buildings and temples were enlarged and expanded during Monte Albán II. The Main Plaza was paved with white stucco and several rows of public buildings were built over original bedrock outcroppings on the mountain top. Three distinct neighborhoods, which may have been established as early as Monte Albán I, flourished within the city; two minor residential areas existed at the base of the hill (Flannery & Marcus 1983). The buildings in the larger areas included two room temples, ballcourts, "altars," a subplaza tunnel, stone masonry tombs with vaulted roofs, and an unusual arrow-shaped building called Temple J. There was also the wide use of slab architecture at the site where large, thin slabs of stone were placed vertically to function as retaining walls, rather than horizontally as normal weight-bearing walls. The builders inclined the slab, with one leaning against the other, and thus created a vault-like thrust that strengthened the structure. If the stones were intended to be carved, they could be carved first and then placed where needed.

As previously noted, the famed arrow-shaped structure known as Temple J was built sometime during this period. It is

66. Temple J, Monte Albán. The arrow-like side of this building points to the southwest, in striking contrast to the north-south axis of the Plaza's other structures; Temple J may have functioned as an astronomical observatory.

the best preserved temple of the Monte Albán II period, and was discovered in 1935 by Alfonso Caso within Mound X, in the northeast corner of the Main Plaza. Its most outstanding feature, other than its curious shape, is a series of more than fifty carved stones set in the building's facade. The glyphs that were carved on the stones identify places conquered by the Zapotecs of Monte Albán, and are called "conquest slabs" (Caso 1938-47, Marcus 1983). In 1947, Alfonso Caso was the first to describe the following identifiable elements that were consistent on each slab: a "hill" sign that identifies place location; a single or compound glyph that names the place; a human head, upside down, with its own unique headdress (Caso proposed that these were the dead rulers of subjugated places, and that the individuality of each headddress may have served to reinforce the place-name data on each stone); and hieroglyphics that include the year sign, month and day relating to the place and event.

According to Marcus (1983), "Bldg. J stones may represent 50-odd landmarks that constituted the limits of Monte Albán's tribute territory in Period II. This is borne out by 16th c. Aztec documents listing places in Oaxaca that paid tribute to the Aztec."

The Aztec scribes of the Codex Mendoza used the *tepetl* or "hill" sign to introduce the names of specific places. Although most of the ancient names have been lost in the 1500 or so years since the decline of Monte Albán, there are at least four identifiable hieroglyphic place names from Building J that closely resemble known place names from Oaxaca in the Codex Mendoza (Marcus 1976). Building J has a northeast stairway orientation which differs from the east-west or north-south orientation of the other buildings in the Main Plaza, suggesting a special purpose for this structure. It has often been referred to as an astronomical observatory and, indeed, investigations of the building's interior, and specifically the tunnel which slices horizontally through the rear of the building, shows that the tunnel itself is directed in such a way that the rising of Capella would have been especially noticeable from this vantage point. Capella was unique among the bright stars at that time because its heliacal rising came precisely on the same day as the first annual passage of the sun across the zenith of Monte Albán. Although the sun and moon positions bore no relation to any portion of Building J, the "point" of the building was directed towards Capella at the time of the zenith, as well as to the setting position of five of the twenty-five brightest stars in the sky (Aveni 1980). Aveni and Linsley, however, caution the reader that there is not enough evidence to conclusively prove its purpose as a true astronomical observatory (Aveni and Linsley 1972).

Monte Albán IIIa: A.D.100-400 This was the time of Zapotec dominance and the florescence of their civilization. Ceremonial grey ware is still very much in evidence, but there was a gradual change in ceramic styles as new forms began to appear exhibiting Teotihuacán influence in style and decoration. Tombs were decorated with vividly colored wall paintings that depicted images of ancestors and deities. Elaborate funerary urns, a particular speciality of the Zapotec, are now included in the burials. There appears to have been a gradual shift at this time from the recording of military conquests to establishing the

67. Clay urn, Monte Albán III. (INAH)

genealogy of Zapotec royalty on the lavishly embellished funerary urns. Construction began in earnest and the main buildings at Monte Albán were completed; a magnificent ball court for the ritual game, which was played throughout Mesoamerica, may date from this time. There were strong political and cultural ties with Teotihuacán during the early part of this period, and one can easily recognize its influence in art and in the architectural style that prevailed. The main buildings have broad ascending stairways, and they were plastered and painted in much the same way as the temples and platforms at Teotihuacán. The architectural format exhibits the same Talud-Tablero profile, and the major groupings of buildings are arranged around central plazas. Although a strong relationship between Monte Albán and Teotihuacán has long been suspected, the discovery of the Oaxaca barrio at Teotihuacán confirms that there were closer ties between the two cities than had

68. Monte Albán. Main Plaza as seen from the north exhibits a general north- south orientation.

earlier been suspected. Indeed, Rene Millon (1973) suggested that Monte Albán and Teotihuacán had a "special relationship."

Monte Albán IIIb: A.D. *400 to 600* At the beginning of this period, cultural ties were still stong with Teotihuacán. Some of the buildings and tomb paintings at Monte Albán reflect this influence. Unlike Teotihuacán, however, which was a large city with a varied social structure, Monte Albán was primarily an administrative and religious center that must have received constant attention from a large resident population that lived in small enclaves close to the administrative/ceremonial buildings, as well as at the foot of the mountain itself. The city was restricted in size by the hilly terrain, and there are no springs to supply water to the mountaintop location. The absence of water alone would have presented an enduring hardship to a large residential population. According to Blanton, a conservative estimate of the population by A.D. 600 is that 15,000 to 30,000 people lived on the mountain. The most densely populated areas covered about 6.5 km. (about four square miles). There were 2004 residences, 35 of which were very elaborate. Nearly all of the visible architecture, tombs, and inscriptions date from this late Classic phase (Blanton 1978).

Monte Albán IV: A.D. 600-950 There was a significant decrease in population during this late Classic period. New construction virtually ceased, and the Main Plaza fell into disuse. Ceramic making activity continued, but the clay objects made during Monte Albán IV are difficult to distinguish from Phase IIIb ceramics because of the similarity in technique and design. Although portions of Monte Albán continued to be occupied, and abandonment never became total, the population consistently declined until Monte Albán was unable to function as an influential decision-making center. It has not been determined why Monte Albán's power diminished; there may have been a combination of factors. It is possible that former residents left for economic reasons, or perhaps the rise in power of other Zapotec cities attracted the Monte Albán residents. Blanton (1983) suggests that the collapse of Teotihuacán in A.D. 700 may have impacted on the polity at Monte Albán; the cessation of power in the Valley of Mexico may have removed the need for an expensive regional authority in Oaxaca. Until more study is completed from this time period, however, our knowledge is entirely speculative. Despite the decline in population, burial activity continued for some time. Areas on the north slope of the city were still occupied, and most of the tombs from this period were found at this location. There are 33 tombs dating from Period IIIb on the north slope, and 40 tombs date from Period IV. It is obvious that the city was still considered an appropriate place for Zapotec burials (Blanton: Flannery & Marcus 1983).

Monte Albán V: A.D. 950-1530 There was a general abandonment of the Main Plaza, and a significant increase in population around the base of Monte Albán after A.D. 950 (Blanton 1983). The remains from this time period include an exceptionally large concentration of pottery, and some burials and burial offerings from the Mixtec occupation. Although much smaller in population size than Phase III times, it may have been used as a small commercial center where people still brought offerings and occasionally buried their dead in the Zapotec tombs. The most famous tomb discovery from this late period is Tomb 7, which was originally a Zapotec tomb that was later used by the Mixtec to bury an important personage (see Postclassic period Mixtec at Monte Albán).

Tombs

Many tombs lie under the courts and plazas of Monte Albán and in the caves that extend into the sharply descending slopes of the mountain itself. The caves were believed by the Zapotec to be the homes of their ancestors, and they were used as sacred burial places. Some of the excavated tombs contain both male and female remains, suggesting that a ruler and his wife, or members of a royal family, were sometimes buried together. The Zapotecs believed that a dead ruler continued to influence the affairs of his people as a "cloud person" who was capable of understanding all aspects of the supernatural. In the Zapotec mind, the deceased ruler became a powerful intermediary between mortal men and the gods (Flannery 1983). An extraordinary amount of creative energy went into the construction and furnishing of the Zapotec tombs. Entire walls were often covered with murals which were stylistically related to the formal murals of Teotihuacán, and elaborate clay urns were placed in the chambers.

Zapotec funerary urns represent the high point of Zapotec art. No other potters in the Americas have been able to master so completely the difficulties of working with wet clay. The Zapotecs created complex images that completely retained their intricate detail after firing. It is believed that many of the urns bear images of Zapotec ancestors; others can be identified as nature gods. The most frequently represented deity was Cocijo, the god of rain and lightning, and a powerful Zapotec supernatural. Cocijo had the power to bring rain, and therefore contributed to the growth of corn. The symbolism repeatedly

69. Monte Albán's Northern Tomb area contains many well preserved burial chambers dating from earliest times up to the Conquest.

associated with him includes a circle of snakes around his neck, fangs, and a mask around the eyes, nose and mouth, including a split Y-formed tongue, which was an ancient symbol of lightning. Cocijo's appearance seems to be related in some ways to the Storm God at Teotihuacán (Marcus: Flannery & Marcus 1983). In addition, the headdresses of these Cocijos frequently display the "Glyph C," which was believed by Caso (1928) to be the stylized representation of the mouth of a tiger, or possibly a vessel holding water. At other times, when the urn has a Cocijo mask with corncobs as part of its headdress, Caso and Bernal (1952) interpret the image as depicting "the God of Harvest of Maize," and is associated in this way with water.

The images on the urns that depict important personages are generally seated in a cross-legged position with their hands placed upon their knees, and wearing elaborate headdresses, large earplugs, bracelets, collars, and capes. Their faces are often covered with stylized masks of gods or totem animals. Although human figures are most frequently represented, animal forms are also depicted—especially the jaguar and the bat. Marcus (1983) suggests that the human urns may represent deceased ancestors. This is supported by the inventory of identifiable Zapotec names on the urns that varies from period to period and site to

70. Clay urn, Monte Albán III.

site in a way that would be unlikely if they were deities. According to Marcus, ancestor worship was an important part of Zapotec religion; the images on the elaborate urns were sacred. Thus, they were important links to the supernatural, and they were kept in temples, tombs, and other important places. After the Conquest of Mexico, the Spaniards found these images and arbitrarily described all of them as "idols" or "gods." Since many names taken from the 260 day ritual calendar were given to human leaders—for example, Three Deer, Eight Deer, Seven Rabbit—and these names were repeated in many villages and during different time periods, the highly individualistic named urns most likely represent those deceased ancestors who became the "Cloud People." (Marcus translation of Espindola 1580:134.)

At the close of the Classic period, the great artistic endeavors that were typical of earlier times slowly disappeared. A continuing decline in Zapotec population after A.D. 1000 saw the

71. Monte Albán's ballcourt is typical of Classic period, I-shaped courts with sloping walls.

abandonment of Monte Albán as an active ceremonial center. From this time on, the site was primarily used for burial purposes. Although the tombs continued to be filled with meaningful funerary offerings, the style that prevailed no longer exhibited the unique qualities and superb craftsmanship that had previously made Monte Albán one of the most artistically prominent cities in ancient Mesoamerica.

After the Conquest of Mexico in the 16th century, the Spaniards referred to both the Zapotec and Mixtec as "The Cloud People." This comes from their translation of the Zapotec and Mixtec names. The Zapotec referred to themselves as the *peni-zaa* (*peni*=people; *zaa* referred to ancestral clouds). The Mixtec lived in *Mixtlan*, which meant "the place of clouds." Even today, some Zapotec refer to their ancestors as *binigulaza*, which means "old people of the clouds." (Flannery & Marcus 1983: xx-xxi.)

72. Geometric designs, Palace of the Columns, Mitla. Light and shadow emphasize decorative qualities of elaborate stonework.

Mitla

After the abandonment of Monte Albán as an important decision making center, other Zapotec sites expanded and began to exert their influence in the Oaxaca valley. One of these late period sites is Mitla, which has generated a great deal of interest because of its palatial buildings and extraordinary architectural style. Unlike Monte Albán, with its simple and undecorated Talud and Tablero format, the buildings at Mitla are all richly decorated with geometric designs that stand out in sharp relief. The dramatic effect of the relief designs creates a visual display that is further emphasized by the changing light and shadow patterns during the day. The builders of Mitla were most likely Zapotec who may have been influenced by the Mixtec (Marcus: Flannery and Marcus 1983).

Fret: an ornamental design consisting of repeated and symmetrical or geometric figures or designs, often in relief, and contained within a band or border.

Frieze: a plain or decorated horizontal band along the upper part of an interior wall. As part of a building's entablature, it is between the architrave and cornice.

There are five separate groups of elaborately decorated buildings at Mitla grouped around spacious plazas and sunken patios. There are **fretwork friezes**, and deeply carved moldings called tablero escapulario (scapular panels) adorning each building. The scapular panels are smooth, horizontal bands of stone, with occasional vertical or "hanging" bands that allow for open spaces between the hanging element and the smooth

73. View of the Fretwork Patio, Palace of the Columns, Mitla.

panels. These open spaces were then further utilized to display a great variety of fretwork patterns, mosaics made of small pieces, and other relief designs.

"The Group Of The Columns" is the name given to two of the five groups of buildings at Mitla. They are the most interesting structures here because of their well-preserved state and richly decorated buildings. The so-called "Palace" in this group is an elaborate structure covered with continuous panels in high relief and fretwork designs. Although the original use of the buildings here at Mitla has not been conclusively proven, they most likely were residences for important personages and places where Zapotec nobles gathered for decision making purposes.

74. Pyramid of the Niches at El Tajín, Veracruz. This 60' high pyramid has 365 niches recessed into its tablero-style tiers.

75. Structure 5. Cornice detail exhibits recurved eaves and squared spiral motifs.

Classic Veracruz Cultures

El Tajín

Many important ceremonial and urban centers flourished in the dense, tropical lowlands of Veracruz during the Classic period. One of the largest was El Tajín, which is located approximately five miles southwest of the present-day city of Papantla. On first impression, the ruins of El Tajín appear to cover a very small area, since the only buildings that have been excavated are grouped together in the center of the site. Closer observation reveals that a great many unexcavated temples and buildings lie hidden under a covering of earth and grass. El Tajín extends for hundreds of acres from the center of the site into the dense tropical growth that covers the surrounding terrain.

Dominating the main central core is the Pyramid of the Niches, a six-tiered, 60 foot high pyramid with 365 niches recessed into the tablero-style exterior. The first tier of the four-sided pyramid has 22 niches per side; each of the five ascending levels decrease in size and have three niches per side fewer than the level below (22, 19, 16, 13, 10, 7 niches from the first level to the sixth), totaling 87 niches per side or 348 for the four sides. When we add to the total figure the 17 niches in the substructure of the temple at the top, we reach a total of 365 niches for the entire pyramid. Although the function of these small apertures has never been fully understood, one cannot lightly dismiss the fact that there are also 365 days in the solar year.

Like most of the buildings at El Tajín, the Pyramid of the Niches was built of stone slabs that were set in mortar and positioned to form a slight slope, or talus. Wide cornices resembling the re-curved eaves of Japanese roofs project over each of the six tiers that form the pyramid; a stairway provided access to the top, where a temple once stood. On either side of the steps are the squared spiral and interlaced designs for which El Tajín is famous. Since the niches, cornices, and design elements continue uninterruptedly under the stairway, we know that the steps were not built until the pyramid was completed. Like many Mexican pyramids, it was built over an older and smaller version of the six-tiered pyramid that we see today.

Overlooking the Niches pyramid are palace-like buildings on a gently sloping hill. Well constructed, with large blocks made from a concrete mixture of sand and finely ground seashells formed in wooden molds this is Tajin Chico. The largest

76. Buildings at Tajin Chico display squared spirals and recurved eaves.

structure has a base measurement of 650 by 295 feet. It is called the Building of the Columns because of the massive columns located near the front entry area. Despite the fact that these columns now lie in broken disarray, many of the large fragments still bear clear images of winged dancers, Eagle Knights, human sacrifices, mythological animals, and glyphs. There are also the double-line, interlaced spiral and scroll patterns that are so identifiable with Classic period Veracruz. They appear on most of the buildings and ballcourts at El Tajín, and have often been compared to motifs found on bronze objects from the Chou period in ancient China. This distinctive art style does not have an identifiable ethnic origin, and we do not know to which ethnic group the inhabitants belonged. However, Olmec influence from earliest times, as well as certain Classic period traditions from Teotihuacán and the Maya, are recognizable in many of the art forms of Classic Veracruz.

Near the Pyramid of the Niches are two major ball courts, and at least nine more have been identified. No other Mesoamerican site has this many courts, and it is apparent that this city may have been the center for the ritual game. The enclosing walls of the South Ballcourt are decorated with six elaborate bas-relief panels. There are elaborate scrolls, reclining and flying figures, and plumed forms. One scene depicts a figure who grasps a bundle of three downward pointing arrows, a gesture signifying war; another panel portrays musicians with drums and rattles. There is no reference to the ballgame on the south wall panels. In contrast, both scenes on the north wall take place in a ball court and describe details of the event. The first panel shows two standing players; between them is the crossed-band war sign of the Aztec. The second scene describes a human sacrifice whereby a seated ball player is held firmly by the arms while a third figure prepares to plunge a sharp knife into his heart. A royal observer is depicted in the background, and the God of Death descends upon the sacrificial victim from above.

The Ball Game

The ancient ballgame of Mesoamerica was played throughout Mexico, in Central America, and at some locations in the northern part of South America as early as the second millenium B.C. Although ballcourts have been found at almost every

77. Ballcourt wall panel describes the sacrifice of a ball player.

ancient site from Early Preclassic times, it is believed that the game was first played south of El Tajín, in the lowlands of the Gulf Coast region where the ancient Olmec built their major cities. According to Michael Coe (1965), the remains of at least one ball court have been discovered at the oldest known Olmec city of San Lorenzo. In addition, clay figures of ball players have been found at Olmec-occupied locations that date from the earliest Preclassic times. Over 1000 ballcourts have been discovered at the aforementioned locations.

Although the ballcourts of Mesoamerica varied in size and shape from one location to another, the earliest courts were simple, elongated earthen playing fields. The courts of the Classic and Postclassic periods were most often shaped like a capital "H" with two short "end zone" arms and an elongated center playing field. The early courts were made of earth; later examples were most often built of stone. By A.D. 400 stone courts predominated, and walls with straight or sloping sides usually flanked the long playing field. On some of the side walls were bas-relief images of ball players and ceremonial scenes that related to the game. The best preserved scenes were found on the walls of the Great Ball Court at Chichén Itzá, the largest ball court in Mesoamerica, and also at El Tajín, where as many as eleven courts are known to exist. The wide distribution of ball court remains indicates that it was a game of significant religious or ceremonial importance, often depicting astronomical events (most probably a tribute to the rising and setting of the sun, which was represented by the ball), a military conquest, an athletic contest, or the birth or death of an important ruler. There are no records to explain exactly how or why the ballgame was played in ancient times. After the Conquest of Mexico in the 16th century, the Spaniards described the ballgame as a contest between two opposing teams who would attempt to score points with a heavy rubber ball. There often were differences in the manner in which the game was played and in the number of players on each "team."

As recorded by the Spaniards after the Conquest, the object of the game was to score by hitting a heavy rubber ball against a marker, or through stone rings that projected from either side wall above the centerline. To knock the ball through the stone rings was extremely difficult, if not almost impossible, since the players were not allowed to touch the ball with their hands. Therefore, we can assume that scoring was relatively rare, or that most of the victories resulted from hitting the ball against a marker or by simply getting the ball into the opponent's scoring area. The game may have been played for pleasure or to demonstrate or improve upon one's skill. (In some examples of Maya art, ballplayers are identified with the Hero Twins from the book of the Popul Vuh.) At other times, gambling was the motivation. The stakes ranged from wagers of valuable goods to the highest stake of all, one's life. Bets were placed, and some gamblers became so addicted to the game that they would play until they lost all of their money and material goods. According to Schele (1986), "When points were scored, the spectators would hastily throw their robes at the players in payment of their bets, and then flee to avoid paying higher losses."

To play the game was an honor, and the people played with great enthusiasm. Players would fall to the ground to get under the ball, taking the full impact of the heavy rubber ball as it descended toward the earth; accidents were common. Some ballplayers died as a result of severe internal injuries in the abdominal area after being hit by the hard rubber ball. Incisions were frequently made to relieve the pressure of blood painfully trapped under the surface of the skin. When the game finally ended, the losing captain is believed to have been the one chosen for the sacrificial rites; his heart was offered to the gods, and occasionally his decapitated head was substituted for the rubber ball and used to play the next game (Schele 1986).

Ritual Objects for the Ceremonial Game

Three stone objects are associated with the sacred ball game and with the ceremonial life at El Tajín: yokes, *palmas*, and *hachas*. The yokes are U-shaped and are believed to be stone replicas of lighter protective belts that were worn around the players' waists. Sculptured bas-relief scenes on the ball court walls show these padded belts being worn by the ballplayers to protect the hips and abdominal area from injury. Tucked into the front of the yoke was a tall fan-shaped object called a *palma*, so named because of its similarity in form to palm leaves. The *palmas* may have been used to deflect the ball. They are notched at one end and have a concave surface at the base; the back is smooth and undecorated. The front surface is carved with a wide variety of subject matter, such as human faces, animals, or purely decorative objects. The sculptured wall reliefs show these

78. Greenstone yoke, El Tajín. Height: 16 inches. (MNYC.)

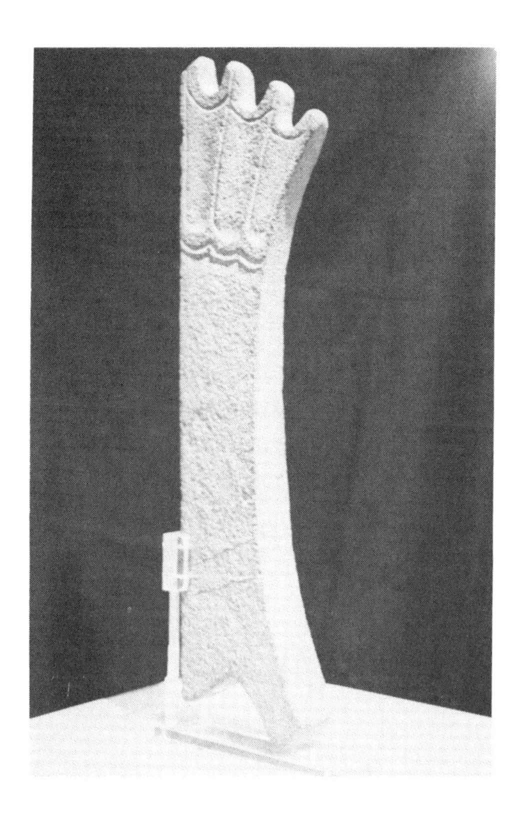

79. *Left*. Fan-shaped stone *palma*. (LSUM.)

80. *Right*. Stone *hacha*. Warrior's headdress depicts animal form, perhaps a deer. (INAH.)

palmas resting on the yokes. Another object associated with the ballgame was the wedge-shaped *hacha*. Like the *palmas* and the yokes, the *hachas* are intricately carved in stone to represent human, animal, or bird forms. Although their function has never been conclusively determined, the *hachas* may have served as markers for the ball game (Miller 1991).

The stone yokes, *palmas* and *hachas* that have been found are far too heavy and cumbersome to have been worn during actual play. Instead, the stone effigies were most likely used during important rituals. The actual playing gear was probably made of an impermanent but lighter material such as wood or leather. According to Fox (1994), "At Tikal, in Guatemala, vestiges of an actual playing yoke have been found, but this polychromed and lime-stuccoed shell of a wooden yoke is one of very few examples of actual playing equipment known at this time." In addition to the well-known yoke, *palma*, and *hacha*, wood and leather knee and elbow guards have been found, along with stone effigies of these protective objects, and *manoplas*, which were rectangular stones with handles. It is believed that the *manoplas* were used to deflect the ball, to protect the player from the impact of the hard rubber ball, or to protect from possible injury when falling to the ground (Fox 1994). Ballgame players depicted on the relief panels of the Great Ball Court at Chichén Itzá hold *manoplas*. One especially clear example is held by the kneeling figure in the central panel. Although widely distributed throughout Mexico and Guatemala during the Classic period, Veracruz was no doubt the manufacturing center of these ceremonial objects.

Remojades

During recent years, excavations have yielded a rich treasure trove of sophisticated clay objects in central and southern Veracruz. Of particular interest are the hand-modeled and mold-made figurines and large clay statues. Traditionally, the figures have been labeled "Remojades," despite the fact that Remojades was only one center of manufacture. A more accurate accounting shows that other areas within the present-day state of Veracruz included Cerro de las Mesas, Los Cerros, Dicha Tuerta, Isla de Sacrificios, and Nopiloa. Other than Remojades, the sites named above have not yet received enough attention, other than in scholarly reports and journals, to be easily recognized by the general student.

The potters of Veracruz exhibited a sophisticated clay technology that included a mastery of two of the major problems inherent in clay: the tendency to shrink and warp, and the potential to explode during firing. Warping results when the clay dries unevenly. To increase porosity and allow the object to dry more evenly, crushed pottery pieces were added to the fine clay. To address the problem of breakage of the larger pieces during the firing process, hollow figures with thin walls between one-quarter and one-half inch thick were made. The potters understood that the moisture-laden air bubbles, which expand and explode during firing, are more likely to form in thick slabs of clay. Therefore, the lightness of the large figures and the thinness of their walls became of primary importance. The mastery of pit firing procedures demonstrates an extraordinary understanding of ceramic techniques.

81. Smiling Figure, Remojades. Clay. Height: 19 inches.

82. Standing Woman. Remojades-style.

83. Woman with cranial performations, Veracruz. (INAH.)

84. Clay Mask, Veracruz. (INAH.)

Veracruz ceramics were skillfully fired under carefully controlled conditions. Although true kilns have never been found in any of the manufacturing regions, it is generally accepted that the ancient technique of pit firing was used to bake the figurines and other clay objects. They were first buried in pits and then covered with fuel and old pot shards. This procedure ensured a high degree of insulation, which maximized heat retention during the final baking. The insulation the shards provided allowed temperatures to be maintained or even increased to a higher level than would have been attained from a simple bonfire-type of firing.

Colors that were used by the ancient potters to paint the figurines were obtained from natural minerals. Unfortunately, these natural colors faded or disappeared entirely when fired. As a result, the clay pieces were usually repainted after firing. A white substance derived from kaolin or calcium carbonate was frequently used, as was black from some plant juices, red from the cinnabar, and two different blue clays. In addition to these colors, a shiny black pigment was used to enhance the features and highlight certain symbolic designs. This substance, found on so many of the Veracruz pieces, consists of a complex mixture of at least six different resins, asphalt, and soot. The resinous material is called *hule* (rubber) and the asphalt is called *chapopote.*

The most well known of all of the Veracruz figurines are the so-called "Smiling Faces." Although there is great similarity in their appearance, there are subtle differences in the construction of the whole figure. They were often solid, but some were made in two part molds. The use of molds to form the bodies is especially characteristic of the Nopiloa figurines. The figures are generally about ten to twenty inches tall, and represent men and women who are dressed in long skirts of richly patterned textiles delicately reproduced in clay. They wear bands around their chests and usually stand with their legs slightly apart, with both arms spread wide. Their wide smiles display filed teeth that are visible because of their joyous expressions. Men, women, and infants are all represented. It has been suggested that these small figures are clay representations of those men and women who were selected to represent the gods during the monthly festivals of the ancient Mesoamerican calendar, and who were sacrificed during the ceremonies (Heyden 1970). Each assumed the

85. Smiling face, clay.
Veracruz. (INAH)

86. Wheeled "toy." Although the wheel was not used for transporting objects or people, the concept of a wheel and axle was understood.

character of the god they were chosen to represent by being dressed and ornamented in his image. The victims were kept happy, as it was essential to present a positive image to the gods. If one became frightened, he or she may have been given an inebriating potion to drink (Duran 1967). The fact that many of these smiling heads are found without bodies may be because many of the human victims were decapitated during the ceremonies. Thus, the ritual breaking off of the heads of the clay figures would have corresponded to the actual ceremony itself.

Many figurines and large-scale heads do not display the famous smile. There are men and women in various poses; some are on swings and others have whistles embedded in their backs. Most of these pieces are highlighted with the black *hule* and *chapopote* that is indigenous to the region. This substance was used to emphasize various symbols and distinguishing features of the figures.

Small clay animals with wheels found here are of great interest because the wheel was never used during this time for transporting either people or objects. Investigators originally called the wheeled figures "toys" simply because there was no other obvious purpose for them. Although the use of the wheel for the small figurines was widespread, one can easily understand why it never became practical to use wheeled vehicles to transport people or large objects. First, there were no large draft animals; the largest domestic animals in ancient Mexico were medium-size dogs. In order to transport goods, humans would have had to pull the large carts, which may not have been a practical solution to the transportation problem. Another factor was the terrain itself. Both the mountainous highlands region and the swampy coastal areas of Mexico would challenge any kind of wheeled transportation. Instead, the ancient Mesoamericans most probably carried their goods on their backs, and used rafts and boats on the rivers and streams.

The archaeological history of El Tajín spans nearly one thousand years, from its earliest beginnings around A.D. 100 to A.D. 1200 when the site was abandoned. Most of the construction took place between the sixth and eighth centuries A.D., including the Pyramid of the Niches and several of the ball courts. New buildings and temples were added, as needed, until about A.D. 1200, when the site was destroyed by fire and subsequently abandoned.

87. Seated Figure. Maya, Mexico or Guatemala. Classic period. Height: 14 inches, wood. (MNYC.)

The Maya

The region in which the Maya civilization developed includes three distinctive geographic locations: the southern area, a mountainous highlands region which includes eastern Chiapas in Mexico, parts of Guatemala, and western El Salvador in Central America; the northern areas of the low-lying Yucatán Peninsula, which includes the Mexican states of Yucatán, Campeche, and Quintana Roo; and the densely forested central area that reaches from the states of Tabasco and southern Campeche in Mexico, across the Peten region in northern Guatemala, to include Belize and the far western area of Honduras. The earliest Maya lived in simple farming communities scattered throughout these regions. Many of the objects excavated from these sites carbon date from about 1500 B.C. and, until recent times, this was the earliest date Maya culture was believed to have developed. However, in 1975 new archaeological evidence emerged during excavations at the northern Belize site of Cuello that dates the beginnings of Maya civilization at least a thousand years earlier than previously supposed.

No stone structures survive at Cuello, only large plaster platforms that probably served as the bases for the typical Maya temple-pyramid structures. Because there are no other physical remains, we can safely assume that temples and residences were built of timber and other perishable materials. One of the largest excavated platforms had obviously been rebuilt many times, as there were several layers of plaster floors under the uppermost platform. One of the more recent platforms, dating from around 400 B.C., shows the emergence of ritual activity. Twenty human sacrifices there may have marked the dedication of the structure that occupied that platform (Hammond 1982). Pottery fragments found at the deepest level were carbon dated from between 1250 to 2600 B.C., and are older than any pottery of Maya origin previously discovered.

The discovery of Cuello has had a profound effect on archaeology in that it may identify an area rich in cultural remains from the earliest settled Maya communities in Mesoamerica. The establishment of this early date for the beginning of cultural development has increased speculation that the Maya could have influenced the beginnings of the great Olmec society rather than the reverse, as has been previously accepted. If further excavations prove this theory, then perhaps the Maya will someday be called the "Mother Culture" of Mesoamerica. For the moment, however, it seems more reasonable to leave the question open, since the time period from 2600 to 1500 B.C. is so poorly understood. The origins of the Olmec lie hidden within the earliest time periods and the secrets of the Preclassic Maya are just now beginning to unfold. But, as noted above, the excavations at Cuello place the emergence of Maya culture at least a thousand years earlier than once believed.

The Growth of Maya Culture: Early Preclassic to Late Classic period

The transition from the Preclassic to the Classic period was not abrupt, as the dating division implies. Rather, it was a long period of gradual growth and cultural awakening. During the Archaic period, as well as in Preclassic times, village life revolved around agriculture and the production of simple pottery. Then, sometime during the Late Preclassic period, Maya culture began to expand and develop in a more sophisticated way. Trade routes were established and the Maya obtained valuable commodities, which were used for ritual purposes and burial ceremonies, from their foreign neighbors. As a result, communities grew and became more prosperous. There was continuous contact with the Valley of Mexico during the early to mid-Classic periods, as evidenced by the Teotihuacán-style dress and ornamentation of major figures on Maya stelae; there was also an noticable increase in building activity. The Maya expanded throughout the homeland areas into new territories in southern Mexico, Belize, and Central America. The ambitious building programs were directed by powerful rulers who effectively guided and controlled a large labor force. There was hieroglyphic writing, the use of calendars, sophisticated sculpture, exquisitely painted pottery, mural painting, and intensive production of religious and ritual objects. These extraordinary advances in art, architecture, religion, and government began to appear by the end of the Preclassic period. Then, during a remarkable span of six centuries, from about A.D. 300 to 900, the Maya reached intellectual heights that no other people in the Western world could match at that time. This is known as the Classic period of the Maya, a veritable "Golden Age" in Mesoamerica. During this time, the Classic Maya were the most advanced civilization in prehispanic Mexico. They built hundreds of ceremonial centers and cities replete with great plazas, pyramids, and palaces, without metal tools or the use of draft animals or the wheel; they also produced masterpieces of sculpture. Especially noteworthy were the large stone monuments, called stelae, that were carved with images of rulers and deities and inscribed with hieroglyphics and symbolic motifs. As impressive as these accomplishments were, however, the intellectual achievements of the Maya in the fields of astronomy, hieroglyphic writing, mathematics, and calendrics were the most remarkable. Using nothing more than fixed lines of sight to study the movements of the sun, moon, and some planets, the Maya were able to make accurate astronomical observations. As a result, they were able to devise several calendars which recorded historical landmarks and references to fixed points in time.

Time Measurement

The Maya perfected calendric systems that recorded time in many different overlapping cycles, each differing in length of time and point of reference. It was as important to the Maya to place situations and events within an appropriate time context as it has been for all peoples, beginning, perhaps, with the emergence of the earliest settled communities, up to the present time. As strange as it may seem to us to read about the many ways in which the Maya marked time, we in the 20th century also refer to events in time in different ways (Schele 1986). For example, we might say, "Sunrise was at 6:02 A.M. the day before yesterday; sunrise was at 6:02 A.M. 63 days after the Winter Solstice; sunrise was at 6:02 A.M. last Tuesday; sunrise was at 6:02 A.M. on February 22, 1995; sunrise was at 6:02 A.M. on 2/22/95; or sunrise was at 6:02 A.M. on my son's birthday this year." Depending upon the speaker's place in time and his or her audience, all of these remarks could refer to Tuesday, February 22, 1995.

A few examples of Maya calendars are the *Tzolkin*, or Sacred Calendar; the *Haab*, or Vague Year; the Solar Year; the Calendar Round; the Long Count; and the Short Count. There is also the Secondary Series of Distance Numbers, which identifies the necessary calculations needed to adjust the Maya calendar to the solar year, and the Lunar or Supplementary Series, which identifies the phases and position of the moon on certain specified dates.

The *Tzolkin*, or Sacred Calendar of the Maya, was based upon a 260 day cycle that combined twenty named days with the numbers 1 to 13. As the day names and numbers were paired, 260 days would pass before each combination again appeared. This ritualistic and informative calendar was basically prophetic in that all important personal and general matters were decided upon according to the fate attributed to each particular day and its respective number. All of the other Maya calendars had to be coordinated with the Sacred Calendar.

The basis of the *Haab*, or Solar Calendar, was the 360 day period called *Tun*, which was divided into eighteen *Uinal* (months) of twenty days each, to which a short month of five *Uayayeb* (days) was added at the end of each year. The calendar was based upon the computation of the length of a year at 365.242 days, which is remarkably close to our calculation of 365.2422 days. (The Maya were also able to calculate the average synodical revolution of Venus at 584 days, as compared with our figure of 583.92 days.)

The basis of Maya chronology was the 52 year cycle, which is commonly referred to as the Calendar Round. Although they did not invent this calendar, the Maya perfected it. By combining the Solar Calendar with the Sacred Calendar, 18,980 days or 52 years had to go by in order for a single date to reappear on both calendars at the same time. If we think of the Sacred Calendar as a wheel with 260 spokes (days), and the Solar Calendar as having 365 spokes (days), the smaller one would have to turn 18,980 times in order to return to the initial pairing (18,980 days divided by 365 days=52 years). Many Mesoamerican groups used the Calendar Round, but only the Maya developed it in such a way that there was never any danger of confusing a date from this calendar with any other. The Maya understood that the calculation of time required a starting point, and they chose the date 13.0.0.0.0. as the beginning date from which to count time. It is not known why this particular date was chosen, but it corresponds to the 13th of August, 3114 B.C. of our calendar.

Appearing at the beginning of an informative inscription is the Long Count, or Initial Series date, which appears as a linear calculation of time beginning with the date corresponding to August 13, 3114 B.C. in our calendar; this was the day when, according to the Maya, time began. Five glyphs identify the time units in this series. They are: *Kin* (day), *Uinal* (a month made up of 20 days), *Tun* (year), *Katun* (20 years), and *Baktun* (20 *Katuns*, or 400 years). A sixth glyph in the inscription identifies the day that is the sum of all of the days recorded, beginning the count with the first day of Maya time.

The Short Count is an abbreviated version of the Long Count. For example, we could write February 22, 1995, or we could simply abbreviate the date as 2-22-95.

The Secondary Series of Distance Numbers identifies the necessary calculation to adjust the 360 day Maya calendar to the 365.2422 day solar year, starting with the date when Maya time began.

The Lunar or Supplementary Series tells the phase or position of the moon on the date recorded on many of the Maya monuments.

None of these calculations would have been possible without a knowledge of mathematics, and the Maya were extremely competent, if not brilliant, mathematicians. With the knowledge of the zero they were able to shape their numbering system into a positional one, with numbers usually recorded in vertical columns. The Maya number system was vegesimal, a unit of progression based on the number twenty; their value was multiplied by twenty in each new position increasing from the bottom to the top, or if they were in a horizontal position, from the right to the left. Therefore, the ascending positions stood for 20, 400, 8,000, 160,000, and so forth. Numbers from one to nineteen were identified by hieroglyphs or by means of bars or dots. A bar represented five and a dot was one. For example, the number thirteen would be written as two parallel bars and three dots above. Numbers twenty and above were placed in ascending columns which increased the number by multiples of twenty. Thus, the first and lowest place notations include numbers 0-19; the next level is the total of the numbers shown x (20 x 20) the step above equals the sum of the 3rd level x (20 x 20), etc. As soon as

The Maya used three symbols for their numbers: a bar for five, a dot for one, and a zero sign which could be written several ways, usually as an oval, shell-like form.

The Maya number system was vigesimal, that is, using base 20 instead of base 10. Base 10 refers to the numerals 0-9 which form the basis of all other numbers. The Maya system of base 20 used just three symbols which could be used in combination to represent the digits 0-19.

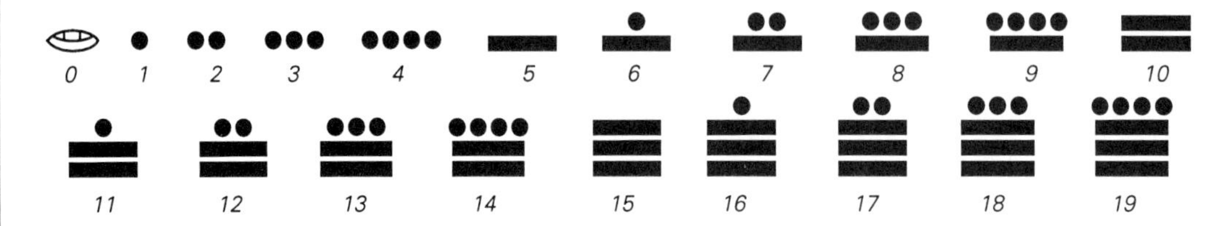

In order to record numbers twenty or above, the Maya counted in steps. On the lowest step were the numbers 0-19, 20-399 would be recorded on the next step where the sum of the numbers shown would be multiplied by 20; on the next step, the sum of the numbers shown would be multiplied by 400 (20 x 20), and so on, increasing by the power of 20 for each succeeding step. Since their number system was based on units of 20, the vertical steps stood for 1, 20, 400, 8000, 160,000, and so forth; each of these was multiplied by the sum of whatever numbers were on that level. The sums of each level, or step, were then added for a final total.

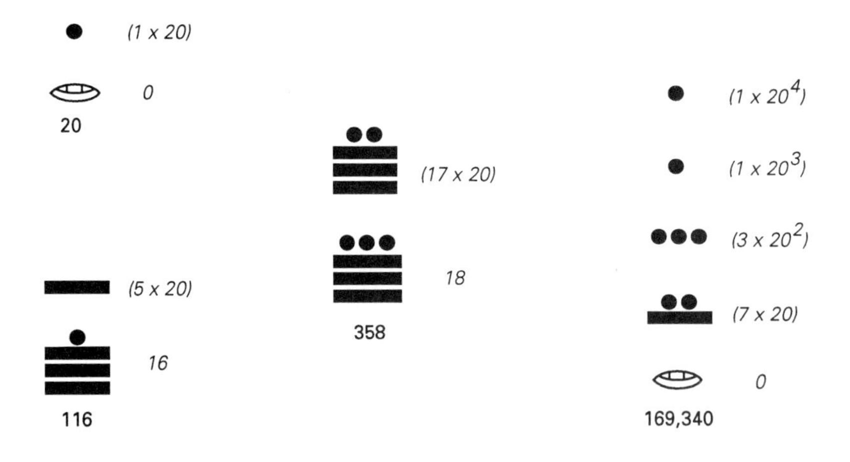

88. The Maya Numbering System.

the desired level was reached, the column was added and the grand total recorded. There was no limit to the number of levels used, nor to the length of the equation.

Maya Glyphs

Of all of the ancient writing systems, the Maya hieroglyphics have proven to be the most difficult to decipher, and it has only been in the last three decades that scholars have recognized the phonetic patterns of the glyphs. Although the writing may have been based upon an earlier Olmec pictographic style, the structure of the Maya glyphs is much more complex and sophisticated than any earlier glyph expressions in Mesoamerica.

All of the information that was recorded by the Maya concerning their history, mythology, religion, astronomy, and mathematics was lost when the civilization collapsed; by the time Cortes arrived in the 16th century, few Maya remained who could read the complicated writing. Fortunately, one of the early Spaniards, Diego de Landa, the first Bishop of the Yucatán wrote down the Mayan hieroglyphics that phonetically corresponded to the Spanish alphabet. For centuries, de Landa's work was discounted by epigraphers because its correlation of glyphs with individual letters was not workable, and provided little, if any, help in decipherment. The breaking of the Maya code seemed impossible until 1952, when a young Russian scholar by the name of Yuri Knorosov proposed that Maya writing was a combination of word signs with signs that represent sound alone (Schele, Miller 1986) . Subsequent studies have confirmed that the glyphs are complete syllables that contain combinations of consonant and vowel sounds. Although it has been proven that the Maya could write everything they wanted to phonetically, they chose not to do this because of the sacredness and prestige of the ideographs or logograms (word signs) that formed a part of the text (Coe 1986). Once the phonetic-logographic nature of the glyphs was recognized, de Landa's original text became useful as an interpretive tool. According to Coe (1986), "We know that the Maya script bears a close typological resemblance to other mixed logographic-phonetic systems of the world, such as Egyptian and Japanese. This resemblance had not been lost to Knorosov, and it probably was the stimulus behind his discoveries."

Ahau "lord," one of several ways "lord" can be written.

In 1958, Heinrich Berlin published a detailed analysis of the inscriptions on the Sarcophagus lid from the Temple of Inscriptions at Palenque, identifying the ten figures on the sides of the sarchophagus by their name glyphs. This was the first time that specific glyphs were identified with the names of rulers and royal families. During the following year, Berlin isolated and named the "Emblem" Glyphs that identify specific locations. In 1960, the noted Maya scholar Tatiana Proskouriakoff determined that some stelae glyphs were clearly intended to introduce the birth and inaugural event dates of the ruler to whom the stela was dedicated. As a result of these early breakthroughs and the continuous advances made by dedicated epigraphers, possibly 75 percent of the Maya glyphs can now be understood. Although the Maya were not the only Mesoamericans with a written language (a simple writing system was used in the Valley of Oaxaca by 600 B.C.), the Maya system was the most complete and extensive. Humor, poetry, and descriptive metaphors emerge from the translations of their language, providing us with detailed and sophisticated descriptions of dynastic lineages, biographies, and accounts of ceremony and warfare. Most of the decipherment of the glyphs has taken place just in the last three decades as linguists have successfully tied the glyphs to the phonetic sounds of two of the current Mayan languages, Chol and Yucatec. Consequently, the translation of some of the ancient inscriptions into English allows many glyphs to be read in a close approximation of their original tongue. An incredible wealth of historical data about the Maya is now available from studying their written language. Although still seeking answers to some of the ancient glyphs, scholars have already gained much new insight into the lives of the remarkable Maya who achieved the greatest cultural development in all of prehispanic America.

Emblem Glyph for Palenque.

Maya Pottery

Throughout their long history of ceramic production, the Maya made pottery entirely by hand, without the use of the potter's wheel. Their vessels were shaped by using long, rolled strips of clay which were layered one on top of the other until the desired height of the product was achieved. The coils of clay were pressed together, and the interior and exterior surfaces were smoothed with the fingertips so that the original spaces between the rolled strips of clay were eliminated. After the vessel was partially dry, and before firing, the surface was carefully scraped and polished. Although this was the most popular method used by the Maya potters during their long history of ceramic production, molds were sometimes used in the manufacture of those items that could be mass produced. Numerous pottery workshops produced distinctive and recognizable styles throughout the Maya region, but styles often overlapped, and the workshop locations are, for the most part, unknown to us; the origins of the majority of pieces we have today are unknown. There are virtually no records from past times that would establish their provenience, and even those items from the burial sites we excavate today could have been moved from a different location by other peoples. Recently, however, an attempt has been made to investigate Classic Maya painted pottery by analyzing both stylistic and chemical components. This work is being carried out by the Maya Polychrome Ceramics Project in the Conservation Analytical Laboratory at the Smithsonian Institution. The project utilizes the highly sensitive technique of Instrumental Neutron Activation Analysis, whereby compositional differences in clays that can reflect their possible sources within a fairly small geographical area are identified (Reents-Budet 1994).

89. Painted Tetrapod Vessel, Maya, Guatemala. Height: 11 inches. (MNYC.)

The earliest known Maya pottery style, labeled by archaeologists as "Swasey Complex pottery," was discovered in 1975 at the site of Cuello in Belize. Swasey ceramics are both unslipped and red and orange **slipped vessels.** Some pieces have incised patterns in simple geometric forms while others were painted with red-on-cream decorations. In addition to the purely utilitarian vessels, a small sampling of whistles and figurines has been found. Radiocarbon analyses of the Swasey ceramics indicate that some of the material may date to 2500 B.C. Although this date is still the subject of some debate, there is no doubt that Swasey pottery is the oldest Maya pottery yet discovered. Mamom pottery appeared around 600 B.C. Despite some regional variation, simplicity was the hallmark of Mamom pottery. Incised, decorative motifs were usually limited to encircling lines, rows of triangles, or checkered motifs, and

Slip: A mixture of clay, water, and a finely ground pigment.

90. Tripod vase, Maya. (MNYC.)

painted in one or two colors. Flat-bottomed plates, thin-walled round bowls, and open-mouthed jars were produced in great abundance.

By the beginning of the Classic period, a pottery style known as Chichanel was in common use throughout the Maya lowlands. Chichanel pieces are easily recognized because of their uniformity of color and shape. They included bowls and plates with distinctive flange-like ridges, and tall urns and small jars that often had spouts or occasionally were fashioned in the form of animals. Although the Chichanel style persisted in most parts of the Maya lowlands, a new ceramic tradition known as "Floral Park" ultimately replaced Chicanel in parts of Belize and along the Rio Pasion in the southern lowlands. With this came an influx of orange clay domestic pottery and unusual bowls that rested on four bulging "Mammiform-like" legs. In addition, and of great importance, true polychrome decoration using three colors in painted designs made its appearance.

Beginning around A.D. 250 and extending into the Late Classic period, new techniques appeared that included the mastery of thinner walled vessels, with taller and more delicate jars and vases (Tzakol pottery, for example). There were also some changes in the clay finishes: surfaces were now glossy and smooth, and the most common slip color of the Late Preclassic period, a dark red, was replaced by a bright orange color. There were covered bowls with scallops or lines of alternating colors; complex symbols and magnificent designs embellished the lids. Polychrome painting included red, orange, black, white, and buff, colors that did not fade during the heat of firing; incising, gouging, and scraping were major decorative techniques. The variety and technical skill involved in the best of the decorated pieces made them artistic creations of the highest quality.

91. Bowl with Lid, Maya. Classic period. (BMA.)

Early Classic figure-painted polychromes included black and red decorations painted over an orange to yellowish base. Maya glyphs, painted figures, and contrasting lines of color appeared on these ceramics; later styles are identified by the use of brighter colors and more complex designs which included overall patterns or repeated motifs. The Maya artist focused on line and form in a naturalistic manner. Images were defined with strong, dark lines. Parallel lines were often used for emphasis. In their efforts to impart realism, without perspective, the Maya artists presented their figures with heads, legs, and lower torso in profile, with the chest and shoulders in a frontal position (Reents-Budet 1994). Although the pictorial scenes were basically two-dimensional, the variation of tone from light to dark, the use of overlapping images, and the degree of slip transparency all were cleverly used to suggest space. Cylindrical vessels displayed religious and mythological scenes. Others dealt with issues of leadership and kingdoms, with named individuals depicted within a recognizable space. These vessels are true reflections of Maya culture during the peak of the Classic period: a time when centers of power expanded and there was an explosive growth of ritual expression. The exquisite pottery was used by the elite, and buried with the dead; it functioned as a symbol of status and power. The artists, who often signed their pieces, were educated in history, science, cosmology, and the writing system. As a result, their pottery is important as a means to examine the culture from a multi-faceted view.

92. Polychrome Plate, Maya. Late Classic period. Height: 13 inches. (MNYC.)

At the end of Maya Civilization and during the Late Classic period (A.D. 800-1000), the quality of painting visibly declined. Multi-color decoration became far less common; colors were faded and poorly controlled. Drawings were more carelessly executed, and the number of creative themes and motifs dramatically decreased. Ironically, it was during this time that the people in the Maya lowlands were exposed to a trade item that was to play an important role in the development of Postclassic ceramics. This was the introduction of Fine Orange ware, which was named both for its color and the fine, untempered clay from which it was produced. The source of the material for these ceramics has been traced to the silty clays found in southwestern Tabasco, an area that has been identified as a center of commerce and the home of the Putun, who were famed as long-distance traders.

The most spectacular pottery made during the Early Postclassic period was Plumbate ware. It was produced from A.D. 1000-1250 along the Pacific coast of Guatemala and traded not only to the Maya lowlands, but as far away as the Toltec capital of Tula, north of Mexico City, and south into Central America. Due to the peculiarities of the clay, the black to grayish Plumbate appears to have a glaze. The most common Plumbate shapes were human and animal forms. During the Late Postclassic period, from about A.D. 1250 to1519, Plumbate ware was no longer made. Red ware was the standard pottery produced, although certain types of Fine Orange continued to be manufactured and traded. Incensarios for household worship and brightly painted effigy vessels were made in great numbers; all were of relatively poor workmanship and design. By the time of the Spanish Conquest, the Maya ceramic tradition had come full circle. It returned to the almost exclusively utilitarian craft that it had been more than three thousand years earlier.

The Cities

One of the most remarkable aspects of Maya culture are the cities that began to appear during the Preclassic period, and were built in great numbers throughout the homeland region. Tikal and Uaxactun in the Peten, Kaminaljuyu in the Guatemalan Highlands, Bonampak, Yaxchilan, and Piedras Negras along the Usumacinta River, Palenque in Tabasco, Caracol in Belize,

Copán in Honduras, and the Puuc Region cities of the Yucatán are but a few well-known examples of the widespread distribution of Maya civic and ceremonial centers. Generally, these cities were where people prepared for religious ceremonies as well as civic functions and administrative detail. The architectural features of the buildings that form the nucleus of the cities are unique to the Maya, and include the following characteristics: temples built on top of stepped, mastaba-like pyramids, with a single steep frontal staircase ascending to the top; elevated stone platforms that support sprawling, multi-roomed complexes (the North Acropolis at Tikal, for example); mansard roofs (not used in later Puuc region architecture); elaborate roof combs made of stucco; and the famed **corbeled arch**. This latter feature was formed after the desired height of the room was achieved, by placing one stone on top of another so that the upper stone projected past the lower one. As the sequence of stones progressed, the distance between the two sides could be bridged by a single slab of stone at the top of the room. All of the temple pyramids were built of solid rubble, mortar, and earth faced with carefully cut and well-fitted stones. The completed buildings were then covered with a white limestone plaster. The corbeled arches and room interiors were often finished with the limestone plaster.

After room height was achieved, one stone would be placed upon another so that the upper stone projected past the lower one. The distance between the two sides could be bridged at the top by a single stone.

Little is known of the purpose of many of the Maya buildings, other than in a general sense. Some were strictly for ceremonial use (such as the small temples on pyramids), some were intended to be funerary monuments to former rulers. Other buildings may have served as dwellings for priests or the upper classes, or functioned as administrative centers. A frequent plan in this latter building group includes a collection of rooms around inner courts; these are commonly called palaces (e.g., Uxmal, Palenque). The small temples on top of the pyramids are believed to have been the most sacred areas, and were entered only by priest-leaders. A single narrow staircase ascends each pyramid, allowing limited access to this sanctuary. Inside the temple are one to three small, dark rooms with thick, windowless walls. Most often they are devoid of decoration; the Temple of the Inscriptions at Palenque is an exception. The architects seemed to be more interested in the outer significance

93. Corbeled Gallery, Palace Complex. Palenque, Chiapas.

94. From left: Temple of the Sun, small ruins, Temple of Inscriptions, and portion of lower Palace Complex at Palenque.

of the building than the inner areas. Roof combs tower over the temples below; they are made of a heavy limestone stucco supported by the thick, corbel vaulted walls below. Some of the roof combs are elaborately carved with religious symbols and likenesses of deities. Others, as at Palenque, are pierced in beautiful, open lattice-like designs. Often they are simply a vertical extension of the front wall of the temple.

The architecture of the various regions in the Maya homeland may also reflect attempts to overcome environmental problems. In areas where earthquakes occur, platform bases are well proportioned, and never very high. Building walls were constructed by alternating courses of large rock with layers of small stones mixed in clay and gravel. The walls were both solid and elastic. In densely forested jungle areas with heavy downpours, there was always adequate drainage, and temples were built upon towering pyramid bases.

The Maya were a paradoxical people. They were able to clear the jungle and build magnificent cities of stone; they produced sculpture and murals of the highest quality. Their carved hieroglyphic inscriptions are so complex that they have not yet been fully deciphered. They used a mathematical notation system more sophisticated than that of their European counterparts, yet they never used the wheel to transport large objects. They achieved their monumental accomplishments with unsophisticated tools—like a Stone Age people. This combination of intellectual and artistic sophistication and technical primitivism is the hallmark of the Maya character.

Tikal
A History of the Excavations

The first official expedition to the abandoned ruins at Tikal took place in 1848. An illustrated account of this trip was published by the leaders of the expedition, Modesto Mendez and Ambrosio Tut, commissioner and governor of El Peten, Guatemala. Their report brought Tikal to the attention of the Western world. Although other groups subsequently visited the city during the 19th century, the most detailed and systematic descriptions of the early expeditions were made by the noted English explorer Alfred Percival Maudslay in 1881 and 1882. Maudslay mapped the site and made detailed plans of the architectural features of many of the temples and buildings. His personal photographs taken over100 years ago are truly extraordinary in their clarity and detail.

Teobert Maler, an Austrian-born photographer and explorer, came to Mexico in 1864 as a member of the Austrian military volunteers who supported the imperial claims of Archduke Maximilian. In 1867, when Maximilian was executed and European forces withdrawn from Mexico, Maler elected to stay and make the country his adopted home. He spent the next eleven years traveling throughout the land, photographing the ancient cities and perfecting his photographic skills. This was to be the beginning of a consuming and passionate interest in Mexico's Precolumbian heritage. In 1885, Maler began serious explorations of the Yucatán. To finance his expeditions, he prepared sets of mounted prints and site plans of the Yucatán ruins. It was at this time that Harvard's Peabody Museum became aware of his work and employed him. He was sent on three major expeditions to Tikal between 1898 and 1905, to complete maps and photograph the site. When he finished the assignments, he refused to submit his work to his superiors, fearing that they would profit from his efforts. As a result, his association with the museum ended, and the great Mayanist, Alfred Marston Tozzer, was sent to finish the project. Despite the initial difficulties, a highly descriptive joint report was eventually published by Maler and Tozzer in 1911. This report, along with Maudslay's pioneering efforts, provided a firm basis for further expeditions.

Four trips to Tikal were made by Sylvanus G. Morley between 1914 and 1928. Morley was head of the archaeological research program at the Carnegie Institution in Washington, D.C. He had a particular interest in Maya writing, and authored numerous papers and books on Maya hieroglyphics. The inscriptions on the Tikal monuments provided much information for Morley's research. From 1926 to 1937 Morley began excavations at Uaxactun, a few miles north of Tikal. His tireless efforts there, as well as his initial work at Tikal, provided invaluable data for subsequent excavations in the Maya area.

In 1956, the University of Pennsylvania and the Guatemalan government entered into a contract to study and excavate Tikal. As a result, what is known as the Tikal Project was born. The original aims of the project were to restore and preserve the buildings, to work out the history of the site, to open the lush rainforest to study by scientists, to establish a scholarly field laboratory, and to create a park that would be a tribute to ancient America. A visit to Tikal underscores the success of the project and gives promise that new challenges will be met in the exploration of this remarkable city.

Tikal is located in a dense and humid rain forest in the northeastern Peten region of Guatemala. It is one of the oldest of the great Classic period Maya cities. Construction started here around 100 B.C. and reached its peak between the 6th and 8th centuries A.D. At that time it was occupied by an estimated 50,000 people. It covered an area of over six square miles. The people were active traders, and Tikal became a prosperous center of trade.

95. Temple I, Temple of the Giant Jaguar. Tikal, Guatemala.

The main core of Tikal has been excavated and restored. It consists of the East, West, and Great Plazas, and the two large complexes of the North and Central Acropolis. Within this core area are five great pyramid structures, several terraces and courtyards, three known ball courts, and many palace-like structures. The Great Plaza, which was started in Late Preclassic times, was probably the most important of the three plazas. The famous Temples I and II are located in this section, and were built around A.D. 700 . Temple I, known also as the Temple of the Giant Jaguar, towers about 145 feet above the Great Plaza. It is a large, mastaba-like pyramid consisting of nine "stepped" platforms of diminishing size. On the ninth level is a three-room, corbel-vaulted temple, topped by a magnificent roof comb. This vertical extension of the temple was ingeniously designed in two levels over a hollow core; this reduced the weight of the whole and still provided enough structural strength to support the heavy stucco, which formed a surface for important imagery. The roof comb, finished with stones arranged to form the image of a seated ruler, has elaborate scrolls and undulating serpent patterns. Since the surface is badly eroded, it is best seen when the temple top and roof comb are bathed in late afternoon sunlight. At this time, details of the composition can clearly be seen.

Like many other large structures at Tikal, Temple I functioned as an important burial monument. During earlier excavations, as interior tunnels were searched, a deep pit was discovered at about Plaza level. In the pit was a high vaulted burial chamber, measuring 14 by 8 feet by 13 feet high, which had been sealed in by the mass of the pyramid above. Placed upon a masonry bench inside the chamber were the remains of a large man, referred to as Ruler A by archaeologists, who died in A.D. 727. Buried with him were jade and pearl objects, some pottery, alabaster, and colorful shells from the sea. The man's head faced north and his body was placed upon an elaborately fringed and decorated mat; jade jewelry adorned his body. In one corner of the tomb were 89 human bone fragments, many of which were intricately carved with iconographic symbols and designs. Four of the bones depict a scene in which a canoe guided by the Paddler Twins in Maya mythology (the Old Jaguar god and the Ancient Stingray Spine God) carries a human who wears an *ahau* (Lord) sign upon his head. Holding his wrist to his forehead in a gesture believed to signal impending death, he is the deceased Ruler A who was buried in the chamber (Schele 1986).

Directly across the Plaza from Temple I is a smaller, 125 foot high terraced pyramid known as Temple II, or the Temple of the Masks. It was named for the large, grotesque masks that decorate the stairway ascending from the pyramid base to the top. The temple has an elaborate roof comb and three small interior rooms. In front of the temple is a large masonry block that may have been used by the priest/rulers of Tikal to stand upon as they addressed the populace in the plaza; the angle of the block would have provided a much clearer view of the person who stood upon it for the people gathered below. Although its function has not been conclusively determined, Temple II may contain the tomb of the wife of Ruler A . Thus, Ruler A and his wife would face each other across the plaza for all time, each in an elaborate memorial structure.

Located between the two temples, and occupying two and one half acres on the northern side of the Great Plaza, is Tikal's single most complex structure: the North Acropolis. It has sixteen large temples and conceals hundreds of earlier platforms and buildings underneath that date from the Preclassic period. Some of these older areas can be reached only by tunnel today. The temples of the North Acropolis appear to have been built as monuments to Maya kings, as numerous tombs have been discovered there. In front of Structure 34, for example, was found the richly furnished tomb of the King "Curl Nose" (so named by archaeologists), whose death date of A.D. 727 was recorded on Stela 4 in front of the tomb.

Tikal's tallest pyramid is just west of the North Acropolis. It is a veritable skyscraper that reaches approximately 220 feet from the base of the pyramid to the top of the roof comb. It is known as Temple IV, and it is the most frequently photographed structure at Tikal. From this area, three causeways lead to other groups of buildings, all of which have vaulted ceilings and elaborate roof combs.

In the Central Acropolis is a large complex that functioned as an official palace and an elite residence; some cooking hearths

96. Temple II with Temple IV in background. Tikal, Guatemala.

have been found here, proving their use as residential quarters. The large, elegant structures were designed so that all of the rooms would open to interior courtyards. Built in the early 8th century, Ruler A of Tikal and his wife may have ordered the building of this palace and residence for their own use.

A large resident labor population consisting of artisans, stone cutters, and unskilled workers labored endlessly to build Tikal. The artisans were architects and master builders; unskilled workers were needed for their basic building abilities. The stone cutters were responsible for keeping a plentiful supply of rock and rubble available for the ongoing construction. Even the terraced bases of the pyramids and palaces were built of massive amounts of limestone, dirt, rubble, and stone. The palaces and temples on top of the pyramids were made of large stones that were fractured with heavy weights or split with wedges and then ground into the correct shapes with pounding tools. Mortar was made from the chemical decomposition of limestone burned over open fire pits. By adding water to this

97. Stele 10, Tikal.

lime, durable mortar and plaster were made. Although most of the temple and pyramid construction at Tikal took place between A.D. 500-900, there is evidence that the Maya were living there by 600 B.C. This would mean that there were ongoing building projects here for about 1500 years.

Despite the fact that almost all of the construction at Tikal is Maya in execution and design, there is some evidence of Teotihuacán influence on monuments and within many of the rich burials. For example, on one side of the fourth century A.D. monument known as Stela 31, a Maya noble is shown; on the other side is a second figure who wears an elaborate feathered headdress and holds a shield in one hand and a spearthrowing weapon in the other. The shield bears the image of Tlaloc, and the weapon is stylistically related to similar weapons from Teotihuacán. In addition to the monuments and stelae, three small platform bases were built, each with distinctive and identifiable characteristics of the Teotihuacán style during the Classic period.

Tikal played a key role in trading with Teotihuacán in the Valley of Mexico, Kaminaljuyu in the Guatemalan highlands, and many of the Maya cities near the Caribbean Sea. By the Middle Classic period, the city had become culturally and politically dominant over most Maya centers in the lowland area, and it may be that this dominance introduced a more commercial lifestyle to the people of Tikal. With luxury items in greater demand, ritual and intellectual life would undoubtedly have faltered. This would explain the cultural decline that prevailed toward the end of the Classic period, when competition and rivalry between rulers and cities greatly increased.

Numerous stelae have been found at Tikal. Many are plain, while others show likenesses of important personages, or are carved with glyphs and dated with the Maya Long Count system of dating. It is believed that the stelae were erected to commemorate important events or to record major accomplishments of the rulers. With a substantiated date of 292 A.D. in our calendar, Stela 29 is the earliest dated stela at Tikal. Stela 4 stands in front of Structure 34 on the North Acropolis, recording A.D. 380 as the date "Curl Nose" ascended to power. Shown in a frontal position, "Curl Nose" wears a plumed Jaguar-face headdress; his dress and ornamentation show Teotihuacán influence, and the frontal face position may indicate a non-Maya. Some of Tikal's stelae were deliberately smashed or broken. No one knows exactly why this destruction occurred other than that it may identify a time when an oppressed working class revolted against excessive demands of the priest/rulers, or when a rival city such as Caracol, in nearby Belize, descended upon Tikal. Indeed, at the time of the Maya hiatus during the middle to late Classic period, most Maya cities had stopped producing; Caracol, however, experienced a meteoric rise in power resulting from military victories, conquest, and sacrifice of conquered kings. Caracol's dynasties flourished while others disintegrated around them.

Tikal's last commemorative stela bears the Long Count date of 8.12.14.8. 15, which corresponds to our date of July 6, 892 A.D. Shortly after this final monument was completed, Tikal was abandoned.

Copán

One of the most important of the southern Maya cities is Copán, which is located on the Copán River, near the Guatemalan border in western Honduras. Situated in a lovely valley some 2000 feet above sea level, the Maya at Copán enjoyed a temperate climate, excellent conditions for agriculture, and many natural resources. There was an abundant supply of trachyite here, which was needed for building projects. Trachyite is a light-green volcanic stone that is easy to cut, but hardens after lengthy exposure to air. The stones could be cut and joined together with great precision before the drying process began; there was an unlimited supply of this material. Building projects here continued well into the Late Classic period. Copán became a great center of learning, especially in the field of astronomy.

Many structural remains occupy the acropolis, which is the ceremonial core of Copán. Although there were many new constructions over older buildings during the Classic period (and the primary functions of the earlier buildings is not known), the later pyramids and temples are believed to have been funerary monuments for the rulers of Copán. Structure 16 is a nine-level pyramid, and it is the largest building on the acropolis. Suggestive of a funerary monument because of its nine levels, it may hold the remains of Smoke Jaguar, a Late Classic Maya king (Miller 1986). Temple 22 on the acropolis may have been the inaugural site of Yax Pac, the last great Copán ruler. Here one climbs a large stairway and enters a rear chamber through a great open monster mouth. The inner door of this temple is carved with human figures seated on skulls and accompanied by supernatural representations. Recent excavations of Structure 18 nearby have revealed an inner chamber that apparently was Yax Pac's burial site. Unfortunately, the chamber was looted in antiquity, and there are no physical remains to substantiate this as Yax Pac's original burial place.

The main ballcourt at Copán is the largest and most beautiful of all Classic courts. Its plan follows the typical elongated H (or capital I) format. There are wide sloping tiers topped by small structures on each of the western and eastern sides of the playing zone. The remains of two earlier courts lie beneath this playing field (Weaver 1972).

Just south of the ballcourt is the famed 90-foot-high, 30-foot-wide Hieroglyphic Stairway. There are 63 steps, and each riser is elaborately carved with glyphs that relate the dynastic history at Copán; there are about 2200 glyphs in all. Five three-dimensional stone figures projecting from the steps in regular intervals may identify rulers from the Classic period. This structure is unique in the Maya world in that here are sculpture, hieroglyphs describing dates and events, and architecture united in one magnificent monument.

Palenque

Palenque lies at the foot of the densely forested mountains in northeastern Chiapas. It is 80 miles inland from the southern shores of the Gulf of Mexico and 65 miles west of the Guatemalan border. In a lush and exotic environment, brilliantly colored parrots and macaws fly through the green jungle. On rainy days, the cries of the howler monkeys can be heard near the abandoned ruins. Palenque is, indeed, a visual treasure in the midst of a unspoiled paradise.

The principal architectural feature of almost all Maya cities is a palace-like complex. Unlike temples, which were small, one-to-three room structures built upon stepped-pyramid bases, the palace-like complexes were composed of groups of multi-room

98. Palace Complex at Palenque.

buildings and corbel-vaulted galleries that were built around interior courtyards. The palaces were the administrative centers for the Maya, and the focal points for their rituals and ceremonies. In these palaces, issues of government were resolved, visiting rulers were received, important captives were arraigned, and tributes were offered. Ritual bloodletting ceremonies for special tribute days also took place in the palaces. Members of the royal household may have lived in some of the palaces, but it is unlikely that the primary purpose of these complex structures was to provide homes for the ruling families. Instead, they undoubtedly functioned as administrative centers for each Maya city. Therefore, the rulers and their families most likely lived in comfortable houses adjacent to the palaces. Unfortunately, these royal residences were built of perishable materials, and nothing remains of them today but a few grass-covered mounds next to the Palace which, in their ruined state, belie their importance as homes for the ruling elite.

The Palace Complex at Palenque was largely completed by A.D 715, and it was the setting for the official functions of the

99. Watchtower or Observatory. Palace Complex at Palenque

100. *Top.* Main Courtyard of the Palace Complex at Palenque.

101. *Bottom.* Detail. Elaborately dressed Mayas are depicted on these upright stones in the main courtyard of the Palace Complex.

102. Temples of the Sun, Cross, and Foliated Cross at Palenque.

families that ruled there. The entire multi-roomed structure was built on a raised platform measuring over 300 feet long by 200 feet wide. It consists of a series of corbel-vaulted galleries and rooms that were built around open courtyards. Along the low inner walls of two of the courtyards are large, upright stones carved with images of men standing with one hand raised to the opposite shoulder. This position has variously been interpreted as a sign of submission or allegiance. The men are elaborately dressed and bejeweled. One cannot help but wonder if they were important political prisoners awaiting their fate, or members of an elite group pledging allegiance to the rulers of Palenque. Towering over all of the courtyards, rooms, and galleries within the complex is a four-storied tower. Beginning at the second level, and circling the interior walls of this tall stone structure, is a spiral staircase. A Venus glyph painted on one of the tower's inside walls suggests that it may have been used as an observatory, as well as a watchtower. Near the Palace Complex are four structures: one small building in poor repair, and three small temple-pyramids of similar design. They are grouped around a secluded plaza on the eastern side of the site, and are called the Temples of the Sun, the Cross, and the Foliated Cross. The three temples rest upon stepped-pyramid bases and are topped by the elaborate pierced roof combs for which Palenque is famous.

The Temple of the Sun conforms to the typical temple plan at Palenque in that the interior of each structure was divided into two horizontal portions, the front section serving as a portico, or large entry, and the area in back divided into two additional small rooms. The most important feature of the Temple of the Sun, and that to which it owes its name, is the magnificent carved panel on the back wall of the primary room. The central figure on the panel is the sun, which is symbolically represented by a round shield and two crossed lances. Two slaves support a throne or altar upon which the shield and lances rest; a priest at each side makes an offering. Flanking this central scene are several columns of hieroglyphs, some of which have been deciphered and convey a date in the Maya calendar which corresponds on our calendar to 642 A.D.

The Temple of the Cross overlooks the Sun Pyramid from a high pyramidal substructure that rises several stories from the floor of the plaza. It resembles, in design, the well-preserved Sun Pyramid, although this building is in very poor condition. Only the towering roof comb displays some of its former beauty. There is a large carved stone on each side of the door leading into the temple. On one stone is the image of an old man wearing an elaborate headdress and a tiger skin garment. He smokes a twist of tobacco while paying homage to a cross which rises from the mask of the Maya Earth God. On the other side of the door is a similarly dressed priest who makes an offering. The hieroglyphs on these panels provide a number of dates, one of which is 642 A.D., the same date that was recorded on the panel found in the Temple of the Sun.

The Temple of the Foliated Cross is directly across the plaza from the Pyramid of the Sun. It lies against a tall, densely forested hill that provides support for the building. The panel that gave its name to the temple still remains inside. It is strikingly similar to the major panel that flanks the doorway into the Temple of the Cross, but differs in that the cross, which is the

103. Temple of the Sun, Palenque.

104. Temple of the Cross, Palenque.

principal motif, is decorated with maize (corn) leaves and human heads. The face of the Sun God and the image of a Quetzál bird wearing the mask of the Rain God are positioned over the cross. The principal date here is 692 A.D.

The Temple of Inscriptions is famous because of a remarkable discovery made in 1952 by the Mexican archaeologist Alberto Ruz. In 1949, Ruz was appointed Director of Archaeological Explorations in the Maya zone for the Mexican National Institute of Anthropology and History. It was at this time that Nelson Rockefeller gave a large grant to the Institute for the excavation of the temples at Palenque. There are eight major structures at Palenque. One of these is the Temple of Inscriptions, which rests on a 65 foot high stepped pyramid base. On the walls of the temple's portico and central room are three panels containing a total of 620 hieroglyphs and dates. The last date recorded on the panels is A.D. 692.

Most floors of Maya construction were made of a fine-grained limestone, but Ruz noticed that the floor of the Temple of Inscriptions was not typical. It was made of tightly fitted stone slabs. He was particularly curious when he discovered that

105. Temple of the Foliated Cross, Palenque.

one slab had a double row of holes neatly plugged with carefully carved stone stoppers. Ruz thought that they looked like finger holes to lift the stone. He also noticed that the sides of the walls in this room did not rest on the floor slabs, but extended down beyond the great stones. When the men lifted the stone with the finger holes, they found a great horizontal stone beam underneath. The beam was embedded into a sloping wall that formed the upper part of a vaulted chamber. It was apparent that Ruz had discovered the top of a vaulted stairway leading down into the interior of the pyramid. It had been deliberately filled with rocks, dirt, and rubble. Because of the extreme heat, excessive humidity, and heavy seasonal rains, Ruz was only able to clear 23 steps during the first year of excavation. It took four years in all to reach the final step 73 feet below.

106. Temple of the Inscriptions, Palenque.

At the bottom of the steps was a chamber that was also filled with rubble. On the floor were the skeletal remains of five or six young adults who probably had been sacrificed. At the far end of the chamber was a huge triangular slab that filled the entire end of the room. When this great stone was moved, Ruz was able to see into a room that had been hidden for over 1200 years. He described a magical scene in a grotto-like room. Moisture had seeped into the room over the centuries and stalactites and stalagmites had formed on the floor and the ceiling from the drippings of mineral-rich water. When Ruz entered the room the beam of his light illuminated the interior, reflecting the moisture and formations as if this were indeed a fairy tale setting. It was the first time in centuries that humans had entered this room. On the walls were nine carved stucco figures, which seemed to surround and guard a massive sculpted stone covering almost half of the chamber's floor space. This magnificently carved slab rested on a limestone sarcophagus that had a hollowed-out depression for the burial of a man of unusually large stature. A life-sized jade portrait mask covered his face; a piece of jade was held in each hand, and another had been placed in his mouth. Two jade figures lay at his side, and two limestone portrait heads were placed on the floor next to the sarcophagus.

According to the inscriptions around the edge of the massive twelve by seven foot sarcophagus lid, the coffin below is the final resting place of Pacal, a great ruler at Palenque who acceded to the throne in A.D. 615 at the age of twelve. The glyphs also confirm that construction on the temple housing his burial chamber commenced around A.D. 675, when Pacal was 72 years old; he died eight years later, on August 31, A.D. 683. There are ten portraits around the sides of the sarchophagus which depict seven of Pacal's ancestors. His mother, father, and great grandmother are shown twice. The death dates of these ancestors are recorded on the lid. Since the sarchophagus containing his remains is larger than the entrance into the subterranean chamber, we can be certain that this room was finished and the sarcophagus made ready before the pyramid above was completed.

After Pacal was buried the room was sealed, and five or six young Maya were sacrificed in the adjoining chamber, in front of the opening to Pacal's burial place. It is not known whether

107. Reconstruction of Pacal's Tomb in the Temple of the Inscriptions. (INAH.)

108. Stucco Head from Pacal's Tomb, Palenque.

they were meant to guard the royal leader from all earthly intrusions, or if their lives were given as offerings to the gods. The long stairwell leading down through the pyramid to the tomb was then filled with rubble in which offerings of jade, pottery, and shell were deposited. A stone tube extended up the stairs to the floor of the temple. The Maya believed that this tube gave the Vision Serpent a path to follow from Pacal's tomb to the living world he had left behind (Schele 1986). After the pyramid and temple were completed, a massive cut stone was lifted into place to hide the stairway that led down into the pyramid and the entrance of the tomb .

The images on the sarcophagus lid describe the instant of Pacal's death and his fall into the maws of the Underworld. At the center of the lid is Pacal, precariously perched and slightly reclining backward, on top of the head of the Quadripartite Monster, the symbol of the sun; he is now in the transitory stage between life and death. His hands are relaxed and his face composed; he shows no fear. In the upper right corner of the sarchophagus lid is a glyph which reads *kin*, or "day" and "sun." In the upper left is the symbol *akbal*, or "night" and "darkness." The entire scene depicts Pacal's passage from life (light and sun) into *Xibalba* (underworld and darkness), and the ultimate journey of Pacal's soul through the underworld to his final destination among his ancestors (Schele 1986). The Maya believed that death was but a transitory stage between one's earthly world and the life that would continue thereafter.

Towering over Pacal's reclining body is the World Tree which, according to Maya mythology, exists at the center of the universe. A double headed Serpent Bar, the symbol of Maya kingship and earthly existence in the middleworld, is wrapped around the branches of the tree. A celestial bird, the symbol of the heavenly realm, sits on the topmost branches. Pacal is below the tree, sitting on the head of the Quadripartite Monster (the sun), who also appears to be in transition between life and death. He is skeletal from the muzzle down, but his eyes have the scroll pupils that identify all living creatures in Maya art (Schele 1986). A date sign and glyph on the head announces that this moment marks the death of the king and the death of the sun (which would be sunset). Poised at the horizon is the sun, ready for its plunge into the dark underworld; the dead king is now ready to make his final journey with the sun. It is interesting to note that at the time of the winter solstice, the sun sets exactly on a line that runs from the center of the Palace through Pacal's tomb. Therefore, on this day each year, the sun falls into darkness (Underworld) through Pacal's tomb as a symbolic re-inactment of the event of Pacal's death.

We know that Pacal had the funerary crypt built during his lifetime to contain his own remains. The secret chamber was completed first. As the pyramid was built, so was the interior staircase leading to the summit upon which a temple was built. Thus, the Temple of Inscriptions, with its mansard-style roof and central roof comb, discretely kept its secret for over 1200 years.

Bonampak

Late in 1945, the photographer-explorer Giles G. Healy was hired by the United Fruit Company to film the Lacandon Indians who live in the mountainous state of Chiapas, Mexico. Healy hired two men to help him with the project: Carlos Frey, who had earlier worked for the well-known Danish explorer Frans Blom, and John G. Bourne who at age nineteen was an inexperienced, albeit enthusiastic, explorer-adventurer. Differing opinions, jealousy, and other incompatibilities soon began to cause tension between the men, and in a very short time the trio split up. Healy returned to San Cristobal de las Casas, and Frey and Bourne went to Mexico City where they began to collect equipment for a return trip to Chiapas. In early February, 1946, Frey and Bourne returned to the rain forest, where they met Chan Bor, a Lacandon Indian who took them to the Bonampak ruins. They saw the large plaza, acropolis, and small temples, but they did not explore the interior of a rather unimposing structure located near the bottom of the acropolis. Unknown to them, this building contained three rooms that were covered from floor to ceiling with exquisitely painted murals. In May of that same year, Healey, continuing his explorations and filming in the jungles of Chiapas, was taken to the same ruins by Chan Bor. Although Frans Blom had passed within a mile of the ancient site the previous year, and Frey and Bourne had been to Bonampak just three months earlier, Healy was the first non-Maya to see the painted rooms inside the Temple of the Murals (Miller 1986).

Bonampak is located in an almost inaccessible area of Chiapas. The word Bonampak literally translated means "dyed or painted walls." It is here, in the building known as the Temple of the Murals, that the Maya created some of the most beautiful prehispanic mural paintings in all of Mesoamerica. Located near the Usumacinta River, in a tropical rainforest bordering Chiapas and Guatemala, Bonampak is a city of still undetermined size, where Late Classic Maya built a number of stepped platform bases to support their temples and monuments. Most of the buildings are grouped around the sides of a large plaza, in the center of which is a tall, carved stela showing a personage of high rank. A man-made terraced acropolis rises approximately 140 feet above the plaza; at the top are several, small temples. The Temple of the Murals, situated at a lower level of the terraced hill, consists of three unconnected rooms covered with the magnificent murals.

109. View of lower plaza from Acropolis at Bonampak, Chiapas.

110. Small temples at the top of the Acropolis at Bonampak.

The Bonampak murals were painted around A.D. 790. They were protected for over a thousand years by a partial covering of calcium carbonite (a white or colorless crystalline compound), which had formed over the paintings from water seepage into the rooms. Experts sent to the site by the Mexican government in 1985 cleaned the walls, revealing a magnificent pictorial narrative of great rituals and celebrations that focused on the presentation of a young heir. There is a detailed description of an important battle, the arraignment of the captives before elaborately robed Bonampak lords, and celebratory blood letting ceremonies. At least 200 almost life-sized human figures adorn these walls. The murals, however, were never finished; hieroglyphic texts on the walls tell most of the story, while other areas prepared for glyph information were never completed.

The story begins in the first room. It is a palace scene, where the ruling family and lords of the court gather to witness and celebrate the presentation of a young heir; the date is 9.18.0.3.4, or December 14, A.D. 790. The royal figures fill the entire wall space, interrupted only by musicians who are shown on the inside surfaces of both end walls in the building. Seated on a throne is Chaan-Muan, the *halach uinic*, or ruler, with his family. Important leaders are attended by servants who carry great plumed fans. They wear elegant clothes, elaborate jewelry, and headdresses made of magnificent Quetzál feathers. There are a total of fourteen figures witnessing the royal ceremonies; many are identified by the glyph *ahau*, or "Lord." This title is used to identify kings, and it is the highest title recorded by the Maya. It is apparent that the royal family is gathered to witness the presentation and pay their respects to Chaan-Muan, their present king. The importance and social position of each figure is clearly understood by clothing, jewelry, and headdress detail. Those who gather to celebrate are dressed in magnificent jaguar skin robes and elaborate headdresses. Their distinctive features suggest that these are portraits of noble lords whose identities remain unknown. (Sections above some of the heads were not completed with the glyphs that would identify the figures.) Beneath the lords are completed glyphs that describe the rites and ceremonies. Shown on the lower bands are nature god impersonators who wear animal, bird, or fish-like masks and

111. *Top.* Temple detail.

112. *Bottom.* Building of the Bonampak murals.

headdresses, perhaps to indicate respect, or to pay homage to the power and life giving forces of the earth, sky and sea. There are also the white-turbaned musicians who blow long trumpets, play drums, or hold rattles. In the center, and apparently leading the procession, are a man and a head musician who seems to be keeping time to the beat of the music. Several glyphs below the two reveal Bonampak's political ties and give recognition to Yaxchilan, an important and dominant nearby Maya city. The date of this celebration was a date of astronomical interest, 9.18.1.2.0, or November 15, A.D. 791, **a day when Venus rose as the Evening Star**. The Maya leaders believed that the first appearance of the Evening Star was a signal of war; they had tables for predicting eclipses and for recording the cycles of Venus.

The Maya believed the first appearance of the Evening Star was a signal for war.

We see scenes of a battle in the second room. It is a heavily forested location, where well-dressed Maya warriors from Bonampak and nearby Yaxchilan, led by Chaan-Muan, aggressively pursue poorly clad or unclothed warriors. The battle was coordinated to occur during an inferior conjunction on August 2, A.D. 792 , when Venus passed in front of the sun. Although most of the figures in the first room display little motion or activity, the battle scene in this room fills the wall space with frenzied movement as the Bonampak warriors pursue their victims. At the end of the battle, the victorious warriors drag the frightened captives away.

The wall paintings clearly illustrate the compositional skills of the artist. Shields, instruments, weapons, and figures are shown at various angles and from different viewpoints; the illusion of depth and perspective is brilliantly achieved, and the intensity of the battle is compelling. The opposite wall shows the captives cowering in fear before nobles who stand above them on a raised, stepped platform. In the center is Chaan-Muan, attired in a jaguar skin vest, sandals, and flowing head-dress of Quetzál feathers. He wears a jade pendant, and jade bracelets encircle his arms. The spear, which is held in his right hand, is covered with a jaguar skin. Some of the captives have already had their fingertips pierced (or nails torn from their fingers) as punishment, mutilation, or blood sacrifice. They hold their bleeding hands and fearfully watch the leaders. One dead captive sprawls across the steps in an incredibly complex,

113. Room One, Bonampak murals

foreshortened pose; a severed head lies near his feet. A prisoner on the upper step faces Chaan-Muan. He holds out his bleeding hand as if to beg for mercy. From the expression on Chaan-Muan's face, it seems unlikely he will deal with the captive in a merciful way. Final scenes describe a victory celebration. Men in towering headdresses of Quetzál feathers dance in triumph to the sound of trumpets.

Blood sacrifice was necessary to honor or to summon the gods, or to bring closure to a successful event or ceremony.

The events depicted in the third room take place in a palace room, and on pyramid steps that resemble the steps of Bonampak's terraced hill. On these walls we see elegant lords, musicians, and **scenes of blood sacrifice rituals**. An attendant waits to assist a seated woman in a blood-letting rite. The lady is tentatively identified, by Miller, as Chaan-Muan's wife, Lady Rabbit. The attendant kneels before Lady Rabbit, a wad of cotton or cloth in his left hand, a sharp blade in his right; the woman brings her fingers to her mouth. She will pierce her tongue, allowing the blood to drip on strips of bark paper which cover the bottom of a large clay vessel. The blood soaked paper will be burned, and the smoke will rise to the gods. Two white-robed Maya ladies sit behind Lady Rabbit on the raised dais, preparing for the ritual. The Maya used thorns, stingray spines, or sharp obsidian blades to pierce their tongues or genitals; cords or vines would sometimes then be pulled through the wound, and the drops of blood would be collected and offered to the gods. Seated on the floor below is a woman holding the young heir. He watches the preparations; perhaps he too will offer his blood in homage to the gods.

The overpowering effect of the Bonampak murals is in the number of figures depicted and the magnificence of color and costuming. The nobles wear towering headdresses of Quetzál feathers and jade ornaments; their clothing is made of feathers, jade, jaguar skins, and beautiful woven fabrics. No verbal or written description can do justice to the technical skill of the artists who created these paintings. In addition to the sheer beauty of the murals, the visual narrative of the event has increased our knowledge of the aggressive nature of the Maya, the social organization and its stratification in a Maya city, and the magnificence of Maya culture during the Late Classic period.

Bonampak is considered an important archaeological site. Not only are the paintings especially significant in terms of their artistic merit, they are also a valuable source of ethnographic and historical data. We do not know the name of the young heir; it is doubtful that he ever ruled at Bonampak, and his fate is unknown. Soon after work on the murals ended, the site was abandoned.

Jaina Island

Jaina is a small island less than a mile in length and only one half mile at its widest point. It is separated from the Yucatán mainland by a narrow channel of water. The distinctive features of Jaina are the swamps, estuaries, and marshes that form a unique geological platform. From a vantage point on the

114. Seated figure with towering headdress, Jaina Island. (CICOM.)

mainland state of Campeche, one would see the island as a land mass whose topography consists of low mounds, small hills, and **various land formations** at the edge of the sea. This is in direct contrast to the sparse and inhospitable Campeche Coast where mangrove swamps, stagnant salt water lagoons, and often submerged land surfaces create a more hostile environment.

It was conclusively established by Ruz Lhuillier in 1948, that Jaina was constructed by artificial means. Land fill was brought from the mainland during the Classic period in an attempt to elevate the level of the land to a point where it could resist the incursion of the sea and swampy waters.

Two principal groups of buildings were established on the island during the Classic Maya period. Unfortunately, little remains of these early structures, because the original building materials such as stone and sascab, which is a soft crumbly form of lime found in limestone deposits on the Yucatán, were frequently removed during later time periods and used for construction purposes on the mainland. The first group of buildings is located on the eastern side of Jaina. It is known as *El Zacpool.* A short distance to the west is *El Zayosal*, the area where the second group is located. During 1941-42, two important archaeological expeditions were conducted by M.A. Fernandez, who was one of several experts commissioned to survey the site by the Instituto National de Antropologia y Historia in Mexico City. Fernandez described the remains of each building on the island. By means of a series of probes into the heart of each structure at *Zayosal*, he was able to prove that there had been three active periods of habitation. He was also able to determine the number of times each building had been reconstructed. For example, at *Zayosal*, the three inner layers of the island's only pyramid were found to correspond in time to the earliest period of occupation, during the seventh century A.D; the fourth and fifth layers were built at a later time, for ceremonial purposes; and the final slope of the pyramid was finished during the third period of occupation. A small platform on the western side of the pyramid was faced with 25 to 30 layers of a stucco coating; Fernandez (1946) postulated that each layer would have lasted for about ten years. From these studies he was able to estimate that the pyramid was probably in use for ceremonial purposes for around 200 years during the last period of occupancy on the island.

During the 1941-42 excavations, Fernandez located 50 previously unknown burial sites. As a result, an exhaustive study of the island's mortuary complex was made, and the archaeological importance of Jaina was conclusively determined. The study confirmed Charnay's earlier report in 1886, that a large burial complex on Jaina may have served the mortuary needs of the mainland areas of Yucatán, Campeche, and Tabasco. Although little remains of either building site on the island that would establish the archaeological importance of Jaina, enough physical evidence concerning Jaina's purpose has been found in the graves there to establish its primary function as an important burial ground.

Many burial sites, complete with figurines, have been located on the Island of Jaina, as well as on the corresponding coast of the Yucatán Peninsula in two areas to the north, and at Jonuta, which lies southwest of Jaina. Despite this broad arc of distribution, there is conclusive proof that the largest number of graves in this region are to be found on Jaina. During excavations in 1966, Gordon Eckholm estimated that 20,000 graves lay untouched on that island, which would indicate that Jaina served as the primary burial site for the Maya during the latter part of the Classic period. The dead may have been brought to Jaina for burial because internment directly into the ground was impossible in some areas of the Yucatán where bedrock lies close to the surface.

There were two types of burials on the island. The first involved internment in a large urn and was usually associated with the burial of small children or infants. The child was placed in a fetal position and wrapped in cloth which was then secured by a cord. The funerary bundle was painted with red cinnabar, and special Jaina-style figurines were placed near the arms. The bundle was then placed in a large ceramic urn. The second type of burial was internment directly into the ground, and appears to have been the accepted method of adult burial. The body was painted with red cinnabar and positioned in a fetal position with the arms either at the sides, across the chest, or near the face. All burial sites were replete with everyday objects which would assure the deceased continued comfort when journeying into the realms of the Maya underworld. Pottery, ornaments, jewelry, tools, and the famous Jaina figurines were found lying either on the body's chest, or in the arms.

115. Maya Noble with elaborate clothing and large hat.

116. Seated Figure, Jaina.

The Figurines

Jaina figurines represent both sexes and are frequently without obvious clues that would conclusively establish their burial function. They range in size from five to ten inches and are made of clays ranging in color from buff to orange. Many figurines exhibit a whitewash and some are painted blue, red, and/or yellow. They are hand-modeled or mold-made, or a combination of both. The figurines are separated by most scholars into three distinct phases which relate to the techniques of manufacture. The most widely accepted classification was established by Corson in 1973:

JAINA PHASE I, c. A.D. 600-800:
The figurines from this period are hand-modeled in wet clay, with pigment applied after drying. They display an astonishing diversity of subject matter and style.

JAINA PHASE II, c. A.D. 800-1000:
Molding techniques are used and there is a gradual abandonment of hand-modeled sculpture.

JAINA PHASE III, c. A.D. 1000-1200:
As the late Classic period ends, mold-made figurines completely replace all individually crafted, sculptural accomplishments.

Phase I: During this time, a rapid spread of religious symbolism throughout the great Maya centers is evidenced in the extraordinary artistic accomplishments of the period. This era represents the height of Maya power: many ceremonial centers were constructed, and there was great emphasis on artistic creativity. This activity culminated in the construction of religious architecture, the growth of the stelae cult, and the production of the extraordinary figurines which were used in burials. The figurines dating from this early period are hand-modeled and display details of extraordinary artistic virtuosity. So clearly have unusual physical types been rendered that the figurines from this phase are often described as genuine "essays in portraiture." Although it has not been conclusively established who is being depicted, it is apparent that these figurines

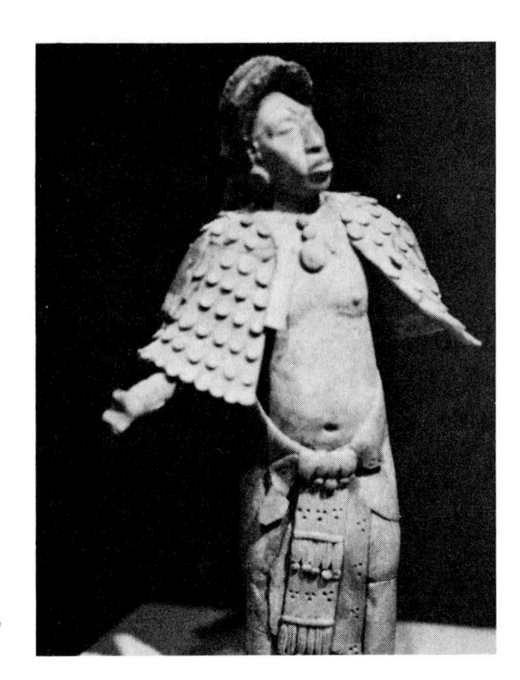

117. Male Noble wearing elaborate cape. Jaina Island. (DYM.)

are not merely cult objects since "cult-type" figurines disappeared from the Maya area with the rise of a dominant organized religion. Instead, many scholars believe that the Jaina figurines are unique in that they were intended to portray likenesses of the gods to whom the burial was consecrated.

Phase II: Toward the end of the Classic period, regionalism became very pronounced. Maya civilization spread from a core region in the Peten west to the lower Usumacinta River and north into Yucatán. Although the tendency to duplicate figurine subjects by using molds began at the end of Phase I, the replication of figurines reached its fullest expression at this later time. It has been sugggested that this change, and a general abandonment of artistic virtuosity, signals a hint of decadence or cultural breakdown in Maya society. These mold-made figurines lack the freely modeled poses that characterize the Phase I groups. There is little emphasis on anatomical detail, and less effort appears to have been applied to the representation of unique figurine types. In addition, arms and legs, which had been treated with great artistic skill during Phase I, are drawn in close to the body and welded to the figure in a solid mass.

Although the introduction of mold-casting techniques resulted in a less detailed and dynamic treatment of subject matter, it is important to note that a repetition of certain figure types continues. The Phase II specimens continue to represent figurines of recognizable religious and mythological subjects and symbolism.

Phase III: The most popular figurine type at Jaina during this late period was a standing woman with hands raised to the sides of her head. This was similar, in a stylistic sense, to the figurines from central Veracruz. The figurines were moldcast and covered with a cream-colored slip that was often painted in vivid colors. Throughout this final phase there is a noticeable reduction in specific physical types. Consequently, as the number of subject types was reduced, the individual expression of each artist became restricted to minor variation in decorative and symbolic elements instead of the variety of dynamic poses and emphasis on the details of anatomical features characteristic of the earlier phases.

118. Clay figures from Jaina Island burial. Height: 6 inches. (MNYC.)

119. *Left.* Maya Woman holding Codex. Earspools, large neckalce, bracelets and Codex suggest high rank. (INAH.)

120. *Right.* Standing Maya noblewoman. Details of clothing, hairstyle and elaborate headdress indicate noble status.

The source of the Jaina figurines is unknown. There is no indication that these objects were produced on the island. Since ceramic molds have not been discovered there and there is no clay on the island, the figurines were undoubtedly manufactured in large quantities in other areas and brought to the island to be used as funerary offerings.

Despite continuing interest in Jaina as a fertile archaeological site and significant burial center, the clay figurines which have been discovered there have received little systematic evaluation in excavation reports or in general summaries of Maya art. Generally, an analysis of the figurines consists of a brief descriptive commentary. There is little evidence to help positively identify the figurines, and there are widely diverse opinions as to their significance, classification, and origin. Despite this lack of conclusive evidence, most scholars agree that Jaina figures were intended to be important burial items even though their specific **iconography** remains somewhat conjectural.

Iconography: symbolic forms that identify a given subject or idea.

Possible Relationships with the Codices

In a survey of Maya pottery completed in 1973, Michael Coe identified some of the scenes on Maya funerary pottery as depictions of the Maya Underworld, *Xibalba*. Coe believes the scenes were derived from the book of Popol Vuh (meaning Council Book), which was written by the Quiche Maya in the 16th century. He suggests that the epics had been handed down from one generation to the next in the ancient codices that described certain beliefs of the Maya. Unfortunately, at the time of the Conquest the ancient Maya codices were considered pagan material and almost all of them were burned by the Spanish clergy. The four that are known to exist today deal with astrology and the Maya cosmos. Coe believes that this limited sampling does not preclude the possibility that certain other codices may have dealt with Maya mythology, particularly with stories that relate to the afterlife and the underworld. In his study, Coe found that certain funerary pottery illustrated a known mythology. Because of this relationship, he believes it is possible to link the Jaina figurines with a common iconography of the myths of the Maya Underworld. Although the Popol Vuh was written by the Quiche Maya in the 16th century and translated into Spanish by Friar Francisco Ximenez after the Spanish Conquest, the stories in the book were of great historical importance to all Maya groups throughout the Yucatán area, and they represented epics that had been handed down from one generation to the next. As a result of his studies, Coe suggests that the stories in the Popol Vuh were also illustrated on pottery and can be applied to the identification of the Jaina figurines.

The Popul Vuh

The stories in the first section of the Popol Vuh relate the Maya myths of creation as described by Quiche Maya writers during the 16th century. The second section focuses on the adventures of twin brothers, Hunahpu and Xbalanque, which take place on earth; this represents the first of two hero cycles in the book. The third section moves back in time to tell the story of Hunahpu and Xbalanque's father, One Hunahpu, and his twin brother, Seven Hunahpu, the Maya Hero Twins, and their experiences in *Xibalba* against the gods of the Underworld. In this section, a woman named Xmucane bears the twins, who grow up to become exceptionally skilled at playing the ritualistic ball game. The commotion the twins make when they play the game, however, soon annoys One Death and Seven Death, lords of the Underworld. They summon the boys and request that they bring their ball game equipment into the Underworld: the kilts, yokes, arm guards, headbands, and **panache** that they, the lords, so desperately wanted (Tedlock 1985). Thus, the twins go into the Underworld, only to be killed by the angry and jealous lords; One Hunahpu is beheaded, Seven Hunahpu is disembowled. The head of One Hunahpu is placed in the branches of a gourd tree, where it looks like one of the fruits growing there. When Xkiq (Blood Woman), the daughter of one of the lords of the Underworld, stands under the gourd tree, the head of One Hunahpu spits a moistureless saliva into her hand and she becomes pregnant. As punishment for this alleged fornication, her father orders her sacrificed, but she escapes and flees to the surface of the earth where she is accepted by her mother-in-law, Xmucane. Together they await the birth of Xkiq's child. Xkiq bears twin sons, Hunahpu and Xbalanque, who eventually descend into the Underworld, slay the evil lords there, resurrect their father, and then ascend into the sky where they remain heroes forever.

Panache: "Probably corresponding to the long bunch of feathers as shown attached to the crowns of the heads of the players in the ball-court relief at Chichén Itzá." (Tedlock 1985.)

Jaina Figurines and the Popul Vuh

There are two categories of female figurines found on Jaina that appear to relate to Xmucane and Xkiq. The first category is represented by groups of Jaina figures depicted in attitudes of quiet patience or resignation. These figurines wear an off-the-shoulder garment known as a *huipil*, with a string of tube-shaped beads around their necks. The hair is parted in the center and there frequently is a V-shaped indentation at the top of the head. It has been suggested that this figure personifies the patience of the ideal Maya mother, which could be Xmucane, mother of One Hunahpu and Seven Hunahpu, and Hunahpu and Xbalanque's grandmother. In the Popol Vuh, Xmucane was instructed by her grandsons to wait patiently and watch for a sign that would indicate their success or failure in their journey into the Underworld. Their instructions to her were as follows:

121. *Left.* Female figure with child on lap. Jaina Island. (INAH.)

122. *Right.* Old Woman. Expression suggests distress or concern. Jaina Island. (INAH.)

> Together we plant this cornstalk for you:
> In the center of our home we plant it
> If it should wither,
> You can say they must be dead.
> If it bears a tassle,
> You can say they are alive.
> Oh our grandmother...

The second group of female figures requires a more complex interpretation. These figurines are usually in an attitude of motion. They are most often shown in a sitting position with a hand extended in a forward gesture. Frequently the head is slightly turned, and the total composition suggests tension or motion. This second type of figurine is most often paired with men, dwarfs, or animals. It may represent Ixchel, the young Moon Goddess, who is described in the Dresden Codex, the oldest and best preserved of the four ancient Maya codices. Ixchel is known as the "whore of heaven" who copulates with many male deities in order to represent the way the moon lines

123. Attentive expression and slight angle of the body enhances the elegant bearing of this Maya woman. (BMFA.)

up with various constellations. In the story of the Hero Twins, Xkiq is anguished at being called a whore by the Lords of the Underworld. However, when she becomes the mother of twins who rescue their father, Xkiq is regarded as a model for childbirth and as the goddess who precipitates the end of the evil lords of *Xibalba* by bearing the sons who slay the reigning leaders. At the close of this section no mention is made of Xkiq; her fate remains a mystery. The general assumption is that Xqik chose to be with her sons when they rose to the sky, one to be identified with the sun, the other to the moon. Thus, as the Moon Goddess known as Ixchel, Xkiq would be able to remain forever with her children.

Since it can be assumed that literacy among the Maya was limited to the scribes and nobles, the codices most likely could not have been read by the common people. However, these same tales could have been available to the lower classes as illustrations on the funerary urns or sculpted into ceramic figurines. According to Michael Coe (1966), "The idea of 'decoration' was alien to the Maya; all elements, including color, design, and composition had meaning to the Maya artist and beholder." Thus, on Jaina Island, the figurines may have become a major medium for ceremonial art in that they brought ritual information to the common man in visual form. Since only the ruling class had commemorative dates incised into stelae, and the codices were most likely the province of the elite, the figurines provided a means by which religious beliefs were recorded. They related in a most meaningful way to the deepest concerns of all of the people.

124. Standing woman holding skein of yarn. (INAH.)

Summary

The Jaina figurine tradition began with great brilliance and artistic expression. The earliest Jaina-style figurines were produced during a period of extraordinary cultural activity in the major Maya cities. Throughout the homeland region artistic production accelerated, and the effects of the great Maya ascendency to power are apparent. Great numbers of Jaina-style figurines were produced for burial, and hundreds of stelae and temple complexes were completed as commemorative monuments and theocratic residences. During this time in these expanding centers, a highly complex and efficient theocracy stimulated and directed the production of all ceremonial and religious structures and artifacts.

At the time the Classic period ended, the Jaina figurines were mass-produced and mold-made. As a result, the figurines lost their individuality and the extraordinary artistic expression seen in the earlier types. This latest period focused on expediency and repetitive subject matter. Undoubtedly this was due to declining inspiration and a lack of organized directives from an all-powerful priesthood, for it coincided with the collapse of the High Maya Civilization. Throughout this final phase, Jaina figurines became increasingly similar. The vitality and diversity of the earlier groups disappeared; and the individual expression of each artist became restricted to minor variation in the decoration of each mold-made figurine. All of this would appear to be truly reflective of the collapse of a once powerful theocratic society.

Uxmal

Toward the end of the Classic period, city construction had stopped in the Central Region, but a small number of magnificent centers were still being built by the Maya in the Yucatán area. Nowhere is this last vestige of architectural glory more evident than at Uxmal, which is located approximately 60 miles from Merida, the present-day capital of the Yucatán. The buildings at Uxmal and the nearby sites of Kabah, Sayil and Labna are some of the finest examples of Puuc-style architecture in the entire region.

Temple buildings at Uxmal were seldom built on level ground, but were situated on artificially constructed, elevated platforms. The platforms were a solid mass of rubble, mortar, and earth which were then faced with carefully cut, dressed stones. The rooms and temples on top of the platform bases were constructed so that the outer walls extended high above the building in a straight line. The top half of these vertical outer walls provided an unbroken facade, which was then embellished with precisely cut pieces of stone applied over the rubble core like tile embedded in cement. When assembled, the stones formed elaborate designs and patterns. Although the exterior line was not as graceful as the mansard roof and roof comb profile of the Palenque type, the vertical facade served better to carry the **magnificently cut stone decoration which is the hallmark of the Puuc style**. The decorative designs are mostly geometric, although human figures, Chac gods, animals, birds, and serpents are also represented.

The top half of the outer walls provided an unbroken facade, which was embellished with precisely cut pieces of stone.

An interesting feature seen on many of the buildings is the stone niche above a doorway. The niches often represent small, decorated houses with two sides and a roof. A seated individual carved from stone or made of stucco is usually inside the niche. These figures may represent the various deities who were worshipped at this time. The use of the mask panel is another noteworthy characteristic of facade decoration at Uxmal. The masks often

125. Courtyard area of the Nunnery at Uxmal, Yucatán.

represent Chac, the Rain God, who is depicted with a long, curved nose. Chac faces are carved one on top of another, and rise to the top of an outer wall or are sometimes wrapped around the corner of a building.

The three largest buildings at Uxmal are the Pyramid of the Magician (sometimes called the Soothsayer's, or Magician's, Pyramid), the Nunnery Complex, and the Palace of the Governor. Among the many smaller structures are the ruins of the Great Pyramid, also called the Dwarf's House, the Dove-cotes, Temple of the Phalli, the Ball Court, and the House of the Turtles. The Pyramid of the Magician is oval in plan and has been expanded five times. Four smaller pyramids lie beneath the present structure and represent earlier periods of construction. One can see openings all along the face of the pyramid leading to the interior buildings. According to legend, this pyramid was built by a hunch-backed dwarf, who was also a magician, in three nights.

The temple at the top of the pyramid is referred to as Temple Number Five, and it represents the last of the five temples. It is 125

126. Entrance into the Nunnery courtyard through corbel vaulted passage.

127. Stacked Chac masks. The Nunnery.

128. Pyramid of The Magician at Uxmal. Unusual oval shape distinguishes this pyramid. Late Classic period.

feet above ground level and can be reached by climbing 150 steep steps that are flanked with masks of the Rain God. The temple has a single row of rooms and a facade decorated with intricate stone designs, serpents, and the image of a simple stone house. Temple Number Four lies beneath, and it is the best preserved of the five temples. Inside is a large mask of Chac, which forms the antechamber to the temple; the entrance is through the open mouth of Chac. The wall surfaces of this sacred room are covered with elaborate decorations . Of even greater antiquity is Temple Number Three, which has a small antechamber and inner temple room. A stairway was built at this time, but it was covered during later periods of construction. Temple Number Two shares a wall with Temple Three. It was the first temple to be built above ground level, about two-thirds of the way to the top of the present temple. Temple Number One lies almost at ground level and is the oldest of the five temples. It consists of four small rooms built around a small courtyard. The complex was decorated with Chac masks, small drums, and intricately decorated pillars.

In addition to the many interesting architectural elements of each of the five temples, some freestanding objects of great beauty were found at Uxmal. One is the well-known "Queen of Uxmal" sculpture that can now be seen at the National Museum of Anthropology in Mexico City. It shows a serpent head with open jaws that reveal the tatooed head of a priest. It was discovered under the main doorway of the primary room that leads into the temple.

The so-called Nunnery Complex is generally thought to be one of the most beautiful groups of buildings at Uxmal. The name "Nunnery" comes from the Spaniards of the Colonial period who thought the buildings resembled nunneries in Spain. It consists of four separate buildings grouped closely together around a large, enclosed courtyard. We do not know for what purpose this complex was intended. The buildings may have been palaces for the rulers, or the individual rooms could have been used by the powerful priesthoood for ceremonial purposes. Like all the buildings at Uxmal, the Nunnery is built of white limestone. The four long buildings are grouped around a large, square courtyard and each structure is richly decorated with the typical Puuc-style mosaic stonework.

129. Stacked Chac masks in profile. The Nunnery.

The Palace of the Governor is considered to be the most perfect example of architecture in the Puuc region, and it closely follows the basic components of the Puuc style. The building has a rather sophisticated design with its facade set back in two stages, and a ten foot high mosaic-like stone frieze that extends across the upper area. The stone patterns provide a dramatic contrast to the smooth, undecorated walls below. Almost 20,000 finished stones, each weighing between 55 and 75 pounds, were used to create this masterpiece. One hundred and fifty masks of the Rain God Chac and over 10,000 stone X's (called St. Andrew's Crosses) have been counted among the most frequently represented motifs. There are also step-frets, Chac masks, and serpents. The Palace of the Governor, with its 24 rooms, may have been the administrative center for the region.

The Maya linked their cities by means of elevated crushed-rock roads called *sacbes*. At one end of each road was a great arch, each distinctively different from the other. Such a monument is the freestanding arch at Kabah, which marks the causeway to Uxmal, a

130. Palace of the Governor at Uxmal. Geometric designs cover the upper facade. This Late Preclassic period structure was built to honor the last ruler of Uxmal. 10th century.

131. Buildings in the Nunnery Complex. Uxmal, Yucatán.

distance of less than eight miles. At nearby Labna is a lavishly decorated arch in pure Puuc style. Perhaps the unique character of each arch served to identify its road and the city to which it was linked, in much the same way as we use street signs and other landmarks to follow our own pathways.

While the Puuc-style architecture at Uxmal seems very different from that of the earlier Maya cities, there are also many characteristics common to all. Ultimately, though, each Maya city, regardless of date, seems to have a unique quality of its own. Puuc region architects created masterpieces in stone decoration, while the builders at Tikal designed and constructed the tallest pyramids deep in the heart of a dense jungle. Where Palenque displays elaborate roof combs, mansard-style roofs, and delicate stucco reliefs, Bonampak boasts beautifully colored murals whose brillance has not dimmed over the 1200 years of their existence. In essence then, it is the unique skill and creativity of the Maya in each region that has made such an extraordinary impact on modern scholars and art lovers throughout the world.

The Collapse of Maya Civilization

After more than a thousand years of extensive construction and development into a sophisticated culture, major cultural activities at the various cities ceased and the Maya civilization collapsed. There were no giant stelae carved with informative and ceremonial data, and there were no temples or palaces built. Within a short span of about 100 years, from approximately A.D. 800 to 909, all of the once populous cities in the central area were deserted. Bonampak was abandoned around AD. 795, Palenque, Yaxchilan, and Copán by A.D. 800. Tikal was essentially a deserted city by 879. At some locations, work ceased so suddenly that most of the buildings were abruptly abandoned as if their occupants had intended to return momentarily. No one returned and the cities were slowly engulfed by the jungles around them. There is no conclusive evidence as to why the cities were abandoned at the very height of their glory, and we can only speculate as to why there was a breakdown of Maya culture. Some theories that have been suggested include frequent earthquakes; agricultural collapse due either to distance or an uncontrolled slash-and-burn system of farming; widespread disease; or large-scale invasions from peoples from the north.

While all of these theories may seem reasonable to the reader, there is no evidence that any one of them could have produced such a wide-scale and catastrophic event as the collapse of the Maya. There is no evidence that earthquakes of an unusual number or frequency occurred; there is substantial evidence that the Maya used land intelligently, building dikes and irrigation canals, terracing steep hillsides, and planting on elevated garden plots; and while there was disease, the most life-threatening diseases from which the native population had no immunity were brought by the Europeans six centuries later. The only substantial evidence we have are the signs of increasing violence and warfare that began to appear around A.D. 800 in areas where cities were abandoned and monuments were smashed. The Bonampak murals from the Late Classic period depict warfare for sacrifice and servitude, and similar scenes on the Late Classic stelae at Yaxchilan describe battle after battle. Indeed, by the end of the Classic period, most of the monuments celebrated war and conquest, instead of the historical events and royal lineages of earlier times. According to Schele and Miller (1986), "War became an event that served individuals rather than systems and allowed small sites and their rulers to achieve status far in excess of their historical position. As more warfare was carried out, it seems to have gained a new scale and purpose, and under the leadership of expansionist kings, some small sites and their lords furthered their status dramatically."

Raymond Sidrys and Rainer Berger of the University of California at Los Angeles suggest a slightly different interpretation of the collapse. They propose that the solution to this puzzle may be found in the framework of the High Maya socio-power structure. Research conducted by Sydrys and Berger indicates that there could very well have been an enormous disruption of a rigid class system, a revolt of the commoners, and a complete socio-economic breakdown with the resulting loss of authority and elitist leadership (*Nature*, Jan. 25, 1979). Their study charted the development over the centuries of three things: the remains of the commoners' homes, the remains of the temple-palace structures associated with the ruling classes, and the frequency of production of the carved stone monuments called stelae. The erection of stelae was an extremely important activity for the Maya. From Early Classic times, the monumental stones were carved with images of rulers, hieroglyphic texts, historical information, descriptions of religious ceremonies, and the date of each of these occurrences according to the Maya calendar. Hundreds of quarry workers, stone masons, carvers, and laborers were needed to produce and erect the important stones. The priest-rulers no doubt were the organizers of this operation, as their primary function was to control and direct all civic and religious activity in their region. Sidrys and Berger discovered that the stelae were erected somewhat infrequently during the third century A.D., but that with each passing century, an increasing number of the commemorative stones were placed in the cities. Between A.D. 613 and 790, when the Classic Maya culture was at its peak, the Maya erected at least 324 of the dated monuments. In A.D. 790 alone, at least nineteen new ceremonial centers were dedicated, more than at any other time. In A.D. 810, however, there is a noticeable decline in organized construction, dedication of commemorative stelae, and an increase in warfare and sacrificial themes. By 830, only one-fifth

132. Tikal's regal buildings bear silent tribute to a former era of growth and accomplishment.

as many stelae were erected as in 790, and by A.D. 909 the activity was virtually abandoned. Studies of temple and palace structures and artifacts of the upper class show a similar correlative rise of production, and then a sharp decline shortly after the last dated stelae was erected in A.D. 909 at Tonina, in Chiapas. Similar studies of the remains of the commoner population sites show no growth increases during the rise of the stelae cult, and no decline at any time after its cessation.

In describing the class structure, it should be noted that the lower classes were not trained to correctly interpret the will of the gods, or to devise the proper means to placate them. Only the priests possessed these "semi-divine" capabilities. They were the absolute rulers in the Maya world. In contrast, the laborers formed the backbone of Maya civilization. Without their efforts, the priest-rulers could not function. Endless labor was required to construct the ceremonial centers, administer to the needs and demands of wealthy nobles or priests, pay tributes, and create luxury goods for the upper classes. In short, the lower classes were kept in a constant state of servitude. Sidrys and Berger suggest that the lower classes may have revolted against the excessive demands of their rulers. Therefore, the collapse of the civilization may have been the collapse of a class structure that had been created over the centuries to maintain and support a demanding hierarchy of rulers.

We do not know for certain whether the collapse of the civilization occurred as a result of an internal revolt, or if tyranical rulers, sated by the luxuries created by their workers, became obsessed with new dreams of territorial expansion. One way or another, warfare and collapse was the end result of a long period of cultural expansion. It does appear, however, that the commoner Maya lived on for centuries in scattered villages throughout the central area; the northern Yucatán cities were the last to be abandoned. For reasons not completely understood, the backbone of Maya culture was broken and the intellectual traditions that had been the achievements of the elite Classic Maya were lost forever.

The Postclassic Period

A.D. 900 - 1521

The Classic period was essentially over by the end of the 9th century A.D. What followed, beginning with the 10th century and continuing for some 600 years, was a period that differed markedly from the former priest-ruled Classic era. Some of the dramatic changes during this time period include full-scale warfare emphasizing human sacrifice, a de-emphasis of religious architecture, the extensive use of the column in architecture, and a new rather rigid art style with a sculptural emphasis on warrior forms and ***chacmool* figures**.

Chacmool: reclining figure with flat, plate-like receptacle on the abdomen. The name means "red jaguar" in Maya. The chacmool is associated with Postclassic sites such as Tula and Chichén Itzá.

At the beginning of the 10th century, groups of Chichimec-Tolteca warriors came down from the north and invaded the central highlands and southern lowlands of Mexico. They brought with them a new and aggressive militaristic manner. In a relatively short time, their leaders replaced the priest-kings of the Classic period and assumed control of most religious and civic activities in the regions they occupied. The newly arrived warrior groups were constantly engaged in acts of aggression and conflict, raiding and plundering villages, and taking victims for sacrificial purposes. Although most of the villagers survived the frequent attacks and continued to develop and expand their communities, their arts and religion began to reflect the new and unfamiliar ways of the invaders. In turn, the warriors adopted many of the villagers' old customs. The result was a merging of the traditional cultural traits that had been carried over from the Classic period with the new rather barbaric customs of the warrior groups.

133. *Opposite:* Standard Bearer. (INAH.)

134. Atlantean Column from Pyramid B, Tula. (INAH.)

The Toltecs

The official record of the Postclassic period begins with the founder of the Toltec dynasty, a powerful Chichimec-Tolteca chieftain named Mixcóatl (Cloud Serpent). According to legend, he was a capable and aggressive military leader who conquered many villages and cities in the Valley of Mexico, and then consolidated the lands he gained into a cohesive Toltec dynasty; the center of his domain was established at Culhuacán. He met a woman whose ancestors were aristocratic priest-leaders; she bore him a son in the year A.D. 947. This year was under the calendrical sign of Ce Acatl, which means "One Reed" in the Nahuatl language of the warriors. The child was given the name of his birth sign, as was the custom of the times, along with the title "Prince." He was thus known as Ce Acatl Topiltzin, which means "One Reed Our Prince." The birth of this special child during the year of the Reed anticipates the fall of Mexico to the Spaniards more than 500 years later, as we shall see in a later chapter.

Little is known about the actual childhood of Ce Acatl, except that after his parents' death he was raised by his maternal grandparents—not in the barbaric-militaristic fashion of his father's people, but in the more gentle Classic period traditions of his grandparents' culture. He studied and learned the ways of the priesthood rather than the ways of the warrior. When Ce Acatl reached adulthood, he began to search for his father's remains. It is said that he found his father's bones on the Cerro de la Estrella (the Hill of the Star) near Culhuacán, and re-buried them with dignity and honor. He was attacked on the hill by his father's assassin, the new leader of the Toltec group. In a personal battle between the two, Ce Acatl killed the man and avenged his father's death. Because of this victory, he was declared the ruler of the Toltecs, thereby assuming his rightful place as leader of his father's people. For reasons unknown to us, Ce Acatl then moved the Toltec capital to Tula, which is some 80 miles north of present-day Mexico City. There he became a strong religious reformer who urged his people away from human sacrifice. The exact date of this transition is unknown. As the High Priest of the Cult of Quetzálcóatl, Ce Acatl Topiltzin assumed the name of the god he worshipped and became known only as "Quetzálcóatl," the living incarnation of the Feathered Serpent Deity.

Tula

By A.D. 986, under Quetzálcóatl's leadership, the Toltecs built an impressive metropolis at Tula. The architectural style was visually dramatic and innovative. Stately columns provided elegant walkways for the warriors who gathered for important ceremonies. The columns were also used as structural supports for the larger temple rooms that were needed for group activities. The temple entrances were framed by great **serpent-columns** that supported massive lintels across each entrance. Their open jaws extended forward to flank the temple doorway, their bodies formed the sides, and their tails swept up in a squared S-shape to support the framework of the door. The transition from the small, exclusive temples of the Classic period to these open, colonnaded structures of the Postclassic reflects the changing times. The new temples were built for active group participation, while the temples of the Classic period were only used by the priests. However, as impressive in design as these new buildings were,

Serpent columns supported massive lintels with their squared, s-shaped tails.

135. Burnt Palace at Tula.

136. Temple B at Tula. Atlantean columns may have supported a roof made with perishable materials.

inferior building materials were used, and the clay bricks and coarse stones soon succumbed to the ravages of time. These Toltec temples were evidently built very rapidly to accommodate the needs of a large population, rather than built painstakingly to last through the centuries.

The best preserved structure at Tula is the Pyramid of Quetzálcóatl in his dual aspect as Venus, the morning and evening star. It is commonly called Temple B, or Building of the *Atlantes*. It is less frequently referred to by its Nahuatl name, Temple of *Tlahuizcalpantecuhtli.* On top of this pyramid are great stone Atlantean figure-columns that may once have supported a roof with their flat-topped heads. In the deliberate destruction of Tula in 1156, these massive columns were broken apart and rolled into a deep trench. Now, after extensive restoration, the columns have been reassembled and returned to their original position on top of the pyramid. Each column is made in four sections which are doweled together. They are over twelve feet high and represent warrior figures. The warrior-columns are richly dressed in military attire and stand stiffly at attention. Their faces have the well-drilled anonymous look of the military. Even the feathers that adorn each headdress project upward in a rigid manner. They hold spearthrowers called *atlatls* in their hands. In contrast to this warrior image is a large butterfly emblem on each chest. The conflict of the times is immediately apparent in this incongruity. As noted before, the priest-king Quetzálcóatl believed only in one god—the ancient Feathered Serpent deity, Quetzálcóatl. The youthful leader was taught to believe that his god did not approve of human sacrifice. He only accepted the offerings of the most precious gifts of life: butterflies, flowers and jade. Thus, the butterfly emblem became the symbol of the priest-king's philosophies, and the rigid warrior columns represented the new military influence of the warrior groups at Tula.

Quetzálcóatl's rivals for leadership of the Toltec nation were those who followed the leadership of the deceiver Tezcatlipoca, who advocated the road to revolution, urging support for the new strong orders of militarism and human sacrifice. The ancient Indian legends ascribe the very invention of war to this cult of the god Tezcatlipoca, for war was no longer a question of raids and defense, but was demanded by their rituals and religious convictions. Great skull racks, called *Tzompantli*, were built next to the temples, and upon these racks were displayed the heads of sacrificial victims. In addition, chacmool figures were carved in stone. They represented the messengers of the gods who held plates on their abdomens for sacrificial offerings.

The followers of Tezcatlipoca saw Quetzálcóatl's gentle philosophies as a threat to their quest for power. Not only did they believe they needed sacrifices to appease their gods, they also needed to have complete control of their subjects in order to maintain their position in the Toltec world. Unfortunately, Quetzálcóatl's thoughts were far too advanced for his time, and he incurred the hatred of the followers of this rival cult. All through his nineteen year reign, the opposing priests attempted to discredit him. In a final act of deception, they forced Quetzálcóatl to drink quantities of an intoxicating beverage when he was ill, and succeeded in humiliating him in front of

137. Ballcourt. Broken *chacmool* lies in the foreground. Tula.

his people, thus forcing his abdication. As a result, he and a group of loyal supporters left Tula in total disgrace, crossed the Valley of Mexico to the Gulf Coast, and set sail eastward on a raft covered with serpent skins. When he left, he promised that in another year of his birth he would return to reclaim his rightful throne.

Quetzálcóatl is the most interesting personality in Pre-Conquest history. He represented the continuation of Classic period ideals, and the legends refer to his reign as the "Golden Age" of Postclassic times. Under his leadership, the Toltecs greatly expanded their cultural and intellectual accomplishments. Those who forced his abdication were the proponents of the bloodthirsty cult of Tezcatlipoca. After Quetzálcóatl left, a series of new rulers carried on for about another 150 years until the final reign of Huemac. During his leadership, there were renewed attacks by barbarians from the north, and Tula was destroyed in 1165. A small group of Toltecs lived among the ruins for some years, but they eventually left and the site was abandoned. The only other noteworthy Toltec group left in the

Valley of Mexico were those who lived in the city of Culhuacán, the first Toltec capital that had been established by Mixcóatl.

The Toltec/Maya at Chichén Itzá

Splinter groups of Toltec warriors began to migrate beyond their territorial boundaries in the Valley of Mexico long before Quetzálcóatl's abdication. There is evidence that their explorations extended as far as the Maya homeland, on the Yucatán Peninsula, several times during the 10th century. According to the Mayan Chronicles in the books of *Chilam Balam*, one very special group of Toltec invaders came to the Yucatán in the year of Quetzálcóatl's abdication and conquered the ancient Maya city of Chichen. They were led by a High Priest called "Kukulcán," the Mayan word meaning "Plumed Serpent." There is no evidence that Kukulcán and Quetzálcóatl were the same person other than the coincidence of time and name, and it is unlikely that they were identical. The records of this invasion indicate that Kukulcán was a bloodthirsty conqueror far different from the gentle leader at Tula. The only proven fact is that a band of Toltec warriors, led by a man called Kukulcán, arrived at Chichén Itzá in A.D. 986.

The Toltecs who came to Chichén Itzá soon began to rebuild and expand a portion of the ancient Maya city they conquered, using architectural details that are unique to the Toltecs. Striking similarities between Tula and the rebuilt areas at Chichen include: the extensive use of the column in architecture, serpent-forms, Toltec columns to flank temple entrances, reclining *chacmool* figures, Tzompantli, and jaguar and eagle symbols identifying the warrior orders of the Toltecs. It appears that the Toltecs brought with them all of their rituals and institutions.

The most impressive building at Chichén Itzá forms the center of the newly-created Toltec section. It is the Temple of Kukulcán, usually called the Castillo (castle). Both Toltec and Maya features blend in this temple-pyramid with its corbeled vaulting and carved reliefs of Toltec warriors. The massive square pyramid rises in nine terraced levels to a height of 75 feet, with a ceremonial staircase ascending each of the four sides to the sanctuary on top. Each stairway has 91 steps; together with the last step of the north platform this adds up to 365 steps, the number of days in the solar calendar. The stairs bisect each of

138. *Top*. El Castillo (Temple of Kukulcán). This nine-leveled structure may house a royal tomb. Chichén Itzá.

139. *Bottom*. Model of The Castillo. Larger pyramid hides earlier temple-pyramid structure (INAH). Preserved inside the earlier pyramid is a *chacmool* and jaguar throne.

140. Detail of The Castillo. Precisely cut stone panels add to the beauty of this pyramid.

the nine levels of the pyramid, creating a total of eighteen sections on each side. This corresponds to the eighteen months of the Maya year. In addition, each side of the pyramid is decorated with 52 panels which represent the 52 year cycle of Venus, the basis of the ritual calendar of the Maya. Inside this impressive structure is a smaller pyramid that dates from earlier times. In its temple was discovered a *chacmool* and a red painted stone throne in the form of a jaguar with eyes of jade, shell fangs projecting from its snarling mouth.

The largest ball court in Mesoamerica is a short distance to the north of the Castillo. The court is 480 feet long by 122 feet wide, with two long walls that flank the sides of the court and rise twenty seven feet in height. There are six bas-relief panels on the walls, each panel having fourteen male images represented, for a total of 84 figures depicted on the ball court panels. The figures represent ball players, or personages associated in some way with the ritual and ceremonies of the ball game. All display a nosebead, a round ear disk into which is inserted a long tubular rod, a back shield, a short tunic, and sandals; arms and knees are padded. Each ball player wears a yoke around his waist, with palmas projecting upward from the front of the

141. The Great Ballcourt at Chichén Itzá is the largest ballcourt in Mesoamerica.

142. The Temple of the Jaguar overlooks the Great Ballcourt at Chichén Itzá.

yoke. The yokes are often elaborate in design, and the palmas are carved as human skulls, or heads of serpents and monkeys. In addition, most of the figures hold *manoplas*, which are flat "box-like" objects with handles. Discovered at many early sites in Mesoamerica, Fox (1994) suggests that these objects were ball game handstones which may have been used to deflect the rubber ball, to steady the player if he lunged after the ball or fell during the game, or to protect the player's hand from injury. A most descriptive, and frequently photographed wall panel shows two ball players opposite one another with a large skull-disk between them. The kneeling player is headless, and has seven serpents sprouting from his severed neck; a third player stands behind the decapitated victim, holding one of the box-like objects. All of the carefully detailed carved stone panels create a dramatic visual narrative of the ball game, its players, and their dress, and the inevitable sacrifice that finalized the contest.

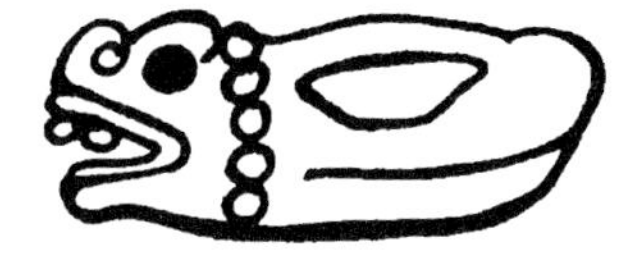

Manopla: drawn from ballcourt relief at Chichén Itzá.

Just next to the Great Ball Court is a *Tzompantli* or skull rack. This is a wall carved with images of human skulls. Although the fate of the game's losers is not certain, there are many indications that they were decapitated and the heads placed on the adjacent *Tzompantli*. The design and concept of this was introduced to the Postclassic period cultures by the Toltec warriors.

The Temple of the Warriors is located to the south of the Castillo. The floor plan of this temple is quite similar to the plan of Temple B at Tula, although larger and more skillfully constructed. The builders at Chichén Itzá were expert Maya craftsmen who used their skill to construct Toltec-style buildings for their new leaders. As at Tula, maximum spaciousness was achieved through the use of colonnaded courts and rooms. In front, and along the side of the temple, is a great walkway of columns and square pillars; some are carved with typical Toltec warrior figures. They are made of stacked, circular or square sections of cut stone firmly joined together by a mixture of mortar and bits of stone and rubble. At the top of the wide frontal staircase is a stone *chacmool* that seems to guard the serpent-columned temple entrance. At the back of the temple are built-in benches, raised platforms, and an altar-like platform supported by small Atlantean figures. Most of the construction

143. *Top.* Front view of the Temple of the Warriors at Chichén Itzá. Recalling Temple B at Tula, connecting colonnades and serpent columns distinguish this building.

144. *Bottom.* Temple of the Warriors. Squared serpent columns once held a massive lintel. Chac masks, *chacmool* figure, and serpent columns reflect Maya-Toltec era.

145. Temple of the Warriors at Chichén Itzá. The stately colonnade may have supported a perishable roof.

at Chichén Itzá consists of cut stones anchored together with rock and rubble and covered with a thick layer of stucco. The finished product was often painted with bright colors and sometimes carved with typical Toltec figures and designs.

At Chichén Itzá is a large well, called a cenote, that was believed to be sacred by the ancient Maya. Cenotes are formed when rainwater seeps through cracks in the earth and accumulates in underground caves. Since the entire Yucatán peninsula is a vast expanse of limestone with no surface water, water is available only from these underground wells. The cenotes become visible when the porous limestone above the water level collapses and exposes the well. There are many cenotes scattered throughout the Yucatán, but the most well known is the largest of two located at Chichén Itzá. Dedicated to Chac, the god of water and rain, it is some 200 feet in diameter with sheer walls that drop straight through the snow-white limestone ground to the water, some 65 feet below. This large well was a major center for pilgrimages during the long period of occupancy of Chichén Itzá, and continuing long after Chichén Itzá was abandoned. The most important written record of the history of the Yucatán, including a vivid description of the famous well, is the detailed chronicle entitled "Relacion de las Cosas de Yucatán." It was written about 1560 by Diego de Landa, a Franciscan friar who reached Yucatán a few years after the Spanish Conquest. This missionary, who later became Bishop of the Yucatán, ordered the burning of Mayan codices and maps at Mani, Yucatán in 1562. Although de Landa has been much criticized for this over-zealous attempt to eliminate "pagan" manuscripts, he partially redeemed himself when his work was published in 1566. In his "Relacion" Bishop Landa wrote:

> Into this well they were and still are accustomed to throw men alive as a sacrifice to the gods in times of drought; they held that they did not die, even though they were not seen again. They also threw in many other offerings of precious stones and things they valued greatly; so if there were gold in this country, this well would have received most of it, so devout were the Indians in this. This well is seven long fathoms deep to the surface of the water, more than a hundred feet wide, round, of natural rock marvelously smooth down to the surface of the water. The water looks green, caused as I think by the trees that surround it; it is very deep. At the top, near the mouth, is a small building where I found idols made in honor of all the principal idols in the land, like the Pantheon in Rome. (Bates translation 1973.)

In 1843, John Lloyd Stephens, a student of ancient cultures, published a book entitled "Incidents of Travel in Central America, Chiapas and Yucatán." The two volumes were brilliantly illustrated by his traveling companion, the noted artist Frederick Catherwood. Stevens described the visit he and Catherwood made to the ceremonial cenote at Chichén Itzá. In 1882, the French explorer Desiree Charnay also recorded his impressions of the cenote in "The Ancient Cities of the New World." He made plans to dredge the well to search for the treasures he was sure he would find, but he never succeeded in carrying out the project.

In 1894, Edward Herbert Thompson was appointed United States Counsel General in Yucatán. At this time, he purchased the archaeological site at Chichén Itzá, which included the sacred cenote, for 200 pesos. Thompson had lived in Yucatán for several years, and he was extremely interested in the history of the ancient Maya. He read the books by Stephens and Landa many times over, and decided to explore the sacred cenote. He learned to handle diving equipment for underwater explorations, had a dredge brought from the United States, and, in 1904 launched one of the earliest underwater archaeological recovery operations. Using the dredge and heavy diving

146. The Caracol as viewed through a corbeled arch at Chichén Itzá.

147. The Caracol at Chichén Itzá. Strategically placed openings suggest planetary observation.

equipment, Thompson and his men began to explore the murky depths of the well. Since they could see nothing in the dark green water, they used their sense of touch to recover golden masks and disks, copper bells, jade objects, pottery vessels, flint knives, figurines, ceremonial scepters and human bones. From 1904 until 1911, approximately 3000 objects were brought from the bottom of the well. Analysis has shown that the gold objects came from Colombia, Panama, and Guatemala; the copper articles came originally from Oaxaca and the Valley of Mexico; and those objects containing tin alone came from Honduras. This was, indeed, a pilgrimage site of great importance to the Maya during the Classic Period. Since Thompson's explorations, there have been many successful attempts to retrieve additional treasure from the cenote. The more recent discoveries are of enormous importance, and have provided us with the most complete archaeological information on the ceremonial and ritual function of the sacred cenote at Chichén Itzá.

One cannot fully describe Chichén Itzá without mentioning the older Maya section. The Caracol, a circular building resembling a conch shell in cross section, is a major structure. So named for its unusual plan, it is a magnificent double-shelled round building with vaulted ceilings and an interior spiral staircase that leads to a small chamber in its tower. Openings in the tower walls are astronomically positioned to allow observation of the movements of Venus, whose cycles as the morning and evening star were of great significance to the Maya. One should also note that the later Aztecs dedicated their round buildings to Quetzálcóatl, who was astronomically linked to Venus. In his manifestation as Ehecatl, the Wind God, Quetzálcóatl was always seen with a conch shell (Miller 1986).

Through the tower openings, one can see the remaining buildings that define Old Chichen: the Nunnery, Temple of the Three Lintels, the Red House, and many other poorly preserved structures. Here we see examples of Puuc-style architectural elements on the buildings that were constructed long before the arrival of the Toltec warriors. The most exquisite example of this style in Old Chichen is the so-called Iglesia (church), a small square building covered with mosaic-like pieces of stone that form many different designs. There are representations of the Rain God Chac, and many images of the four creatures who, in Maya mythology, were believed to hold up the sky: an armadillo, a turtle, a crab, and a snail. These were called Bacabs by the Maya. The "Nunnery" is a 70 foot long, Maya-style building with many rooms. It has two main wings built upon a long platform of rock and rubble. A second floor and temple were added at a later date.

Although the Toltec influence at Chichén Itzá is unmistakable, Maya features were never completely eliminated. The new innovations were Toltec, but construction techniques were Maya. Religions blended; we find the cult of the Feathered Serpent mingling with the worship of the Maya long-nosed, Rain God, Chac. Corbeled vaulting and interior columns were

148. Iglesia (church) at Old Chichen. Named by the Spaniards because of its beauty, the ornate patterns in stone are reminiscent of the Puuc-style.

both used in temple construction, and Jaguar and Eagle warriors are shown on relief sculpture side by side with Maya chieftains.

There is little doubt that the Toltecs established a firm base of power at Chichén Itzá. After Uxmal and other Puuc cities were abandoned, the Toltecs soon dominated most of Yucatán. Then, for unknown reasons, in the year 1224 the Toltecs left Chichén Itzá. Details of their existence from that time on vanish from the records. It is probable that they dispersed throughout the Yucatán and completely merged into the Maya way of life. From 1224 on, the few remaining inhabitants of Chichén Itzá are referred to as the Itza Maya, and the base of power shifted to the nearby city of Mayapán.

149. Carved Skull from Tzompantli at Chichén Itzá.

The Maya in Late Postclassic Times

After Chichén Itzá's abandonment in the 14th century, most of Yucatán came under Mayapán's jurisdiction. Originally founded by Hunac Ceel, who had led a rebellion against Chichen, Mayapán became a city of considerable size with many residential and administrative complexes. Only a few religious temples were built within the walled city, and all of the buildings were poorly constructed. Instead of the finely cut stones used during the Classic period, the Mayapán builders used crudely cut stones covered with thick layers of stucco. There were no great colonnades built; the corbeled arch was largely abandoned, and so was the ceremonial ball game. There were six ball courts at Chichén Itzá, but not one has been found at Mayapán. The tomb offerings consisted only of a few crude vessels instead of ritual objects of great beauty. Also, the burials of chieftains were marked by unprecedented mass slaughter. In one grave alone, the remains of 41 persons have been found interred with their leader. A change of values had taken place. It appears that burying masses of servants to serve the dead in the afterlife was considered more important than the inclusion of ritual offerings for the gods.

There also began a period of continuous warfare between rival cities and dynasties. When the Spaniards began the conquest of Yucatán in 1541, hatred between the remaining Maya cities had reached such intensity that many Maya joined the Spanish forces rather than join their rivals against the Spaniards. A similar development took place among the few remaining Maya in Guatemala. In this area, Toltec warriors started their invasions at the beginning of the Postclassic period, and introduced a new militaristic rule. The new empire that resulted from this aggression eventually collapsed, as it did at Chichén Itzá, and the peoples of the region became hopelessly locked in petty warfare that lasted until the Spaniards arrived in the 16th century. Both Yucatán and Guatemala quickly fell under Spanish control in the 16th century. In only a few remote jungle regions of Peten and Chiapas did Maya independence persist for another 150 years. The last Maya community to fall was a city on a small, remote, easily defended island in Lake Peten. Here, descendants of the Itza dynasty of Chichén Itzá successfully resisted the Spaniards until 1697. Then, they also succumbed to the Spanish invaders.

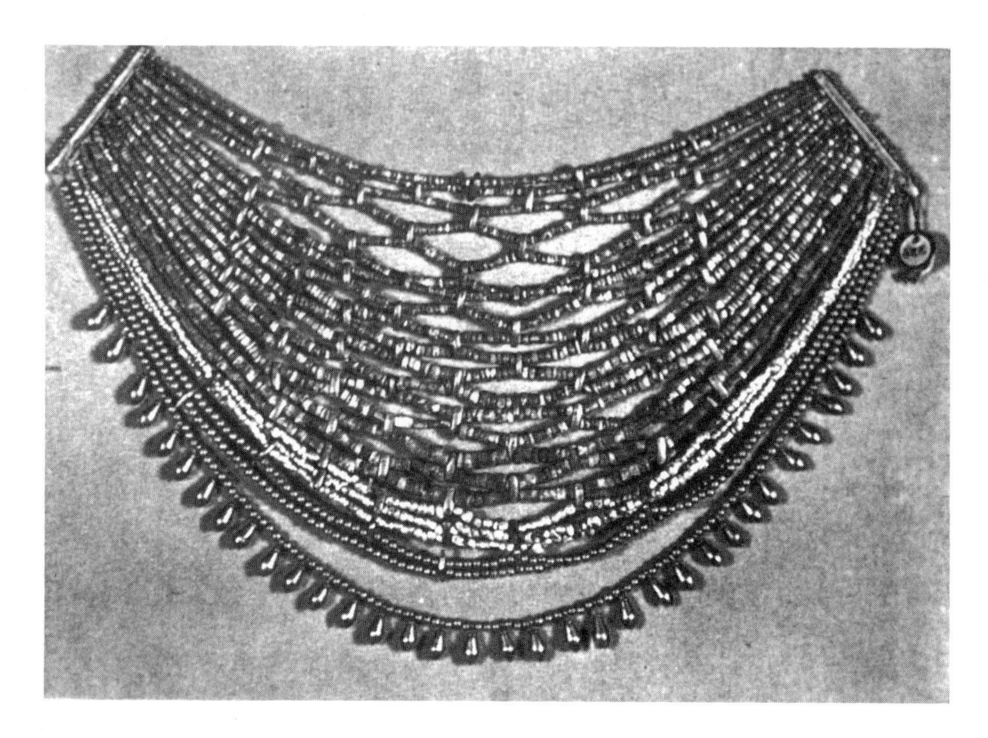

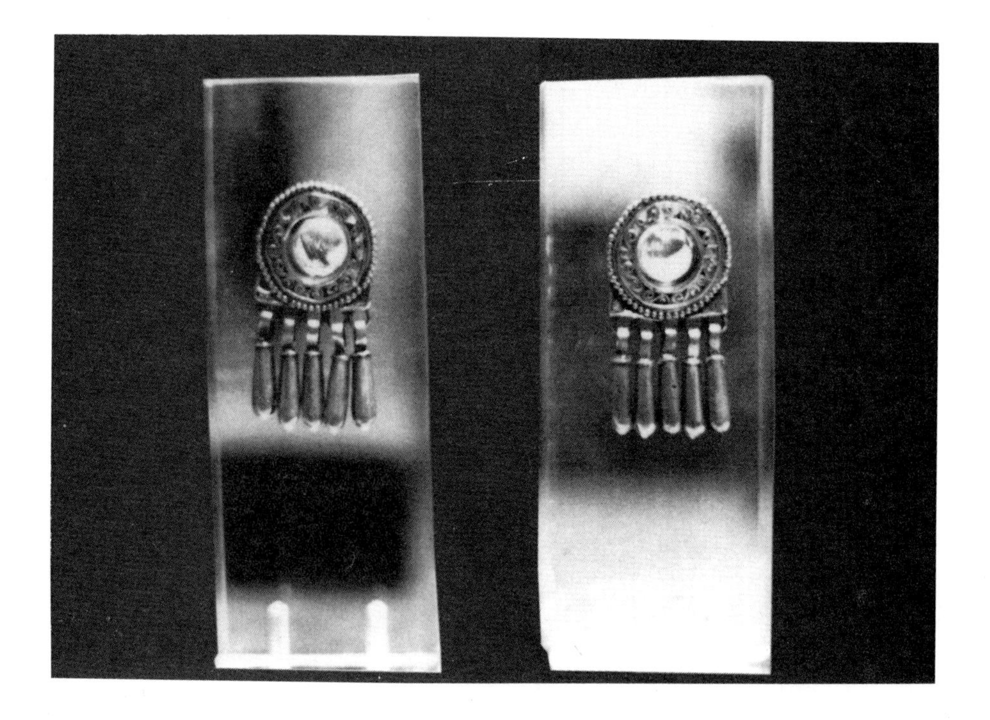

The Mixtec

Monte Albán V

During this late period, Monte Albán no longer functioned as a regional center where important decisions were made. The Main Plaza lay abandoned, and most of Monte Albán's Mixtec inhabitants now lived in large settlements around the base of the mountain. The site became more commercially focused than it had been in earlier Zapotec times. Many workshops and large concentrations of pottery have been discovered here that date from this later period. Trade was established with the peoples of Central America, and local products were bartered for gold from the southern areas. The Mixtecs became extraordinary gold workers as well as committed historians who filled their codices with descriptions of events and chronologies of the Postclassic era. Despite these changes, however, the site continued to serve as a sacred place where the Mixtecs lived and buried their dead in the Classic period Zapotec tombs.

We know very little about the early traditions of the Postclassic Mixtecs, as it was not until the 8th century that they began to record their history. We know of only one major accomplishment dating from an earlier period: the development of a magnificent red-on-cream polychrome pottery. Although it has been previously believed that this early ware may have been a product of the Mixteca-Puebla culture in Cholula, which lies northeast of Mexico City, there is growing support for the theory that the fine ware may first have originated with the Mixtecs of Oaxaca and then spread northward to the people of Cholula (Bernal 1965). Positive attribution is difficult because the elaborate Cholula pottery is almost indistinguishable from the beautiful wares manufactured by the Mixtecs in Oaxaca. We do know, however, that after this early red-on-cream ware ceased to be made in Cholula, it continued to be manufactured in the Mixtec region in Oaxaca. Many splendid examples of the painted pieces have been found, and colorful drawings of the exceptional pottery can be found in Mixtec codices.

The Mixtecs of Postclassic times lived in three distinct regions in the state of Oaxaca: the Mixteca Baja in western and northwestern Oaxaca, the coastal areas called the Mixteca de la Costa, and the high fertile valleys of the Mixteca Alta. It was in the Mixteca Alta that Mixtec culture reached a high level of development, and it was from there that their culture spread into

150. *Opposite, top.* Gold, mother of pearl, and red and blue coral necklace from Tomb 7 at Monte Albán. Museo de Santo Domingo, Oaxaca.

151. *Opposite, bottom.* Gold Earrings from Tomb 7. Museo de Santo Domingo, Oaxaca.

the adjacent Valley of Oaxaca to co-mingle with the remaining Zapotecs. The Mixtecs did not build a major ceremonial center in the valley, but instead occupied many well known Zapotec cities including Monte Albán, Mitla, and Yagul. Lesser known but historically important sites of possible later Mixtec construction in this region include Coixtlahuaca and Tilantongo.

Mixtec Kings were dominant rulers who provided political and religious leadership and were responsible for the general defense, well being, and even recreation of their subjects. According to Spores, the ruling Mixtec aristocracy "represented the kingdom in negotiations and contracts with other political units or groups. The leader was in control of the Polity. The populations owed allegiance and obedience as well as tribute and service to the ruler." (Spores: Flannery & Marcus 1983.)

The Codices

The Mixtecs were exceptionally accurate historians. Their colorfully illustrated codices record the development of their people and rulers from the 8th century on. Although the history is primarily in picture form, it is possible to interpret from the narrative-style illustrations when a King was born, when he died, what his victories were, and other relevant details of his life. The Mixtec scribes used different types of symbols to explain their stories. **Iconographic symbols** were pictorial representations of people, situations, and objects. **Ideographic representations** are pictures that imply certain ideas. **Phonetic symbols** refer to sounds or words. In contrast to the Maya codices, which covered a wide range of intellectual data, the Mixtec books deal primarily with genealogies and historical information that related to the Mixtec dynasties. The lavishly illustrated and colorful codices give us names of rulers, cities, and dates, as well as descriptions of dress, weapons, palaces and important ceremonies that provide valuable ethnographic data about these Postclassic people. From the codices we also know that the Mixtec placed the utmost importance on birth order and royal lineage. Whereas Aztec rulers were chosen by a council of noble elders, their choices limited to any eligible royal offspring, the Zapotecs disregarded birth order and frequently passed leadership to the most competent prince. However, the Mixtecs valued their main trunk descent so highly that rulers occasionally married their full siblings to ensure the high rank of their offspring. Among the descendants of the Mixtec Lord Eight Deer Jaguar Claw alone there are four cases of brother-sister marriages (Dahlgren de Jordan 1954).

The lives of many important rulers are described in the codices, but the most famous leader to be included in these books was the great conqueror, Eight Deer Jaguar Claw. It was the custom, throughout Mesoamerica, to name children after the day of their birth. Thus, Eight Deer was named after Eight-Deer day, the day in the Mixtec calendar upon which he was born. When he reached manhood and became an important prince, the distinguishing name Jaguar Claw was added.

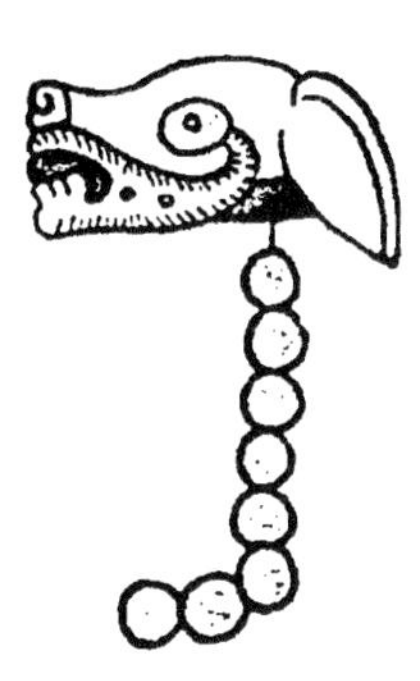

152. Eight Deer Jaguar Claw is always shown with eight circles attached to a deer's head, and adjacent to a jaguar's claw.

Eight Deer was born in A.D. 1011 in Tilantongo, a small city that still stands in the state of Oaxaca. The codices tell of his many wives, his voyages by land and water, his military prowess, and his exceptional abilities as a leader who brought the Mixtec people together to form a consolidated nation. He accomplished these remarkable feats by attacking and conquering neighboring cities, or by arranging strategic marriage contracts with the chieftains who ruled in neighboring regions. We know that for many years Eight Deer won all of his battles. The codices tell us that he killed the males of the ruling families he conquered, and then he or his sons married the widows and women of the defeated aristocratic families. In this way, he consolidated the scattered city-states and extended his domain until at the age of 52, and after losing a battle, he was sacrificed to the gods.

The life of Eight Deer is preserved in several illustrated books called codices. In addition to the genealogical records, we learn that the class structure of the Mixtecs was one of the most highly stratified social structures in Mesoamerica. There was a privileged group headed by the ruler and members of his immediate family; next in rank were the commoners, followed by the servants and slaves. By the Late Postclassic period, the lords of the influential city of Tilantongo were so powerful they could appoint members of their royal families to rule in nearby villages or cities when the ruling *cacique* (lord) had no legitimate heir. The codices also tell us that marriages were arranged to strengthen alliances, and each community formed a distinct political entity; the rise and fall of other great societies in Mesoamerica, and the continuing expansion of the Mixtec empire are all recorded. According to Bernal (1966), "The end of Toltec control in about A.D. 1160 was the event which allowed the Mixtecs to expand into several areas, one of which was the Valley of Mexico" (Marcus and Flannery 1983).

Tomb 7

The Mixtecs developed an extraordinary art style in gold casting that was to impact on all of Mesoamerica throughout the Postclassic years up to the time of the Spanish Conquest. Some of the finest examples of Mixtec gold craftsmanship were discovered in 1932 by Alfonso Caso in the North Cemetery at Monte Albán; this was the area where many important Zapotec rulers of the Classic period were buried. Caso excavated numerous tombs here before he discovered Tomb 7, a tomb which contained a burial of the greatest archaeological importance. The tomb had originally been built for burial purposes by the Zapotecs during Monte Albán IIIb. It consisted of two east-west chambers, connected to each other by a large vestibule (Marcus 1983). During the Postclassic period, the Mixtecs partially cleared the burial chamber and reused the tomb for internment of one of their important leaders (the skeletal remains of at least nine individuals were found within the tomb). The ruler was about 55 to 60 years old; his skull showed evidence of cranial deformation, possibly due to head binding in infancy; his teeth were filed. Included with the human remains were over 500 finely crafted objects which included silver, rock crystal, jade, obsidian, pearl, gold objects, and jewels. The gold had been created by using the *Cire Perdue* method of gold casting (also called the "lost wax" process). The Mixtecs learned the art of metal casting from the gold workers of Panama and Costa Rica, and excelled in this technique. Using gold, copper, and occasionally silver, they created an enormous variety of exquisite jewelry. No finer gold work has ever been found in the Americas than the beautiful funerary offerings included with the dead leader at Monte Albán.

Although the Mixtec and Zapotec cultures mingled and overlapped in certain areas of Oaxaca during the Postclassic period, each had a very individual development. The Zapotecs remained rooted in their Classic period religious traditions and the Mixtecs developed a secular rule. The Mixtecs were more aggressive than the

153. Gold Necklace from Tomb 7 at Monte Albán. Museo de Santo Domingo, Oaxaca.

Zapotecs, and they built numerous defensive sites on mountaintop locations. Their effective war strategies were recorded in the codices.

Toward the end of the Postclassic period, the Mixtecs banded together with the remaining Zapotecs to push back the encroaching Aztecs. But eventually, in the 15th century, the greater part of the Mixtec region fell to the forces of Tenochtitlán. At this time, the Aztec Emperor Motecuhzoma conquered the city of Coixtlahuaca, where the richest tributes in the Mixteca Alta were stored. From that time on, the Mixtec rulers were allowed to retain their power, but they were required to send their people to the Aztec capital at Tenochtitlán bearing rich tributes to the Aztec kings. In everything they did, Mixtec artists and craftsmen were greatly admired. Their accomplishments and style were held in high esteem all throughout Mesoamerica. Even at the end, when Cortes marched into the Aztec capital at Tenochtitlán and proclaimed it the most extraordinary city he had ever seen, it was the Mixtec gold that filled him with the greatest sense of awe and wonder.

154. Coyolxauhqui, "The Face Decorated with Bells." Diorite. (INAH.)

The Aztecs

The story of the Aztecs' rise to power is one of the most remarkable in Mesoamerican history. Known to posterity as the Aztecs, they were first called the "Mexica," a relatively unknown group of people who came to the Valley of Mexico during the13th century A.D. Within two hundred years, long before the Spaniards arrived in 1519, they rose from complete obscurity to become the most powerful force in the Mesoamerican world.

We know very little about the early Aztecs because most of their history was not recorded, but passed along by word of mouth from generation to generation. Some of the surviving legends depict them as a nomadic and uncultured group from an unidentified island called Aztlan, meaning "White Place." Other myths tell us that the Aztecs were created in Chicomoztoc (Seven Caves), and that they were one of seven groups of people who spoke Nahuatl. Although these two legends seem in conflict, one explanation for the apparent contradiction is found in the illustrated Aztec codex *Tira de la Peregrinacion*, commonly referred to as the "Migration Scrolls." Here we see their departure from Aztlan, which is shown as an island in a lake with seven temples in the center of the island. The Aztecs believed they were a "chosen people" who had been told by their protector god, Huitzilopochtli, to search for a new homeland. They were to look for an eagle holding a snake; it would be found perched on a prickly pear (nopal) cactus growing from a rock, or in a cave surrounded by water. Therefore, it may be that an island location similar to their homeland became the focus of their search.

It is uncertain exactly when the people from Aztlan first became known as the Aztecs. First known as the Mexica, they were later referred to as the "Culhua-Mexica" when they became associated with the Toltecs at Culhuacán. It should be noted here that all of the people who lived in central Mexico during the Postclassic period are usually referred to as "Aztecs" even though there were at least five separate groups speaking a variety of languages and functioning independently within locally governed city-states. The five groups include those people of Chichimec ancestry; descendants of the Toltecs; a large group of settled peoples; barbarian outsiders; and high culture outsiders (Pazstory 1994; Carrasco 1971).

The earliest Aztecs were a poor and ragged group who reached the Valley of Mexico sometime during the 13th century. Existing on stolen food, snakes, and vermin, they were rejected by everyone they encountered. They stayed briefly at Coatepec, and then wandered to Tula. An attempt was made to settle at Chapultepec, but they were soon driven out by the neighboring Tepanecs.

During the 14th century, the Aztecs fought as mercenaries for ruling lords in the valley. The aristocratic King of Culhuacán used them as warriors, and the Aztecs married into Culhuacán families. It was here that they became known as the Culhua-Mexica. In a short time, however, the king of Culhuacán became repulsed by their barbaric customs and uncultured habits, and he ordered them to leave his domain. Led by four priest-rulers, the Aztecs searched for a place where they could build a city in honor of their god, Huitzilopochtli. History tells us that Huitzilopochtli spoke to Tenoch, who was one of their leaders, and told him to watch for an eagle on a cactus; there they would find their place of refuge. Tenoch led them to the Valley of Mexico, where they found the eagle on the cactus. A simple earth and thatch temple to honor Huitzilopochtli was built first, then a ballcourt; the city was named Tenochtitlán, the city of Tenoch. Although historic legends place the founding of the city at 1325, Kirchhoff (1949) suggests that the date of this event may have been as late as 1369.

Tenochtitlán

In its earliest stages of development Tenochtitlán was just a marshy island with limited resources, a few reed and thatch huts, and some small temples. Life was undoubtedly difficult in this undesirable location, for there would have been a constant struggle to produce food for the city on the swampy land. In addition, tension continued between the Aztecs and the neighboring mainlanders who still rejected them. Despite these difficulties, however, the Aztecs worked hard to improve the quality of their lives. They adopted an ancient agricultural technique called the *Chinampas* system of farming, and, in a relatively short period of time the swampy site was transformed into a fertile and highly productive island. To form the *Chinampas*, grass and other organic material was woven into reed frames which were then thickly covered with silt from the lake bottoms. Although they floated at first, the grass and organic cuttings soon rooted, thus anchoring the mats in the shallow water. Fast growing willow trees were sometimes planted on the edges of the banks to control erosion; farmers continuously added layers of organic material and mud from the bottom of the canals to the surface of the plots. Fruit, flowers, and vegetables flourished in the rich, moist soil. The agricultural technology of the Aztecs was, indeed, the most advanced in the central valley.

Despite the increase in food production, life was still very difficult for the early Aztecs. They continued to hire themselves out as mercenaries to the kings of the neighboring regions to supplement their modest existence. And as the empire expanded, specialized craftsmen and common laborers were brought to Tenochtitlán to build residences and religious buildings. Because of the marshy and somewhat unstable soil, the builders had to drive large wooden stakes into the soft ground to provide secure footings for new walls and buildings; the lightweight and plentiful volcanic stone called *Tezontli* was used as the primary building material. Despite these precautions, however, the larger temples and palaces would often sink below normal ground level or settle unevenly. As a result, the older buildings continuously needed repair, or new structures were rebuilt over the older core. The city was divided into four sections, with ceremonial buildings in the center of the island, and reed and thatch homes for the commoners in the peripheral areas.

The Aztecs knew that in order to gain the respect of their neighbors they would have to select a leader of royal lineage. Therefore, after Tenoch's death in 1376, they chose a man of Culhua-Mexica parentage to rule as their king. His name was Acamapichtli. Related to the last rulers of Culhuacán, Acamapichtli's lineage extended back to the reign of the great Toltec ruler, Quetzálcóatl. With the selection of Acamapichli as their first true king, the Aztecs were able to claim descendancy from the ancient Toltec bloodline. Unfortunately, they also inherited the fateful prophecy that Quetzálcóatl would return in another year of his birth to reclaim his rightful throne.

By the end of the century the Tepanec kingdom of Atzcapotzalco was still the ruling power in the Valley of Mexico. The Aztecs fought for the Tepanecs, receiving land and tributes as pay for their military services. As a result, the Aztec kingdom began to grow and prosper (Pazstory 1994). Many important changes occurred during the 15th century. Under Itzcoatl's leadership the military strength of the Aztecs greatly increased, and the small group of mercenaries was transformed into a powerful and highly disciplined military force. Independence from Azcapotzalco was declared in 1428, and the Aztec Empire expanded further. There were important social reforms, and alliances were formed with neighboring regions. It was also a time for building. Tenochtitlán grew and prospered. This was known as the "Period of Great Expansion."

After Itzcoatl's death, Motecuhzoma I became the Aztecs' fifth king. He formed an alliance with Texcoco, and Tlacopan. Tenochtitlán was the dominant force and its power lasted until the

155. Double Pyramid at Tenayuca, in Mexico City's suburbs. The Great Temple at Tenochtitlán was patterned after this structure.

Spanish conquest in the16th century. All of the cities in the Valley of Mexico were controlled by the Aztecs, and their empire extended east to the Gulf Coast and as far west as Oaxaca.

A great double pyramid was formally dedicated by Motecuhzoma's son, Axayacatl, during his reign in 1487. The massive structure honored Huitzilopochtli, the god of sun and warfare, and Tlaloc, the deity of rain and sustenance. According to 16th century descriptions recorded by the conquering Spaniards, the Great Pyramid was a large structure of four or five stepped levels. It faced west and had two stairways which gave access to the temples of Tlaloc and Huitzilophtli. Of the temple itself, Sahagun writes: "In the center and higher than the other temples of the city the principal temple was dedicated to the god Huitzilopochtli. This was divided at the top so that it looked like two; it had two sanctuaries or altars, each of which was topped by a tall roof which bore distinct insignia or devices. In one of those, the principal one, stood the statue of Huitzilopochtli...in the other was the image of the god Tlaloc. In front of each one of these statues was a round stone, like an executioner's block, upon which they killed all those whom they sacrificed in honor of that god. From the block to the ground was a pool of blood from those who were killed on it, and this was true of all the temples. They all faced west and had very narrow and steep steps leading to the top" (Sahagun 1956). Construction of the temple first started around A.D. 1390. By 1487, the Great Pyramid had been enlarged on all sides seven times. The first level of construction is almost intact, but the seventh was virtually razed by the Spaniards in the 16th century. The second epoch of construction contains the remarkably complete pyramid that supported the temples dedicated to Huitzuilopochtli and Tlaloc.

The Great Temple was the most important structure in Tenochtitlán. It formed the nucleus of the city. Ceremonies lasting for four days marked its dedication, and thousands were selected to give their lives as the ultimate gift in honor of the two gods. In front of the Huitzuilopochtli sanctuary we find the sacrificial stone, called a *techcatl.* On the Tlaloc side is a *chacmool.* A massive stone bearing the sculpted image of

156. Standing Warrior Figure. INAH, Tenochtitlán.

Huitzilopochtli's mother, Coyolxauhque, was found in the middle of the lower platform.

By the late 15th century Motecuhzoma's empire covered so much territory that his expanded campaigns became unmanageable. The armies could not remain in the field for any length of time: Motecuhzoma's men could not feed themselves off the land, and there were no draught animals or carts to carry the necessary supplies. There were signs of dissension throughout the empire, as the people became more and more resentful of excessive demands placed on them by the Aztecs. The rulers continued to press for military expansion to obtain victims for sacrifice and tributes. Tributes were collected every 80 days and sent to Tenochtitlán to be divided among the members of the alliance. Tenochtitlán and Texcoco each received two-thirds of the tribute items, and one-fifth went to Tlacopan. The tributes supported the alliance, providing luxury items for Aztec royalty and gifts for noble guests. The gifts were lavish; even the Spaniards wrote of the quantities of luxurious goods and valuable commodities that were obtained by tribute (Pasztory 1994). Toward the end of the century, the commoners' resentment increased, and the iron control that had characterized Aztec rule in earlier times began to disappear.

Culturally, all of the arts flourished in the 15th century. Magnificent stone sculptures were created, and lyrical poetry reached a high level of expression. The most remarkable poet-philosopher of this century was Netzahualcoyotl, a respected ruler of the powerful neighboring kingdom of Texcoco. Netzahualcoyotl was an original thinker who was concerned with the meaning of life and death and the endless questions concerning eternal life. The following poem beautifully expresses his sense of the ephemeral nature of life:

> Is it true that we live on earth?
> Not forever on earth; we are only a little while here.
> Even jade will be broken,
> Even gold shall be crushed,
> Even Quetzál feathers will be torn apart.
> Not forever on earth; we are only a little while here.

King Netzahualcoyotl of Texcoco
1402-1472

157. Sanctuary of Tlaloc and Huitzilopochtli, Tenochtitlán.

The triple alliance united Texcoco, Tacuba and Tenochtitlán.

Despite the fact that Netzahualcoyotl lived at a time when human sacrifice was at its peak, he was not comfortable with the ritual and discouraged it as much as possible within his kingdom. Although he is best known as the poet-king of Texcoco, history also recognizes his engineering genius in the design and construction of a ten-mile stone dike across Lake Texcoco. Twenty thousand workers completed the dike under the supervision of Motecuhzoma I and Netzahualcoyotl. The dike was complete with drawbridges and sluice gates that successfully halted the lake's annual flooding of Tenochtitlán. Although Netzahualcoyotl was actively engaged in many building projects, and acted as an advisor in the military campaigns of the **Triple Alliance** that united Texcoco, Tacuba, and Tenochtitlán, his primary pleasure appears to have come from his philosophical poetry, which focused on the fragile interaction between man and nature. Netzahualcoyotl lived through the reigns of Itzcoatl and Motecuhzoma I; he contributed greatly to the development of the arts, successfully experimented with hydraulic engineering projects, and was partly responsible for the strength and success of the Triple Alliance in the Valley of Mexico.

By the early 16th century the Aztecs occupied an area of about 35 square miles of islands and *chinampas*; an estimated 200,000 persons inhabited Tenochtitlán. There were impressive botanical gardens with samples of almost all species of plant life in the land, carefully tended zoos where all the animals and snakes of the country were represented, royal palaces, residences for the nobles, and special districts for the commoners. The city resembled Venice, with its interlaced canals and canoes that carried the trade-oriented merchants; paved footpaths paralled the canals. The four major districts of the city were served by avenues ending in four wide causeways that joined the island city to the mainland. Drawbridges spanned the canals; these could be removed for defensive purposes. The island was easily defended and difficult to attack. It had indeed been positioned in a strategically ideal location. For example, in 1520, when Hernan Cortes was forced to flee the city after his first attempt at conquest, causeway bridges were destroyed by the Aztecs and many Spaniards were ambushed and drowned.

Religion and Sacrifice

It was human sacrifice more than anything else that appalled the Spaniards at the time of the conquest. Although human sacrifice had been practiced by most of the Indian groups of Mesoamerica, it was the Aztecs who carried it to new heights. When Cortes and his men marched into Tenochtitlán, they were horrified by the sight of thousands of skulls exhibited upon *Tzompantlis*. Calling them heathens because of their ceremonies, the Spaniards ignored the "religio-magical" element that was the dominant force in Aztec philosophy. (As macabre as the rite of human sacrifice may seem to the reader, one should note that it is equally horrifying for us to hear of the tales which followed the arrival of the Europeans when "civilized" Spaniards massacred and tortured the Indians with a perfectly clear conscience because of their greed for gold and land for the expansion of their colonies.)

The Aztecs saw themselves as a chosen people who were especially favored by the gods. They believed their gods watched over everything and were all-powerful. The gods had created the universe, and they controlled the fate of the people: they withheld

158. Model of Tenochtitlán at the time of the Conquest. (INAH.)

rain and sunshine, guarded every hour of the day and night, and influenced even the most trivial aspects of daily life. In return, the people did what they believed was expected of them. They honored their gods and provided nourishment to insure their own survival. It was believed that the sun itself would cease to exist unless it received the nourishing blood that was lost each day in the battle with the forces of darkness.

The growth of Aztec power, and the resulting accumulation of new lands, was a direct result of shrewd political alliances and warfare. The wars for land and power were an equally important source of captives necessary for sacrificial rites. In effect, war was a religious as well as a military and political necessity. The warriors did their utmost to kill as few men as possible on the battlefield so that the captives could be sacrificed to the gods. Far from being an act of barbarism, the Aztecs felt that the offering of blood was a holy act and a religious rite that was necessary to appease and nourish the gods. They believed that four successive "worlds" or "suns" had existed before their own time, and the gods had destroyed each world in turn by jaguars, hurricanes, fire, and flood. Believing they faced the same destiny, the Aztecs provided human sacrifice to appease the gods. Without this ritual, the world in which they lived, the World of the Fifth Sun, would again be destroyed.

The foundation for this belief is more clearly understood by evaluating one aspect of native folklore. It is the story of Huitzilopochtli, who was the son of the Mother Goddess, Coatlicue. Huitzilopochtli, the most important of all Aztec gods, was a warrior god who was identified with the sun. He battled against the forces of darkness each night so that the sun would be reborn again the next morning. The people believed that if Huitzilopochtli were ever to grow weak and feeble the sun would not rise, darkness would triumph, and the universe would again come to an end. Therefore, it was vital that he should remain strong and vigorous with nourishment provided for him in the form of blood offerings. This alone would save their world. In the minds of the Aztecs, the struggle of the sun against the powers of darkness was not only a struggle of the gods, it symbolized the struggle of good against evil. Therefore, the most precious and meaningful offering that one could provide was life itself.

Other reasons for the Aztecs' willing participation in human sacrifice included the belief that it would appease an angry god, or that it could secure special favors from one of their gods; they also used sacrifice as penance for a perceived wrongdoing. Their goal was to win the favor of the gods and achieve the ultimate in harmony between the gods and man. In addition to the benefits human sacrifice would bring to the people, the Aztecs saw it as a means of assuring eternal life. The victims believed that they would live in the afterworld in the House of the Sun, and accompany Huitzilopochtli on the first part of his journey each day. After four years of serving Huitzilopochtli, they would return to earth in the form of hummingbirds and live forever sipping honey. Those who were sacrificed to the rain god, Tlaloc, believed they would go directly to his watery paradise. In some cases the most honored victims were lavishly fed, adorned with flowers, and dressed in special garments so that they could be sacrificed as earthly representatives of the gods themselves.

159. Aztec Mother Goddess, *Coatlicue*, "Serpent Skirt". Two serpents shape her head, human hands and hearts form her necklace. (INAH.)

The spirit of the Aztec people as revealed in their traditional customs, festivals, and ceremonies creates doubt that they were simply a brutal culture ruled by a bloodthirsty priesthood. All levels of society participated in the religious ceremonies, not just the elite warrior class or the priests. Even the lowly merchants who dealt in slaves were allowed to make sacrifices of them during the month that was sacred to Huitzilopochtli. Each individual group of workers would join together to buy a victim to honor the great national deity. Those who were selected for the religious rites did not rebel; this manner of death seemed inevitable. Even those who were born under certain signs of the ritual calendar were predestined for this fate. Regardless of their station in life, those selected for sacrifice were a privileged lot who were groomed and ornamented, and treated as if they were earthly manifestations of the gods. For a brief time they were the gods. Even the prisioners of war accepted their destiny, and the warrior who brought the prisoner from the battlefield to die knew that sooner or later he might experience the same fate.

In summary, human sacrifice among the Aztecs was inspired by neither cruelty nor hatred. There was the need to maintain cosmic order, and human sacrifice was the Aztecs' response to existence in a continuously threatened world. Blood sacrifice was necessary to save their world; the victim was a privileged intermediary who would be sent in dignity to the gods. Thus, human sacrifice was only a means by which life was made out of death.

Poetry

The Aztec poets were the philosophers of the ruling class. Their views are expressed in poetry that is remarkably intelligent and sensitive, considering the Aztecs are usually thought of as blood-thirsty barbarians. The belief in the destiny of a total world collapse during the World of the Fifth Sun greatly affected the Aztecs; a feeling of pessimism prevailed. They knew that the sun would ultimately be defeated, the people would perish by catastrophic earthquakes, and the powers of evil would prevail. Convinced of the transitory aspect of their world, the poets expressed their concerns in a most profound way. If life on earth was simply a time of transition between one world and the next, then truth (reality) must be found in the depths of one's mind, in an ephemeral or semi-real state. Some of their most deeply felt questions reveal the insecurity of the

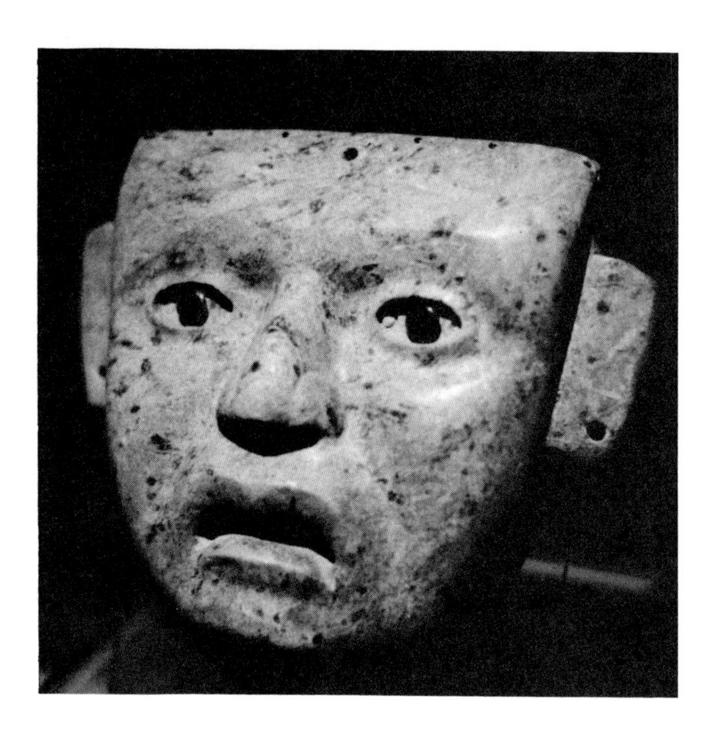

160. Stone Mask (INAH, Templo Mayor.)

Aztec world: "On earth, is the striving for anything really worthwhile?" "Do we speak any truth here?" "Are men really true?" These searching questions were given impetus by the need to find answers before the imminent end of their world. Pessimism appears in the vigorous and awesome sculpture of the Aztecs, and comes to light in the profound sadness that prevails in their poetry.

Most Aztec poetry begins with a question and ends with at least a partial answer or solution. The verses are filled with fatalistic thoughts about the end of life. The poets also suggest that life may be but a "dream" from which death brings reality.

> By chance is there truth to our words here?
> It seems so like a dream; do we rise from this sleep?
> Only on earth do our words remain.

and,

> We merely came to sleep,
> We merely came to dream
> It is not true, no, it is not true
> That we live on the earth.

161. Teotihuacán-style mask with inlaid shell and stone teeth. Templo Mayor, Tenochtitlán.

Why might the Aztecs have viewed life as unreal? The main reason they lived, fought, and sacrificed to their gods was to keep the world from ending, as their religion prophesied. Life to them was truly unreal—a transitory existence that enabled them to fulfill their mission to the gods and to look to a "real" life after death. The poets also described their need to acknowledge their existence on earth. In some poems it was a profound plea to be remembered.

Am I perchance a shield of turquoise,
will I as a mosaic be embedded once more in existence?
Will I come again to the earth?
Will I be shrouded in fine mantles?
Still on earth, near the place of the drums,
I remember them.

Cacamatzin, last king of Texcoco. c. 1519
Romances de los senores de Nueva Espana.
Translated by Leon-Portilla.

Merely like this shall I leave
Like the flowers that died?
Shall nothing be left of my name?
At least flowers, at least songs.

Cantos De Huexotzingo

162. Abandoned warrior figures lie on the steps of the double pyramid. Templo Mayor.

These are philosophical concepts voiced by pensive, sophisticated people who pondered life and death just as poets have done throughout the ages. The only difference is that the Aztec poets believed they lived in a transitional world with a predestined end. Life to them was but a dream, and death an awakening to reality.

> The sadness is that we must leave,
> and it is only here on earth
> that there are songs and flowers.
> Well, then they will bring us joy,
> they will be our ornament...
> We will take happiness from them while we can.

The Aztecs were an enigmatic people. They were war-like and had a religion of shocking intensity, yet they spent their rare moments of peace philosophizing about the meaning of life. Theirs was an endless search for beauty in life that to them was as elusive and fragile as a butterfly. Even the name of the Aztec god, Huitzilopochtli means not "Killer of Thousands" or "Bloodthirsty God" as you might expect. It means "The Hummingbird of the South."

Sculpture

A powerful new art style emerged during the mid-15th century that had its greatest expression in stone carving. It was a revival of the superior stone carving techniques that were used by the Olmecs, but largely ignored by most later groups in Mesoamerica (Teotihuacán is an exception). The Aztecs carved basalt and other hard stones into ritual and funerary masks, warrior figures, images of deities, realistic representations of insects and animals, and thrones for royal leaders. The largest and most unusual example of Aztec stone carving is the Rock Temple at Malinalco, near Mexico City. Built early in the 15th century, the temple was hewn out of solid rock and dedicated to the military orders of the Jaguar and the Eagle.

The Aztec Calendar Stone (sometimes called the "Sun" Stone) was found buried near the southeast corner of the main plaza in Mexico City; it is now displayed in the city's great Museo Nacional de Antropologia. Dedicated in 1487 in our calendar time, the elaborately carved basalt monument measures twelve feet in diameter and weighs approximately 25 tons. In the center of the stone is a human-like face, possibly depicting the Sun God, Tonatiuh. The stone was never meant to function as a calendar. It was, instead, a record of the cosmos as interpreted by the Aztec. There is an *Ollin*, or "movement," sign near the center of the stone containing the four dates that identify four previous "worlds" or "suns" of the Aztec. The Aztecs believed that the world of the Fifth Sun would end on the date 4 Movement; this is inscribed on the stone. There is also the symbol for earthquake which, according to legend, is the natural catastrophe that will destroy the world of the Fifth Sun. The four cardinal points of the compass, and the twenty day signs of the Aztec months appear on outer bands. Around the border of the stone are the signs of the heavens. Two serpents circle the edge of the gigantic monument.

163. *Left*. Xochipilli, the Aztec Flower Prince. Stone. (INAH.)

164. *Right*. The Aztec Calendar Stone did not function as a calendar; much of its composition refers to their four previous worlds (Suns) of the Aztecs, and describes the ultimate end of the world in the time of the Fifth Sun. (INAH.)

An even more dramatic example of large-scale Aztec stone sculpture is the massive figure of Coatlicue (Lady of the Serpent Skirt), who was, according to Aztec myths, the mother of Huitzilopochtli. She is shown wearing a necklace of sacrificed hands, hearts, and skulls, and a skirt of interlaced serpents; huge claws are her feet, and her head consists of two fanged serpent heads that face each other above powerful shoulders. According to legend, Coatlicue found a ball of down feathers while she was sweeping on top of the Hill of Coatepec (Hill of the Serpent). She placed the ball of feathers in the bosom of her dress, thus conceiving her son, Huitzilopochtli. Her daughter, Coyolxauhqui, and her 400 sons were filled with shame when they learned of their mother's pregnancy. Coyolxauhqui killed their mother by cutting off her head, and Huitzilopochtli was born as she died, fully grown and dressed as a warrior. He drove away his 400 brothers and decapitated his evil sister, Coyolxauhqui.

The statue of Huitzilopochtli's mother, Coatlicue, was discovered near the Great Pyramid. Most probably it was meant to be placed before his shrine on the temple top; in 1978, a second monumental stone was discovered at the foot of the pyramid, carved with the image of the dismembered Coyolxauhqui. Thus, a permanent reminder of Coyolxauhqui's treachery against her mother and Coatlicue's devotion to her son, Huitzilopochtli, were permanantly established at the shrine. Huitzilopochtli was both the warrior god and the god of the daytime sky; Coatlicue was an earth-mother goddess. Her 400 sons were the stars, and Coyolxauhqui the moon. According to Pazstory (1994), the legend of Huitzilopochtli's miraculous birth reinforced the Aztec belief in the victory of day over night; as the sun died in the west, it was reborn each day in the east.

The stone bearing the relief of Coyolxauhqui weighs approximately eight tons. It depicts a dismembered woman, with her decapitated head laying backwards at right angles to her shoulders. On the severed head is a headdress of feathers; her cheeks have raised rectangular strips, each bearing several carved bells. This detail gives Coyolxauhqui the name "the one with bells on the cheek." Her turquoise earplugs are carved with solar symbols; the dismembered arms and legs show images of snakes; on her waist are the skull and snake representative of the duality of life and death.

The Great Temple recreates the Hill of Coatepec where, according to legend, Huitzilopochtli's conception took place. Here the events of the myth were brought to life, and repeated over and over again in the sacrifices that took place on top of the temple. The sacrifices were the re-enactment of the myth: the everyday struggle of light against darkness; of day and night; of good versus evil. This was a continuous reminder of the myth that honored Huitzilopochtli's birth and his first appearance as the warrior god; and of the fact that his birth was a metaphor for the sun's rising each day.

Another example of Aztec stone carving of the highest quality and complexity is the Stone of Tizoc. It is a cylindrical stone some eight and one-half feet in diameter and three feet high. A sundisk with eight rays is on top, and a sky border of stars appears on the side. The gaping maw (opening) of the earth monster is on the bottom. Fifteen warriors are depicted on the side, each holding a captive. Although it was once believed

165. Vase (INAH, Templo Mayor.)

that the warrior figures were multiple images of the 15th century ruler Tizoc, only one has been positively identified as this ruler. He wears the hummingbird helmet of the god Huitzilopochtli, and his name glyph, a "leg" symbol, is shown next to his head. The other costumed figures may be his warriors. Pasztory suggests that the stone commemorates conquests that created the Mexica empire, and acknowledges Tizoc by including him among the fifteen rulers that made major conquests. According to Pasztory (1994), each newly selected ruler had to fight a battle and bring back prisoners before he could succeed to the throne. Although Tizoc was known as a cowardly ruler who lost most of his military campaigns, he is also remembered for his large-scale rebuilding of the main temples of Tenochtitlán. The Stone of Tizoc may have been intended for the newly rebuilt ceremonial center.

166. Vase (INAH, Templo Mayor.)

The 15th century was a highly productive period when tremendous artistic contributions were made. In addition to stone sculpture, the Aztecs produced quantities of finely crafted ritual figures made out of clay, and exquisite pottery; there were also feathered masterpieces made from rare feathers, with gold, turquoise, and mother-of-pearl accents. Historical records describe many illustrated codices. Unfortunately, none survived the Spaniards' attempt to destroy the "devil's" history. There are only fourteen known books dating from Postclassic times, and these are Maya and Mixtec manuscripts. The Aztec codices we have today are duplicates of earlier works that were destroyed. They were written after the conquest, when the Spaniards allowed some Christianized natives to re-record certain historical and religious information.

The Aztecs established a tight line of succession. Each king was selected from the royal lineage by a council composed of nobles, warriors, and priests. Leadership would usually be passed first from brother to brother before it went on to the next generation. Listed below are the known Aztec rulers, the probable dates of leadership, and their relationship to the preceding leader, if known.

Acamapichtli: (1372-1391)	was the first true king of the Aztecs, of Culhua-Mexica parentage, and descended from the Toltec royal lineage that could be traced back to the rulers at Tula.
Huitzilaihuitl: (1391-1417)	was the son of Acamapichtli, and father of Motecuhzoma I.
Chimalpopoca: (1417-1426)	is believed to have been the grandson of Acamapichtli. Under his leadership the people served as mercenaries to Tezozomoc, a ruthless but gifted leader of the neighboring Tepanecs. Chimalpopoca died in a mysterious fashion, possibly at the hands of the Tepanecs from whom he had become estranged at the end of his reign.
Itzcoatl: (1426-1440)	was related to Acamapichtli. When Tezozomoc died in 1426, theAztecs broke with the Tepanecs. Independence from Azcapotzalco was declared in 1428 and Tenochtitlán, Huejotzingo, and Texcoco formed an alliance. Itzcoatl's political advisor was a brilliant man named Tlacaelel, who suggested that all early recorded history of the Aztecs be burned and history be rewritten beginning at this time. Tlacaelel served as advisor to Itzcoatl and the next two kings. There was a new cultural awareness in Aztec society. Itzcoatl and the "Poet King" Nezahualcoyotl, of Texcoco, greatly encouraged the development of the arts.
Motecuhzoma I: (1440-1468)	was Huitzilhuitl's son. He formally established the TripleAlliance which united Tenochtitlán, Texcoco, and Tacuba. Most of the Mixtec territories were conquered during his reign, and tributes flowed to Tenochtitlán. This time was known as the Period of Great Expansion. Motecuhzoma built botanical and zoological gardens where every known plant, animal, and bird was collected and observed. Beset by many natural disasters such as storms, floods, and drought, many people left the valley. Human sacrifice dramatically increased and a ceremonial kind of perpetual warfare called "Flowery Wars," provided the necessary sacrificial victims.

167. Seated Aztec Standard Bearer. Sandstone, height: 31 inches. (MNYC.)

168. Kneeling female Figure, Aztec. Stone with traces of paint, height: 21 inches. (MNYC.)

Axayacatl: (1468-1481)	was Motecuhzoma's son. He reconquered lost territories and suppressed rebellion within Aztec territories. He brought the wealthy trading district of Tlatelolco, which included the largest trading market in the empire, under Aztec control.
Tizoc: (1481-1486)	was the brother of Axayacatl and Ahuitzotl. It is said that he was an ineffective ruler who knew little of warfare.
Ahuizotl: (1486-1502)	was Motecuhzoma's son, and father of Cuauhtemoc. He was aggressive and warlike, and a gifted military leader who expanded Aztec territory to the Guatemalan border. His reign officially began with the dedication of the main temple at Tenochtitlán in 1487.
Motecuhzoma II: (1502-1520)	was the son of Axayacatl, and grandson of Motecuhzoma I. He is remembered largely for his surrender of Tenochtitlán to the Spaniards. He was a well educated and capable but demanding leader who had been trained for leadership since childhood. He was extremely superstitious and believed in the legend of Quetzálcóatl. He transformed the city into a beautiful cultural metropolis, but demanded heavy tributes from the cities around him. When distant provinces rebelled, the empire began to show signs of weakening. Aztec retaliation against the recalcitrant neighboring regions was swift and harsh. As a result, many of the provinces, especially the nearby Tlaxcalans, joined forces with the Spaniards against the Aztecs during the seige of Tenochtitlán. Motecuhzoma II died in1520 in the midst of a bloody battle against the Spaniards.
Cuitlahuac: (1520)	was Motecuhzoma II's brother; he ruled only four months, and died of disease brought by the Europeans.
Cuauhtemoc: (1520-1524)	was the son of Ahuitzotl, and cousin of Motecuhzoma II and Cuitlhuac. He was the last of the Aztec kings and the bravest of all. He fought valiantly against the Spaniards in defense of Tenochtitlán. Refusing to disclose the location of Motecuhzoma's treasures, he died in 1524 when he was unjustly tortured and hanged by the Spaniards.

The Conquest of Mexico

Is it true that we live on earth?
Not forever on earth; we are only a little while here.
Even jade will be broken,
Even gold shall be crushed,
Even Quetzál feathers will be torn apart.
Not forever on earth; we are only a little while here.

King Nezahualcóyotl of Texcoco
1402-1472

Motecuhzoma II was selected from the royal lineage in 1502. With jurisdiction over all of the Aztec territories, he was a demanding ruler who extracted excessive tributes from his subjects, and enjoyed a luxurious lifestyle. It is said that hundreds of servants attended his needs, and no fewer than 100 different dishes would be prepared for each of his meals. He was interested in all religions, and quite knowledgeable about his country's past history. His respect for tradition and his belief in ancient legends and superstitions were factors in his successful rule, as well as key factors that contributed to the final collapse of the Aztec state. He lived with total conviction that the great leader Quetzálcóatl would someday return to reclaim his rightful throne.

There were many strange phenomena that occurred during Motecuhzoma's reign; all were interpreted as bad omens. There were comets that flashed through Aztec skies, mysterious reports of lake water boiling, the sound of a weeping woman at night, and unusually violent lightning storms. All created fear in the hearts of the people. Wise men and philosophers told stories of strange dreams that predicted the arrival of strangers who would alter the course of Aztec history. Motecuhzoma was filled with a sense of helplessness and resignation; he felt that the omens anticipated the return of Quetzálcóatl.

169. *Opposite.* Plaza of the Three Cultures, Tlatelolco, Mexico City. In foreground are the Aztec ruins where Cuauhtemoc fought against the Spaniards; in the center is an early 16th c. Catholic Church; modern, 20th century apartment buildings are in the background.

170. Aztec Noble.
(INAH.)

In the spring of 1519, Motecuhzoma was advised that fair skinned and bearded foreigners had landed on the shores of Veracruz. It was the year of One Reed—and Quetzálcóatl had been fair skinned and bearded. News of the Spaniards' arrival greatly disturbed the king. Messengers were sent from Tenochtitlán to seek out the leader of the foreign group to determine if he was indeed the great Quetzálcóatl. If the leader was the reborn priest-king, the Aztec emissaries were instructed to plead with him to stay away from Tenochtitlán until Motecuhzoma's death, at which time he could reclaim his rightful throne. The Aztecs placed gifts of food and gold along the shore opposite the boats and waited to see what the strangers would do. The Spaniards took the gifts and asked the Aztecs to accompany them to the lead ship to meet Hernan Cortes, personal representative of Charles V of Spain, the most powerful country in Europe at that time.

Cortes

Hernan Cortes was born in the Spanish town of Medellin, Spain, in 1485. He was the frail and often sickly son of an upper middle class family. At the age of fourteen, he was sent by his parents to the University of Salamanca to study law, but poor health forced him to leave school before his studies were completed. After some deliberation, Cortes decided to pursue a clerical position in the Spanish army.

Cortes sailed to the West Indies in 1504, at the age of nineteen. He was appointed personal secretary to Diego Velazquez during the Spanish conquest of Cuba, in 1511. At the end of the successful campaign, Velazquez was appointed Governor of Cuba; he named Cortes head of the King's Treasury. Velazquez also gave him substantial landholdings in Santiago de Baracoa, the first Spanish town in Cuba, and a large number of Indian slaves. Cortes used the slaves to work his mines, mining enough gold to start a successful trading operation. Although he became a respected member of the community, serving twice as mayor of Santiago, he was also known for his many amorous affairs, from which he contacted syphilis, an incurable disease.

In 1518, Velazquez appointed Cortes as leader of an expedition to Mexico to seek gold, claim land, and develop trade with the Indians. Two earlier attempts to establish contact with Mexico had not been particularly successful in achieving their primary objectives. Cortes accepted the new assignment and began his preparations. It was not until the expedition was fully organized that Velazquez had second thoughts about Cortes. Suspecting him of excessive ambition, he ordered Cortes to stay in Cuba. Cortes ignored the order and set sail for Western Cuba, where he picked up additional supplies and men. He departed for Mexico on February 18, 1519. He was only 34 years old at the time.

Cortes sailed from Cuba in eleven ships with 550 soldiers, some 200 Cuban Indians, a few small cannons, and sixteen horses. He crossed the turbulent seas and landed his ships on the island of Cozumel, off the Yucatán Peninsula, where friendly natives led him to two previously shipwrecked Spanish sailors. The sailors were useful to Cortes as interpreters; they could speak the Mayan language and had become familiar with local customs. Invaluable as translators for the newly arrived Spaniards, they also advised them on issues of protocol. After a brief stay, Cortes left the island, taking one of the previously shipwrecked sailors with him. (The second Spaniard decided to stay with his Maya wife and children.) Cortes continued his journey around the peninsula and eventually landed at Potochan, where the Spaniards were attacked by hostile natives. Many of Cortes' men were wounded, but only two died in the battle; the Indians lost 200 warriors. As a result, the Maya became convinced that the Spaniards were indestructible. Twenty young Indian women were given to Cortes as a respectful parting gift when the Spaniards left Potochan. He sailed along the Gulf Coast to San Juan de Ulua, near the present city of Veracruz, where the inhabitants spoke an entirely different language. Fortunately for Cortes, one of the women could speak their language. She translated what they said to the shipwrecked sailor, who translated the information into Spanish for Cortes. Called Malinche by her people, Cortes renamed her **Doña Marina**. She became Cortes' interpreter, advisor on local customs and legends, and mistress.

Doña Marina was Cortes' mistress, advisor and interpreter.

Cortes founded the town of La Villa Rica de Vera Cruz (modern Veracruz) in the name of the King of Spain. He appointed the necessary municipal officers to govern the town and assumed the title of Captain General, with responsibility in all military matters. His primary motives for settling the city in the King's name were to establish a base for the conquest of the country, and to gain favor with the Spanish ruler, gambling that his original disregard of the orders issued by Velazquez would be overlooked in the event of a total and successful conquest. He wrote to the King of Spain and asked for additional support and financial assistance. As an unsolicited but clever gesture of good will, he also sent all of the treasure he had accumulated.

Some of Cortes' men became frightened by the difficulties that faced them in this alien land and plotted to seize the ship to keep the letter and the treasure from reaching their destination. When he learned of their plans, Cortes hanged the two major leaders of the conspiracy against him and had the feet of a third cut off. All of the other participants in the mutinous plan were given 200 lashes. Cortes was now even more determined to let nothing interfere with his decision to conquer the new land. To ensure this, he ordered his men to burn and sink their ships. His decisive but extreme action brought the men close to mutiny, but they now lacked the means to return to Cuba. There was no choice left but to conquer the country or die in the attempt.

Motecuhzoma was constantly aware of Cortes' actions, and gave careful thought to each of the Spaniard's moves. He sent valuable presents to the Europeans, but said he could not make the long journey to Veracruz to meet Cortes because of illness. He hoped that a polite refusal would discourage Cortes, but the Spaniard sent a messenger to the Aztec king stating that he had a personal message from the Spanish king, and would come to Tenochtitlán to deliver it in person.

The March to Tenochtitlán

Cortes began the arduous journey to Tenochtitlán, across rugged mountains and deserts, and through dangerous and hostile territory. The Spaniards were treated in a courteous manner by the natives they met, for Motecuhzoma had ordered his subjects to be friendly to the foreigners. The only disastrous opposition Cortes encountered during the early part of his journey was when a small band of Tlaxcalans attacked the Spaniards. A short battle took place, and two of Cortes' horses were killed. The Indians had never seen horses and were terrified by the large animals, thinking them immortal monsters. When the horses died, the Indians realized that the great beasts were only flesh and blood. The god-like qualities of Cortes and his men began to be questioned.

Motecuhzoma sent word to Cortes asking him to proceed to the city of Cholula and await instructions. When the Spaniards reached the city, they were welcomed and given food and gifts. Shortly thereafter, Motecuhzoma sent word to the Cholulans that the "guests" were to be kept in the city by force, if necessary, and

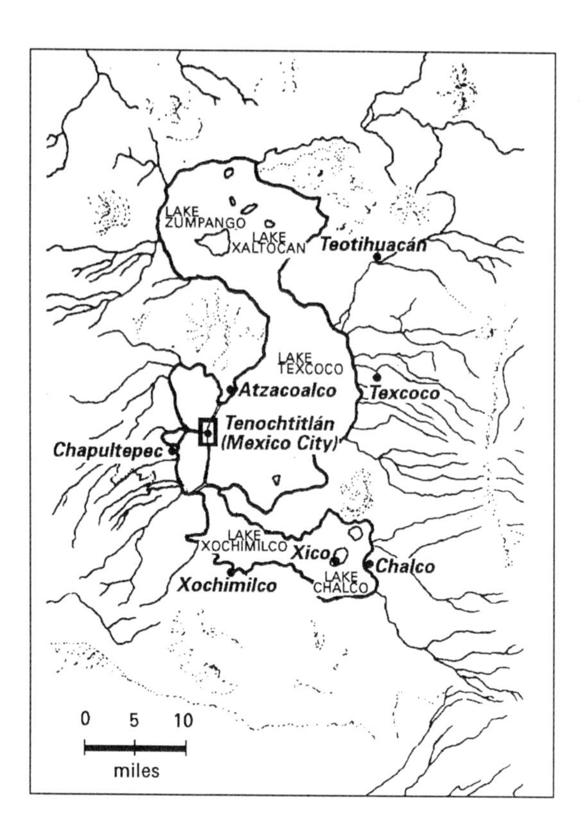

171. The Valley of Mexico at the time of the Conquest.

they were not to be given any more food. He was determined to subject the foreigners to one more test to determine if the men were truly gods. Dona Marina told Cortes of the plan; he became so enraged he had some of the nobles executed, and ordered his men to shoot into the main plaza of the town. In the five hour battle that took place, approximately 6000 inhabitants were brutally slaughtered. Cortes' name has never been vindicated for his role in this violent and unprovoked attack.

Greatly encouraged by their victory at Cholula, the Spaniards marched on towards Tenochtitlán. They climbed the pass between the snowy mountain peaks of Popocatepetl and Ixtaccihuatl and began their descent into the valley. Below them spread the incredibly beautiful city of the Aztecs. They proceeded along one of the wide causeways, and crossed the final drawbridge that gave access to the city. There, under a great canopy, was the Emperor Motecuhzoma. He was clothed in the

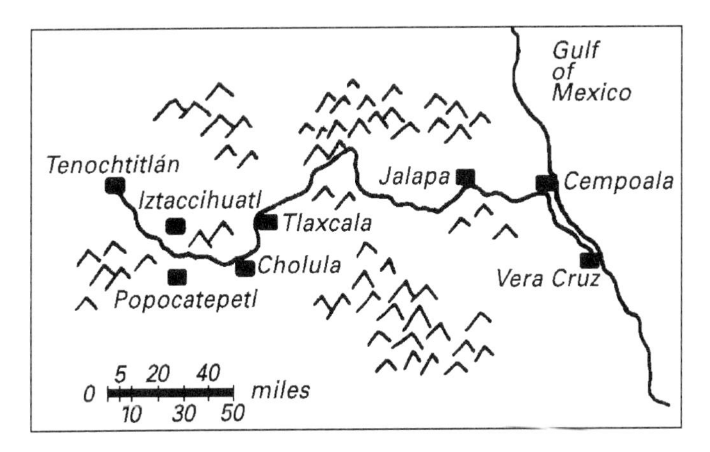

172. Map showing Cortes' initial journey from Veracruz to Tenochtitlán.

finest fabrics, adorned with magnificent jewelry, and attended by many servants. The Aztec king greeted Cortes; they saluted each other and exchanged necklaces. Motecuhzoma addressed Cortes as "Quetzálcóatl," and welcomed him back to reclaim his rightful throne. It was November 8, 1519.

Cortes and his men were treated in a courteous manner by the Aztecs, and comfortably housed in Motehcuhzoma's father's magnificent palace. A large quantity of gold was found in the palace; it would ultimately be melted down into bars and sent to the King of Spain. The Spaniards were pleased by their reception, but uneasy in the knowledge that their good luck could change at any time; thousands of Aztecs could turn against them at a moment's notice. After much thought, Cortes decided to confine Motecuhzoma to his quarters, thus assuring their continued saftey. It was one of the most disastrous mistakes Cortes made. Motecuhzoma protested that his people would never accept such an outrage, but he finally agreed to continue his role as leader in this restricted manner. Realizing his people were becoming angry and disenchanted with the foreigners, he announced to his subjects that he was not a prisoner, but under Cortes' authority because it was the "will of the gods." Though kept under guard, advisors were free to visit him and he was allowed to worship at the Great Temple. The Emperor seemed strangely resigned to his fate. The people grudgingly accepted this turn of events, even though many of the Aztec began to question the "divinity" of the Spanish intruders. A noticeable undercurrent of unrest could be detected at this time, and some of the people began to look to Motecuhzoma's brother, Cuitlahuac, for support. There was also bitter opposition to Cortes' demand that human sacrifice cease.

Intervention from Cuba

Diego Velazquez became increasingly bitter when he heard reports of Cortes' success, as he had come to view the man as an insubordinate and rebellious soldier. When he was finally appointed Governor of all controllable Yucatán territories, Velazquez used his extended jurisdiction to assemble an expedition of about 1000 men, headed by a Spaniard named Panfilo de Narvaez, to bring back the recalcitrant captain. When Cortes learned of their arrival he experienced a sense of foreboding, and correctly suspected the soldiers were sent by Velazquez to take him back to Cuba. He told his men that the troops from Cuba were there to take what he and his men had won. Selecting some volunteers to accompany him to Veracruz, he asked Motecuhzoma to guarantee the safety of the Spaniards that were left to guard Tenochtitlán. The Emperor agreed, and even offered the use of Aztec warriors to Cortes. Leaving Pedro de Alvarado in command of about 80 men, Cortes took the remaining soldiers and departed for the coast. He arrived in Cempoala, Veracruz at night, and immediately launched a surprise attack against the newly arrived Spaniards. After a frenzied skirmish, the newcomers from Cuba surrendered. This decisive action of Cortes enhanced his position among the Indians, as well as with Narvaez' men, who immediately joined his group. With his ranks now greatly increased, Cortes returned to Tenochtitlán.

La Noche Triste— The Sad Night

While Cortes was away, Alvarado gave permission to the Aztecs to conduct a ceremony in honor of their god Huitzilopochtli, as long as human sacrifice was not practiced. According to Spanish accounts of the incident that followed, Alvarado was told that the Aztecs planned to sacrifice the Spaniards who had been left in charge. Alvarado reacted to these rumors without considering their authenticity, and slaughtered 200 Aztec nobles in the midst of their religious ceremony.

Cortes found a strangely silent city when he returned from his victory at Cempoala. He entered Tenochtitlán with over 1000 soldiers, including reinforcements from Cuba. They marched toward Motecuhzoma's palace. It was unusually quiet, because the Aztecs had set a trap and were waiting for him to enter the heart of the city.

Within the open areas of the Great Temple Complex, the Spaniards had little protection from the Indians who attacked from hidden positions on top of the buildings. Even though Spanish cannons and crossbows quickly killed and maimed many Indians, the Aztecs continued to pour into the area from their hiding places among the temples and palaces. They came in wave after wave, and the Spaniards were quickly overwhelmed. Greatly alarmed by the turn of events, Cortes persuaded Motecuhzoma to plead with the Aztecs to halt their attack. The ruler emerged from his quarters, but in the confusion of battle the outraged Indians threw stones at the palace. One of the stones struck the emperor in the temple; he died three days later. Some accounts say that Motecuhzoma was stoned to death by his own people. Other reports indicate that he was killed by the Spaniards (Pazstory 1994).

Motecuhzoma's brother, Cuitlahuac, assumed leadership, and the Aztecs continued their violent thrust. The Spaniards retreated; their food and gun powder were almost gone, and there were many wounded men. Cortes attempted to negotiate a truce, but the Aztecs rejected his offer.

Cortes realized his position was impossible, and planned a retreat. He had his men quickly build a portable bridge that could be used in their escape, since the Aztecs had removed the bridges that spanned the gaps in the canals. Each man was given as much treasure as he wished to carry. They left the palace on the night of June 30, 1520. Advancing cautiously, they placed their portable bridge over the first canal, and crossed successfully. But they were spotted by the Aztecs before they could cross the second span of water. Thousands of Aztec warriors came pouring out of the city in pursuit. The portable bridge was placed over the second canal, and Cortes and some of his men were able to get across. The remaining foot soldiers panicked; the flimsy bridge broke, and hundreds of men were drowned

173. Excavations of the Templo Mayor, with the Cathedral of Mexico City in background.

because of the weight of the treasure they had so greedily stuffed into their clothing. The most dramatic reversal of Spanish fortune occurred on that night: at least 450 Spaniards died, and more than 4000 Indians also perished. The survivors reached the mainland where, according to authenticated records, Cortes was so exhausted and drained by the disaster he sat under a tree and wept. That night was called *La Noche Triste,* the sad night.

The Fall of Tenochtitlán

Because of their defeat at Tenochtitlán, the Spaniards were uncertain of their reception by the previously supportive mainland Tlaxcalans. They were greatly encouraged when they were greeted with friendliness and reaffirmation of loyalty. Had it not been for the continuing support of these Indian allies, Cortes would not have conquered Mexico.

Cortes conceived an ingenious plan for securing the island city of Tenochtitlán. He decided to use **Brigantines**, which would be far superior in strength and speed to Aztec canoes. His carpenters built the boats in sections that could be carried across the mountains. They would be assembled and fitted with sails and oars on the shore of Lake Texcoco.

Brigantine: a two-masted sailing ship used for skirmishes.

Cortes and his army re-entered the Valley of Mexico in November, 1520, establishing headquarters in the city of Texcoco. Supporting him were over 100,000 Indian warriors who had become disenchanted with Aztec rule. They marched toward Tenochtitlán with their portable boats, and assembled them when they reached the lake. Each vessel held about a dozen armed men. As they approached the island city, they attacked the approaching Aztec canoes with such speed and fury that many of the Indian boats were swamped or crushed. Although the Spaniards were able to penetrate sections of Tenochtitlán, they could not hold their positions because of the ferocious counterattack by the Aztec warriors. In addition, the advantage of the Spanish horses and cannons was greatly reduced because of the close-in street fighting. As a result, Cortes gave the order to systematically destroy all of the buildings, great temples, and palaces that gave protection to the Aztecs. These were demolished as he proceeded, so that none remained in his path. Unknown to the Spaniards, Cuitlahuac had died from disease

174. Excavations of the Great Temple show double stairway and chronological periods of construction.

brought by the Spaniards. His cousin, Cuauhtemoc, was now the Aztec leader.

The Aztecs defended the city for 80 days, suffering heavy casualties. Finally, amidst a horror of destruction, death, and rubble, the city fell. Cuauhtemoc was taken prisoner at Tlatelolco, where he had made his last courageous stand against the Spaniards; the date was August 13, 1521. Cuauhtemoc was destined to remain a prisoner for the rest of his life. He was kept under constant guard, and brutally tortured when he refused to divulge the location of Motecuhzoma's gold. At least 200,000 Aztecs died in the conquest. These included warriors, members of the priesthood, and thousands of Tenochtitlán's inhabitants. Visiting chiefs were later shown the wreckage of their empire. Newly arrived Spanish ships brought wine and pigs for the Spanish victory celebration (Pazstory 1994).

The Aztec civilization rose to power because of its brilliant military strategies. The character of the Aztecs' downfall was consistent with their rise: warfare was their historical strength, and military battle resulted in their ultimate collapse. The effect of the excessive tribute and tax demands on the people and constant warfare for expansion ultimately weakened the empire.

The last great warrior-king was Cuauhtemoc, whose name means "Falling Eagle." Since the eagle was representative of the all-important sun, it might be appropriate to say that in a symbolic sense, the collapse of the empire came at the time of the death of the Setting Sun.

A Question to Ponder

The question of who ultimately caused the collapse of the Aztec empire is a powerful one. Was it the invaders, or was it the role played by religion and superstition, and the resulting effect on society? Perhaps it was not Cortes who defeated the Aztecs, but Motecuhzoma's belief in the promised return of the priest-king, Quetzálcóatl. The Aztecs' entire life activity centered on their religious convictions, and on the excessive demands of their leaders. Both of these constrained their cultural growth. Cortes brilliantly capitalized on these traditions, and because of this was able to conquer the country.

Epilogue

On October 15, 1522, Charles V appointed Hernan Cortes Governor of "New Spain," as the country was now called. This title gave Cortes an opportunity to test his abilities as an administrator and colonizer. During the first years after the conquest, the Spaniards successfully expanded into adjacent territories and destroyed small pockets of hostile Indians throughout the land. Within a few years, the Spaniards controlled all of what is now central and southern Mexico.

Major building programs were started, and homes and churches for the Spaniards were quickly constructed. Hospitals were also needed; the Hospital of Jesus, which still stands in Mexico City, was built at this time. Indian labor was used for construction, and to make the bricks and tiles for new buildings. (It should be noted here that large quantities of stones from the ruins of Indian temples were also used for new construction. Mexico City literally emerged from Tenochtitlán's rubble.) So much Indian labor was used that only five months after the conquest, Cortes wrote the King of Spain that the (new) city was "already very beautiful." After three years, he wrote, "So well and so quickly does the work go...that many of the houses are mostly large and comely" (Cortes 1986).

Father Motolinia, one of the earliest and most reliable of the church men to record events of this time, described the feverish rebuilding in this way:

> So many were working on the buildings...that a man could hardly pick his way through the streets...Many were killed by falling beams or by falling from a height: others lost their lives under buildings they were taking down in one place to put up in another, especially when they dismantled the chief temples of the devil. Many Indians died in this work, and many years passed before these temples were completely destroyed (Toussaint 1967).

The Spaniards immediately began to convert the native population to Catholicism. Franciscan, Dominican, and

175. *Opposite*. Dominican Church at Acolman, Valley of Mexico. Basilican church and Open Chapel served the religious needs of Spaniards and Indians.

176. Interior courtyard at Acolman, Valley of Mexico.

177. Acolman, Valley of Mexico. 16th century fresco, *The Resurrection of Christ*. Probably painted by Indian artists.

Augustinian friars came to the new land in groups of twelve to accomplish this goal. Some of the friars advocated forced conversion to the new politics and religion. Other more humane and educated holy men preferred a slower and more peaceful conversion. Irrespective of which course of action was taken, however, failure by the Indians to accept the new order and "true" God resulted in torture, or war against them. Hundreds of monasteries were constructed for the newly arrived religous groups, and open-air chapels were built for the converted Indians. The open-air chapels, which the Spaniards called "Chapels of the Indians," were used by the indigenous population throughout most of the Colonial period.

Most earlier art forms did not survive after the conquest. Disease, despair, and forced labor took a devastating toll on the Indian population, and there was little time for the arts. (Roughly twenty million Indians lived in Mesoamerica at the time of the conquest; by the end of the 16th century, the indigenous population numbered about one million.) Only feather paintings and illustrated manuscripts continued to be produced, at the request of the Spaniards. Once the Franciscan friars realized the importance of understanding the Indians' legacies, they encourged some educated natives to record their histories. Thus, earlier works destroyed by overzealous Spaniards were later re-recorded on illustrated manuscripts by Indian nobles, or by concerned Spaniards who translated and recorded many of the ancient legends to Spanish or Latin. One of the most important documents of pre-conquest times is Father Bernardino de Sahagun's twelve-volume endeavor, *The General History of the Things of New Spain.*

In 1524, Cortes headed a difficult expedition to the jungles of Honduras, where he spent two frustrating years that gained him nothing but damage to his health and position. He took Cuauhtemoc with him, because he was convinced the Aztec leader still had a great deal of power and influence over the surviving Indian groups. It was during this expedition that he finally tortured and hung the brave ruler. Upon his return to Mexico City, Cortes found that his name had been discredited and his property seized by the officials left in charge. Further reports of the cruelty of the Spanish administration in this new colony were beginning to arouse concern in Spain. From the records of the Spaniards themselves, we know that the Conquest of Mexico was a brutal time that brought about a total change in the structure of the centuries-old country; we also know that the Spanish Inquisition functioned here in the name of the Catholic faith as a harsh and unsympathetic high court. Although many Spaniards were well educated and humane in their treatment of the indigenous population, others were cruel and sadistic in their quest for a new Catholic country under Spain's jurisdiction.

Cortes returned to Spain in 1528, and was warmly received despite the unfavorable reports that had preceded his arrival. Charles V awarded him the titles of Captain General and Marquis of the Valley of Oaxaca, but refused to reconfirm Cortes' position as Captain General of New Spain. Instead, he was given title to 22 prosperous towns and 23,000 Indian slaves for his part in the Conquest of Mexico. A disappointed Cortes returned to Mexico and remained there for the next ten years, managing his estate and undertaking new expeditions which he hoped would bring back his fading power. His efforts were unsuccessful, however, and in 1540, he returned to Spain where he lived until his death seven years later. In accordance with his final wishes, his remains were returned to Mexico where they still lie today in the Church of the Hospital of Jesus in Mexico City, an institution he had founded.

Gods of Mesoamerica

A selected list

Chac: Maya god of water, see **Tlaloc**.

Chalchiuhtlicue: "She of the Skirt of Jade" or "Precious Woman"—goddess of all ground waters.

Cihuateteo: "Deified Woman"—the goddess of all young mothers who died in childbirth. She also helped to carry the sun across the sky.

Cocijo: Zapotec god of water, see **Tlaloc**.

Coatlicue: "She of the Serpent Skirt"—mother of **Huitzilopochtli** and many other gods.

Huehueteotl: "The Old Fire God"—often shown as a toothless and wrinkled old man with a fire brazier on his back or on his head.

Huitzilopochtli: "Hummingbird on the Left"—War and Sun association. Aztec god of war and chief deity of Tenochtitlán. He can be identified by his weapon, the fire serpent.

Mictlantecuhtli: "Lord of Mictlan, Land of the Dead"—god of death who resided in the underworld darkness.

Quetzálcóatl: "Feathered Serpent" or "Precious Twin"—The Feathered Serpent Deity was the god of learning and of the priesthood. His many different aspects include: god of wind, the morning star, the evening star; was credited with bringing to man all knowledge of the arts, agriculture, and science. Called **Quetzálcóatl Ehecatl** by the Aztec.

Tezcatlipoca: "Smoking Mirror"—major god of Toltec and Nahuatl groups. Associated with the rulership, and night; god of fate.

Tlaloc: "Water God" and "Earth Lord"—He was associated with water, rain, flooding, hail, and the serpent; probably one of the oldest deities and is traceable to the Olmec culture; rings around the eyes, fangs, and a volute over the mouth are frequent distinguishing characteristics; called **Chac** by the Maya and **Cocijo** by the Zapotec.

Tonatiuh: "He who makes the day"—The sun god of the Aztec and closely associated with **Huitzilopochtli**; his face is in the center of the Aztec calendar stone.

Xipe Totec: "Our Flayed Lord"—God of springtime, seeding, and planting; he symbolizes the renewal of all vegetation and life. He wears the skin of a sacrificial victim to symbolize the continuous renewal of life.

Selected Bibliography

ABRAMS, ELLIOT M.
1994 *How the Maya Built Their World.* Energetics and Ancient Architecture. Austin: University of Texas Press.

AVENI, A.F.
1981 Tropical Archeoastronomy. *Science,* V 213.

BADA, JEFFREY L., and PATRICIA MASTERS HELFMAN
1975 Amino Acid Racemization Dating of Fossil Bones. *World Archaelogy.* Vol.7, no.2. pp.160-175.

BEADLE, GEORGE
1977 The Origins of Zea Mays. *Origins of Agriculture.* Edited by Charles A. Reed. Chicago: Aldine Publishing Co. pp. 615-35.

BENDITT, JOHN
1988 Ritual on Wheels: or why Mesoamericans never got on a roll (Toltec Civilization Used Wheels Only on Ritual Figurines). *Scientific American,* pp. 31,32.

BENSON, ELIZABETH ed.
1973 *Death and the Afterlife in Pre-Columbian America.* A Conference at Dumbarton Oaks. Washington, D.C.: Dumbarton Oaks Research Library and Collections.
1977 *The Maya World.* New York: Thomas Crowell
1981 *The Olmec and their Neighbors.* Michael D. Coe and David Grove, Organizers.Dumbarton Oaks Research Library and Collections. Washington, D.C.

BERGER, RAINER
1975 Advances and Results in Radiocarbon Dating: Early Man in America. *World Archaeology,* vol. 7, no. 2 , pp. 175-184.

BERNAL, I.M., COE, G. EKHOLM, P. FURST, W. HABERLAND, G. KUBLER, H.B. NICHOLSON, J. ERIC THOMPSON, G.R. WILLEY
1973 *The Iconography of Middle American Sculpture.* New York: The Metropolitan Museum of Art.

BERNAL, IGNACIO
1968 *The Olmec World.* Berkeley, Los Angeles, London: University of California Press.
1973 *Mexico Before Cortez: Art, History, Legend.* New York: Anchor Books.

BERRIN, K., AND ESTHER PASZTORY, Ed.
1993 *Teotihuacán.* New York: Thames and Hudson.

BLANTON, R.E.
1978 *Monte Albán: Settlement Patterns at the Ancient Zapotec Capital.* New York, London: Academic Press.

BORHEGYI, STEPHEN
1980 *The Pre-Columbian Ballgames: A Pan Mesoamerican Tradition.* Milwaukee, Museum Publication.

BROWN, HANBURY
1978 *Man and the Stars.* London: Oxford University Press.

BRUNDAGE, BURR C.
1972 *A Rain of Darts: the Mexica Aztecs.* Austin: University of Texas Press.
1979 *The Fifth Sun-Aztec Gods, Aztec Worlds.* Austin: University of Texas Press.

BURLAND, C.A.
1967 *The Gods of Mexico.* New York: G.P. Putnam's Sons.
1975 *Feathered Serpent and Smoking Mirror.* New York: G.P. Putnam's Sons.

BUSHNELL, GEOFFREY
1965 *Ancient Arts of the Americas.* New York: Praeger Publishers.

CABRERA, RUBEN
1982 "El Projecto Arqueologico Teotihuacán" Mexico: INAH.

CABRERA, COWGILL, SUGIYAMA AND SERRANO
1989 "El Projecto Templo de Quetzálcóatl" Mexico: INAH.

CASO, ALFONSO
1959 *The Aztecs: People of the Sun.* Norman: University of Oklahoma Press.

CHASE, DIANE and ARLEN CHASE, editors
1992 *Mesoamerican Elites: An Archaeological Assessment.* Oklahoma: University of Oklahoma Press.

CHODKIEWICZ, JEAN-LUC
1995 *Peoples of the Past and Present.* Readings in Anthropology. Canada, Ltd: Harcourt Brace and Company.

CLEWLOW, CARL WILLIAM, Jr.
1970 Comparison of Two Unusual Olmec Monuments. *Contributions of the University of California Archaeological Research Facility,* no. 8, pp. 35-40. Berkeley.

COE, MICHAEL D.
1962 *Mexico.* New York, Washington D.C.: Praeger Publishers.
1965 Archaeological Synthesis of Southern Veracruz and Tabasco. *Handbook of Middle American Indians,* Vol. 3, part 2, pp. 679-716: Austin.
1965 *The Jaguar's Children.* Greenwich, Connecticut: New York Graphic Society.
1967 Olmec Civilization, Veracruz, Mexico: Dating of the San Lorenzo Phase. *Science,* Vol. 155, pp. 1399-1401.
1968 *America's First Civilization.* Princeton: Van Nostrand Press.
1987 *The Maya.* New York, Washington, D.C.: Praeger Publishers.
1992 *Breaking the Maya Code.* New York: Thames and Hudson.

COE, MICHAEL D. and RICHARD A. DIEHL
1980 *In the Land of the Olmec.* Austin: University of Texas Press.

CORDY-COLLINS, ALANA and JEAN STERN
1977 *Pre-Columbian Art History:* Selected Readings. Palo Alto, California: Peek Publications.

CORSON, CHRISTOPHER
1973 Iconographic Survey of Some Principle Figurine Subjects from the Mortuary Complex of Jaina, Campeche. *Contributions of the University of California Archaeological Research Facilities,* No. 18, pp. 51-64.

CORTES, HERNAN.
1970 *Letter of Account to King Charles V of Spain.* Hispanoamericana Antololgia e Introduccion Historica. New York: Holt, Rinehart, and Winston.

CORTES, HERNAN. Ed. by Anthony Pagden.
1986 *Letters From Mexico.* New Haven: Yale University Press

COVARRUBIAS, MIGUEL
1957 *Indian Art of Mexico and Central America.* New York: Knopf Publishers.

CYPRESS, SANDRA MESSINGER
1991 *La Malinche in Mexican Literature.* Austin: University of Texas Press.

DANIEN, ELIN and ROBERT SHARER, editors
1992 *New Theories on the Ancient Maya.* Philadelphia: The University Museum.

DAVIES, NIGEL
1973 *The Aztecs.* London: Macmillan Publishers.

DIAZ DEL CASTILLO, B
1944 *Historia Verdadera de la Conquista del la Nueva Espana.* Mexico, D.F., Pedro Robredo, 3 volumes.

DOCKSTADER, FREDERICK J.
1964 *Indian Art in Middle America.* Graphic Society: Greenwich, Conn.

DOOLITTLE, WILLIAM E.
1990' *Canal Irrigation in Prehistoric Mexico.* Austin: University of Texas Press.

DURAN, DIEGO
1967 *Historia de las Indias de Nueva Espana e Islas de las Tierra Firme.* Two volumes. Mexico.
1971 *Book of the Gods and Rites and the Ancient Calendar.* Horcasitas , Fernando and Doris Heyden editing. University of Oklahoma Press.

EASBY, D.T.
1956 Ancient American Goldsmiths. *Natural History,* Vol. 65, pp. 401-99

EASBY, ELIZABETH K. and JOHN F. SCOTT
1970 *Before Cortez: Sculpture of Middle America.* New York Graphic Society: Catalogue published by the Metropolitan Museum of Art.

EMMERICH, ANDRE
1965 *Sweat of the Sun and Tears of the Moon.* Seattle, Washington: University of Washington Press.
1983 *Art Before Columbus.* New York: Simon and Schuster.

FASH, WILLIAM
1991 *Scribes, Warriors and Kings. The City of Copán and the Ancient Maya.* London: Thames and Hudson, Ltd.

FLANNERY, KENT V.
1968 Archaeological Systems Theory and Early Mesoamerica. *Anthropological Archaeology in the Americas.* Washington, D.C: The Anthropological Society of Washington.

FLANNERY, KENT V. and JOYCE MARCUS ed.
1983 *The Cloud People, Divergent Evolution of the Zapotec and Mixtec Civilizations.* New York: Academic Press.

FLANNERY, KENT V., ed.
1986 Studies in Archaeology. *The Early Mesoamerican Village.* San Diego, California: Academic Press.

FOLAN, W.J.
1979 Social Organizations of a Maya Urban Center. *Science,* Vol. 204, pp. 697-701.

FOX, JAMES
1994 *Ulama: Game of Life and Death in Early Mesoamerica.* Stanford, California Stanford University Museum of Art Exhibition Catalogue.

GALLENKAMP, CHARLES AND REGINA JOHNSON
1985 *Maya Treasures of an Ancient Civilization.* New York: Abram Publishers in association with the Albuquerque Museum.

GAY, CARLO
1967 Oldest Paintings in the New World: Juxtlahuaca Cave, Mexico. *Natural History,* Vol. 76, pp. 28-35.

GAY, CARLO
1972 *Xochipala: The Beginnings of Olmec Art.* Princton: Princton Art Museum.

GIFFORD, J.C.
1974 *Recent Thought Concerning the Interpretation of Maya Prehistory.* Austin: University of Texas Press.

GOODMAN, JEFFREY
1981 *American Genesis.* New York: Summit Books.

GROVE, D.C.
1969 Olmec Cave Paintings: Discovery from Guerrero, Mexico. *Science,* Vol. 164, pp. 421-23.

GYLES, ANNA BENSON AND CHLOE SAYER
1980 *Of Gods and Men.* New York: Harper and Row.

HARDOY, JORGE
1968 *Urban Planning in Pre-Columbian America.* New York: George Braziller.

HEIZER, R.F.
1968 Agriculture and the Theocratic State in Lowland Southeastern Mexico. *American Antiquities* 26: pp. 215-222.

HEIZER, R.F.
1971 Commentary on: The Olmec Region-Oaxaca. *Contributions of the University of California Archaeological Research Facility*, no. 11, pp. 51-69. Berkeley.

HENDERSON, J.S.
1981 *The World of the Maya*. Ithaca, New York: Cornell University.

Heyden, Doris and Luis Francisco Villasenor
1984 *The Great Temple and the Aztec Gods*. Mexico, D.F.: Minutiae Mexicana.

HEYDEN, DORIS
1970 A New Interpretation of the Smiling Figures. *Ancient Art of Veracruz: Exhibit Catalog*. Los Angeles County Museum of Natural History.

HOUSTON, STEPHEN
1993 *Maya Glyphs*. Berkeley: University of California Press.

JORALEMON, P.D.
1971 A Study of Olmec Iconography. *Studies in Pre-Columbian Art and Archaeology*, no. 7. Washington, D.C.: Dumbarton Oaks.

KLOR DE ALVA, J.JORGE, H.B. NICHOLSON, ELOISE QUINONES KEBER editing
1988 *The Work of Bernardino de Sahagun*. Austin: University of Texas Press.

KRUPP, DR. E.C.
1977 *In Search of Ancient Astronomies*. New York: Doubleday.

KUBLER, GEORGE
1962 *The Art and Architecture of Ancient America: The Mexican, Maya, and Andean Peoples*. Maryland: Penguin Books.

KURTZ DONALD V.
1987 The Economics of Urbanization and State Formation at Teotihuacán. *Current Anthropology* 28:329-53.

LAUGHLIN, WM.S. AND ALBER B. HARPER editing
1979 *The First Americans: Origins, Affinities, and Adaptations*. New York, Stuttgart: Gustav Fischer.

LEON PORTILLO, MIGUEL
1963 *Aztec Thought and Culture, A Study of the Ancient Nahuatl Mind*. Norman: University of Oklahoma Press.
1992 *Fifteen Poets of the Aztec World*. Norman: University of Oklahoma Press.

LOTHROP, SAMUEL K.
1964 *Essays in Pre-Columbian Art and Archaeology*. Harvard University Press.

LUCKERT, KARL
1976 *Olmec Religion, A Key to Middle America and Beyond.* Norman: University of Oklahoma Press.

MACNEISCH, RICHARD: PAUL C. MANGELSDORF: WALTON GALINAT
1964 The Domestication of Corn. *Science*, Vol. 143, pp. 538-545. Washington, D.C.
1964 Origins of New World Civilization. *Scientific American*, Vol. 211, pp. 29-37.

MARCUS, JOYCE
1976 The Origins of Mesoamerican Writing. *Annual Revue of Anthropology* 5:35-67.
1992 *Mesoamerican Writing Systems*. Princeton: Princeton University Press.

McANANY, PATRICIA
1995 *Living With The Ancestors. Kinship and Kingship*. Austin: University of Texas Press.

MILBRATH SUSAN
1979 A Study of Olmec Sculptural Chronology. *Studies in Pre Columbian Art and Archaeology*, no. 23. Washington, D.C. Dumbarton Oaks.

MILLER, A.G.
1973 *The Mural Painting of Teotihuacán*. Washington, D.C. Dumbarton Oaks.

MILLER, M.E.
1986 *The Murals of Bonampak*. Princeton.
1986 *The Art of Mesoamerica from Olmec to Aztec*. New York: Thames and Hudson.

MILLER, M.E. and DAVID JORALEMAN
1975 *Jaina Figurines*. Princeton: The Princeton Art Museum.

MILLON, RENE
1973 *Urbanization at Teotihuacán, Mexico*, vol. 1. Austin: University of Texas Press.
1981 Teotihuacán: City, State, and Civilization.In *Handbook of Middle American Indians, Supplement I*, edited by Jeremy A. Sabloff with the assistance of P.A. Andrews, pp. 198-243. Austin: University of Texas Press.

MOCTEZUMA, EDWARDO MATOS
1980 The Great Temple. *National Geographic*, Vol. 158, pp. 767-775.

MORLEY, S.G.
1956 *The Ancient Maya*. Stanford, California: Stanford University Press.

NICHOLSON, IRENE
1967 *Mexican and Central American Mythology*. London: Hamylin.

NUNO, RUBEN BONIFAZ
1981 *El Arte en el Templo Mayor*. Mexico, D.F.: Instituto Nacional de Antropologia e Historia.

PASZTORY, E.
1974 *The Murals of Tepantitla, Teotihuacán*. New York: Columbia University Press
1978 *Middle Classic Mesoamerica A.D. 400-700*. New York: Columbia University Press.
1983 *Aztec Art*. New York: Columbia University Press.

PASZTORY, E. ed.
1978 *Middle Classic Mesoamerica A.D. 400-700*. New York: Columbia University Press.

PAYON, J.
1957 *El Tajín, Gira Oficial*. Mexico: INAH.

PINA CHAN, ROMAN
1968 *Jaina*. Mexico, D.F.: Instituto Nacional de Antropologia e Historia.

PROSKOURIAKOFF, T.
1960 Historical Implications of a Pattern of Dates at Piedras Negras, Guatemala. *American Antiquities* 25:454-75.
1963 *An Album of Maya Architecture*. Norman: University of Oklahoma Press.
1993 *Maya History*. Austin: University of Texas Press.

RENSBERGER, BOYCE
1981 Black Kings of Ancient America. *Science Digest*, pp. 74-77,122.

REENTS-BUDET, DORIE
1994 *Painting the Maya Universe: Royal Ceramics of the Classic Period*. Durham: Duke University Press.

ROBERTSON, DONALD
1963 *Pre-Columbian Architecture*. New York: George Braziller.

ROBERTSON, M.G.
1983 *The Sculpture of Palenque V.1.* The Temple of Inscriptions. Princeton.

RUPPERT, J., ERIC S. THOMPSON, TATIANA PROSKOURIAKOFF
1955 *Bonampak, Chiapas, Mexico.* Washington: Carnegie Institution Publication 602.

RUST, WM. F. AND ROBERT SHARER
1988 Olmec Settlement Data from La Venta, Tabasco, Mexico. *Science*- Vol. 242 pp.102-104.

SAHAGUN, FRAY BERNARDINO DE
1956 *Historia General de las Cosas de Nueva Espana.* Mexico City: Edicion Porrua.
1950-59 *General History of the Things of New Spain.* Monographs of the School of American Research, No. 14. Santa Fe, New Mexico.

SANDERS, W.T. AND B.J. PRICE
1968 *Mesoamerica: The Evolution of a Civilization.* New York: Random House.

SHARER, J.
1974 Prehistory of the Southeastern Maya Periphery. *Current Anthropology*, Vol. 15, pp. 165-187.

SCHELE, LINDA
1986 *Notebook for the Maya Hieroglyphic Writing Workshop at Texas.* Austin: Institute of Latin American Studies, University of Texas.

SCHELE, LINDA with MARY ELLEN MILLER
1986 T*he Blood of Kings.* Fort Worth Texas: Kimbell Art Museum.

SCHELE, LINDA and DAVID FREIDEL
1990 *A Forest of Kings.* New York: William Morrow and Company, Inc.

SIDRYS, RAYMOND and RAINER BERGER
1979 Lowland Maya Radiocarbon Dates and the Classic Maya Collapse. *Nature*, Vol. 277.

SOUSTELLE, J.
1966 *Arts of Ancient Mexico.* New York: Viking Press.

SPORES, RONALD
1961 *The Mixtec Kings and their People.* Norman: University of Oklahoma Press.

STEPHENS, JOHN L.
1843 *Incidents of Travel in Yucatán.* Two Volumes. New York: Harper & Brothers.

STUART, GEORGE and GENE STUART
1992 *Lost Kingdoms of the Maya.* Washington, D.D.: National Geographic Society.

TAUBE, KARL
1993 *Aztec and Maya Myths.* Austin: University of Texas Press and British Museum Press.

TEDLOCK, DENNIS
1985 *Popol Vuh.* New York: Simon and Schuster, Inc.

THOMPSON, J. ERIC S.
1927 A Correlation of the Mayan and European Calendars. *Field Museum Natural History, Anthrol. Series 17*(1).
1937 *Mexico before Cortez: an account of the daily life, religion, and ritual of the Aztecs and kindred peoples.* New York: C. Scribner's Sons.
1970 *Maya History and Religion.* Norman: University of Oklahoma Press.

THOMPKINS, PETER
1976 *Mysteries of the Mexican Pyramids.* New York: Harper and Row.

TOUSSAINT, MANUEL.
1967 *Colonial Art.* Austin: University of Texas Press.

VAILLANT, GEORGE
1962 *Aztecs of Mexico.* New York: Doubleday and Company Inc.

VON WINNING, HASSO AND O. HAMMER
1972 *Anecdotal Sculpture of West Mexico.* Los Angeles.

WAUCHOPE, R. ed.
1965-84 *Handbook of Middle American Indians.* Austin: University of Texas Press.

WEAVER, MURIEL PORTER
1972 *The Aztecs, Maya and their Predecessors.* New York: Seminar Press.

WILKERSON, S. JEFFREY
1980 "Man's Eighty Centuries in Veracruz." *National Geographic*: August, 1980.

WILLEY, GORDON R. and JEREMY A. SABLOFF
1980 *Readings from Scientific American Precolumbian Archaeology.* San Francisco: Seminar Press.

Index

D

E

N

O

P

Q

U

V

W

X

Y

Z